The Concise Companion Human Resource

This *Concise Companion to Strategic Human Resource Management* contains ten selected chapters from the full, 30-chapter version of the *Routledge Companion to Strategic Human Resource Management* edited by John Storey, Patrick Wright and Dave Ulrich (2009). The chapters in this shorter edition have been selected to meet the needs of students studying the Open University's B827 course in Strategic Human Resource Management.

John Storey is Professor of Management at the Open University Business School, UK. He regularly consults for both public and private sector organisations. He is Chairman of the IPA and also Chaired the B827 Course Team at The Open University Business School.

Patrick Wright is Professor of Strategic Human Resource Management at Cornell University, USA. He has published widely in leading international journals and has helped the world's leading firms to align their HR with business strategy.

Dave Ulrich is Professor of Business at The University of Michigan and a partner and co-founder of the RBL Group. He has been ranked by *BusinessWeek* as the Number 1 Management Educator and was listed in Forbes as among the "world's top five" business coaches. His HR models have hugely influenced organisations in many countries.

The Concise Companion to Strategic Human Resource Management

Edited by
John Storey,
Patrick M. Wright
and Dave Ulrich

OU
Business
School

Routledge
Taylor & Francis Group

LONDON AND NEW YORK

First published 2009
by Routledge
2 Park Square, Milton Park, Abingdon, Oxon OX14 4RN

Simultaneously published in the USA and Canada
by Routledge
270 Madison Ave, New York, NY 10016

Routledge is an imprint of the Taylor & Francis Group, an informa business

In association with
The Open University,
Walton Hall,
Milton Keynes MK7 6AA,
United Kingdom.

Typeset in Bembo
by Keystroke, Tettenhall, Wolverhampton
Printed and bound
by the MPG Books Group in the UK

British Library Cataloguing in Publication Data
A catalogue record for this book is available from the British Library

Library of Congress Cataloguing in Publication Data
The concise companion to strategic human resource management / edited
by John Storey, Patrick M. Wright and Dave Ulrich.
p. cm.
Includes bibliographical references and index.
1. Personnel management. I. Storey, John, 1947– II. Wright, Patrick M.
III. Ulrich, David, 1953–
HF5549.C71157 2009
658.3'01—dc22
2009024727

ISBN10: 0-415–57719–4 (pbk)
ISBN13: 978–0–415–57719–1 (pbk)

Contents

CONTENTS

Illustrations

Figures

Tables

Contributors

John W. Boudreau is Research Director at the Center for Effective Organizations, and Professor of Management and Organization at the Marshall School of Business, University of Southern California. He is recognized worldwide for over twenty-five years of breakthrough research on links between human capital and competitive advantage. A Fellow of the National Academy of Human Resources, he has received scholarly contribution and research innovation awards from the Academy of Management. He consults and conducts research worldwide, with organizations as diverse as the Global 100, early-stage entrepreneurial companies, and the U.S. Navy. He is the co-author of *Beyond HR* and *Investing in People*, as well as over fifty scholarly articles and chapters.

David E. Bowen is the G. Robert & Katherine Herberger Chair in Global Management at the Thunderbird School of Global Management. His work focuses on HRM organizational behavior issues associated with delivering service quality. His book, *Winning the Service Game*, with Benjamin Schneider, has been published in five languages. He is a past recipient of the Scholarly Achievement Award from the Human Resource Division, Academy of Management, and the Best Paper Award, Academy of Management Perspectives.

Wayne Brockbank is Clinical Professor of Business at the Ross School of Business at the University of Michigan. He is a faculty director and core instructor of its Human Resource Executive Programs. Over the past eighteen years, these have been consistently rated as the best HR executive programs in the United States and Europe by *BusinessWeek* and *Fortune*. He is director of the Michigan Human Resource Executive Programs in Hong Kong, Dubai, Singapore, and India. His research focuses on links between HR practices and business strategy, high-value-added HR strategies, and implementing business strategy through people. He has published many academic and popular articles on these topics. He is the co-author with Dave Ulrich of *Competencies for the New HR* and the *Human Resource Value Proposition*. Among his clients have been General Electric, ICICI Bank (India), Harley-Davidson, Citicorp, Cisco, General Motors, Saudi Aramco, Texas Instruments, BP, Goldman Sachs, and Hewlett-Packard.

David A. Buchanan is Professor of Organizational Behaviour at Cranfield University School of Management. He holds a degree in business administration and another in organizational behaviour from Heriot-Watt and Edinburgh Universities respectively. He has also held positions in universities in Scotland, Canada and Australia. He is the author of numerous books, book chapters, and papers on various aspects of organizational behaviour. Research interests include the management of change, change agency, factors influencing the sustainability and spread of new working practices in healthcare, and the management experience and use of organization politics. Current projects include a study of links between corporate governance arrangements and performance in healthcare organizations.

David Coats has been Associate Director (Policy) at The Work Foundation since February 2004. He is responsible for TWF's engagement with the public policy world, seeking to influence the national conversation about the world of work. David was a member of the Low Pay Commission from 2000 to 2004 and was appointed to the Central Arbitration Committee (the UK's industrial court) in 2005. He also serves on the National Stakeholder Council, advising the government on the implementation of the Work and Well-Being Strategy.

Barry Gerhart is Professor of Management and Human Resources and the Bruce R. Ellig Distinguished Chair in Pay and Organizational Effectiveness, School of Business, University of Wisconsin-Madison. His research interests include compensation, human resource strategy, international human resources, and employee movement. Professor Gerhart received his B.S. in Psychology from Bowling Green State University and his PhD in Industrial Relations from the University of Wisconsin-Madison. He serves on the editorial boards of the *Academy of Management Journal, Human Relations, Industrial and Labor Relations Review, International Journal of Human Resource Management, Journal of Management and Organization, Management Review,* and *Personnel Psychology*. Professor Gerhart is a past recipient of the Scholarly Achievement Award and of the International Human Resource Management Scholarly Research Award, both from the Human Resources Division, Academy of Management. He is also a Fellow of the American Psychological Association and of the Society for Industrial and Organizational Psychology.

Manuel London is Associate Dean of the College of Business, Director of the Center for Human Resource Management in the College of Business, and Professor of Management and Psychology at the State University of New York at Stony Brook. He received his PhD from the Ohio State University in industrial and organizational psychology. He taught at the University of Illinois at Champaign before moving to AT&T as a researcher and human resource manager. He joined Stony Brook in 1989. He has written extensively on the topics of 360-degree feedback, continuous learning, career dynamics, and management development. He is co-author with Marilyn London of *First Time Leaders of Small Groups: How to Create High-Performing Committees, Task Forces, Clubs, and Boards* (2007) and, with Valerie Sessa, *Continuous Learning: Individual, Group, and Organizational Perspectives* (2006).

Edward M. Mone has more than twenty-five years of experience in career, leadership, and organization change and development. He is currently Vice President for Organization Development at CA, Inc. He was previously vice president for organization development at Cablevision and director of people processes and systems at Booz Allen Hamilton, Inc. He was HR division manager for strategic planning and development at AT&T, where he also held a variety of human resource and organization development positions. He is an adjunct faculty member in the College of Business, State University of New York at Stony Brook. He holds an MA in counseling psychology, and has completed doctoral coursework in organizational psychology, as well as individual, team, and organization learning at Teachers College, Columbia University. He has co-authored and co-edited books, book chapters, and articles in the areas of human resources and organization development, including *HR to the Rescue: Case Studies of HR Solutions to Business Challenges* (1998) and *Fundamentals of Performance Management* (2003).

S. Douglas Pugh is an Associate Professor of Management in the Belk College of Business at the University of North Carolina at Charlotte, and an Associate Professor in the interdisciplinary program in organizational science. Previously he was a faculty member at San Diego State University. He received his PhD degree in organizational behavior from Tulane University's A. B. Freeman School of Business. His research includes the study of organizational climate in service organizations and on the emotional labor demands of service work. He has published his research in outlets including the *Academy of Management Journal, Academy of Management Executive, Journal of Applied Psychology, Journal of Occupational and Organizational Psychology, Journal of Business Ethics,* and *Organizational Behavior and Human Decision Processes.*

Peter M. Ramstad is Vice President, Human Resources and Business Development of the Toro Company, a role that includes leadership of the human resources function. Formerly at Personnel Decisions International (PDI), a global leader in helping organizations build superior strategies that provide a competitive advantage, he also served as the firm's CFO for several years. Prior to joining PDI, he was a partner in the consulting division of McGladrey & Pullen and specialized in information technology and financial consultation. He has served as an executive education faculty member at several universities and is published in Harvard Business Review and other periodicals.

Anthony J. Rucci is Senior Lecturer in the Department of Management at Ohio State University. He was an executive officer for twenty-five years with three international companies: Baxter International, Sears Roebuck and Co., and Cardinal Health. His roles have included global responsibility for corporate strategy and development, legal, human resources, information technology, quality and regulatory affairs, media and investor relations and corporate branding. He has been Chairman of the Board of Sears de Mexico and Dean of the College of Business at the University of Illinois at Chicago. He has published over twenty-five journal articles and book chapters, and has delivered over 125 invited keynote addresses at major conferences over the past ten years. He holds Bachelors, Masters and PhD degrees in organizational psychology from Bowling Green State University.

Scott A. Snell is Professor of Business Administration in the Leadership and Organization area at the University of Virginia. He is the author of over fifty publications in professional journals and edited texts and has co-authored three books: *Management: Leading and Collaborating in a Competitive World, Managing Human Resources,* and *Managing People and Knowledge in Professional Service Firms.* Professor Snell has worked with companies such as American Express, AstraZeneca, CIGNA, Deutsche Telekom, Shell, and the World Bank to address the alignment of human resource issues and strategic management. He was formerly professor and director of executive education at Cornell University's Center for Advanced Human Resource Studies.

John Storey is Professor of Human Resource Management at the Open University Business School and Chairman of the Involvement & Participation Association (IPA). He is an Elected Fellow of the British Academy of Management, a Fellow of the Higher Education Academy and a member of the UK Government's Leadership & Management Panel. He was Editor of the *Human Resource Management Journal* 1994–2000. He was the Principal Investigator on the ESRC project "Manager's Roles in the Evolution of Knowledge" which was part of the ESRC Programme on The Evolution of Business Knowledge; he is currently Principal Investigator on the three-year NHS-funded project on "Comparative Governance and Comparative Performance". His books include: *Developments in the Management of Human Resources*, *The Management of Innovation*, and *Leadership in Organizations*, and he co-authored *Managers of Innovation*. He has extensive consultancy experience at senior management and board level.

Dave Ulrich is a Professor of Business at the Ross School of Management at the University of Michigan and a partner in the RBL Group (www.rbl.net). He has published over a dozen books and hundreds of articles on issues of leadership and HR. He has created award-winning databases and consulted in hundreds of companies. His work centers on defining and delivering value to internal and external stakeholders. He likes the pursuit of ideas with impact as he bridges theory and practice.

Theresa M. Welbourne is Adjunct Professor of Executive Education at the Ross School of Business, the University of Michigan. Prior to her adjunct work with Michigan, she was a full-time professor at the University of Michigan and at Cornell University. She is the founder, President, and CEO of eePulse, Inc., a technology and management research company delivering web-based leadership tools that transform real-time business information from employees into real-time results for organizations. With over twenty-five years in the HR field, her particular focus is on understanding how various human resource, communication, and leadership strategies can harness employee and customer energy to improve firm performance. Her research has been featured in popular publications such as *Inc. Magazine*, *Wall Street Journal*, *The Financial Times*, *BusinessWeek*, *New York Times*, and *Entrepreneur Magazine*. Her work has been published in several books and in journals such as the *Academy of Management Journal*, *Journal of Management*, *Human Resource Planning*, *Journal of Organization Behavior*, *Compensation and Benefits Review*, *Journal of Applied Psychology*, and *Journal of High Technology Management Research*. She is the Editor-in-Chief of *Human Resource Management*.

Patrick M. Wright is the William J. Conaty GE Professor of Strategic Human Resources in the School of Industrial and Labor Relations, Cornell University, and Senior Research Fellow in the School of Social Sciences at Tilburg University. He holds a BA in psychology from Wheaton College, and an MBA and a PhD in Organizational Behavior/Human Resource Management from Michigan State University. Professor Wright teaches, conducts research, and consults in the area of Strategic Human Resource Management (SHRM), focusing particularly on how firms use people as a source of competitive advantage. He has published over sixty research articles, twenty chapters in books and edited volumes, co-authored a leading HRM textbook (now in its 6th edition), and co-authored or co-edited six books.

Introduction

John Storey, Dave Ulrich
and Patrick M. Wright

Strategic Human Resource Management is concerned with the constellation of policies and practices relating to the interaction between people and organization designed to enable an organization to achieve its purposes. As such, it is both a field of practice and a field of study.

This *Concise Companion* is designed to bridge research and practice. It does not speculate about why there may be a divide or propose what might be done about it, rather, it seeks to show how there is much of mutual relevance between current theory and practice. Practice anchors theory and theory informs practice. One without the other is incomplete.

Strategic HRM and performance outcomes

The fundamental premise underpinning any serious discussion within SHRM is that a causal connection exists between HR practices and organizational performance (measured in various ways and against various outcome criteria). Without such an assumption, the only rationale for allocating time and effort in HR from a management point of view would be to comply with prevailing employment laws or to meet minimum operational requirements in hiring, firing and labour deployment and the like.

At the most basic level, scholars have sought to measure the statistical correlations between the existence of certain HR practices and a range of performance outcomes. While such statistical relationships may be fairly crude measures and subject to all manner of caveats they provide a starting point to show the relevance of HR research.

Investments in HR impact on individuals and organizations. At the individual, or human capital level, investing in HR practices may increase either competence or commitment of the individual employee. Competence is comprised of knowledge and skills including tacit knowledge as well as formal knowledge. This 'human capital' embedded in individuals can be enhanced through education, training and development, or aligned compensation system. Individuals may become more competent in delivering an organization's financial or strategic goals (e.g., learning to do business in China). Commitment deals with engagement or application of knowledge to a particular condition or setting. Regardless of competence, individuals may be more or less committed to the extent that they dedicate their energy and attention to a particular set of goals. HR practices may focus and enhance how much individuals attend to a particular set of issues through staffing, compensation, or training.

Commitment deals with 'effort'. This has always been a point of focus for HR, labour relations and staff management of all kinds. Human capital is unique in the inherent variability with which it can be deployed. No matter how regulated the job, people tend to have degrees of *discretionary effort* which they can withhold or commit. As a result, a great deal of time has been spent in thinking about how managers can 'motivate' and how they can 'engage' workers so that they will be sufficiently committed as to go the extra mile in their work. This attempt to win hearts and minds has long been core to HRM. Much recent discussion of the theme when applied to the application of effort towards organizational-wide rather than 'merely' task focus is based on the concept of 'organizational citizenship behaviour'.

However, individuals do not usually work in a vacuum. They are surrounded by co-workers; peers, subordinates, and managers in their work group, as well as in other work groups across the organization. Often, the effectiveness of one's own contributions depends upon the network of relationships s/he has with others around the firm. Competitive advantage can derive from a combination of social capital and human or intellectual capital. The implication is that SHRM needs not only to tackle the resourcing and development of individual abilities but in addition to attend also to the fuller utilization and development of shared and *complementary capabilities*.

SHRM has to deal holistically with a range of variables. In dealing with the range of variables, theorists and practitioners have developed a number of analytical frameworks to guide thinking and decisions about the linkages between HR, strategy, and various individual and organizational outcomes.

Analytical frameworks

Contemporary SHRM is the confluence between diverse streams of academic work. The field of HRM has various roots in economics, sociology, and psychology, and similarly SHRM has evolved as a somewhat multidisciplinary field of inquiry. The resource based view of the firm has been especially influential. The resource based view focuses on the valuable and unique internal resources and capabilities that firms possess that enable them to outperform their competitors. Building from this framework many early authors focused on the concept of 'human capital' or the talent pool as having the potential to be sources of competitive advantage. Different human capital pools within the firm vary in terms of the value and uniqueness of their skills, and these differences imply different HR systems to manage them. Moving another step forward in this train of thought, Boudreau and Ramstad (see Chapter 1) contend that the part of HR focused on talent is ripe for upgrading into a more sophisticated 'Decision Science'.

An additional set of analytical approaches tends to not only focus on how individuals perform but also on how organizations perform through the capabilities embedded in an organization. This is examined in the course through units on organization culture and building organizational capability. Chapters 4 and 5 in this volume add depth to these discussions.

The nature and purpose of strategic HRM does not stand still. It is honed and shaped by global, national and local currents and is thus ever-changing. Hence 'solutions' are time specific. These currents are multiple in nature including political, legal, economic, social and cultural. Key changes impacting massively on HRM include globalization, technological changes, migration and demographic changes, ownership structures, and customer expectations to name just the salient ones.

Globalization undoubtedly has been one of the major factors driving organizational change. As transportation has enabled the movements of goods and people more quickly and easily, companies have been able to expand their products and services into other markets. Early on, globalization required HR to understand how to manage people from different countries and geographies, but the work in each was largely the same. However, the recent advances in telecommunications have enabled the mass migration of work to whatever area of the globe provides the necessary skills to perform that work at the lowest cost. The phenomenon of 'globalization' takes numerous forms including off-shoring, relocation of headquarters, changes in corporate ownership, challenges of immigration, new strategic alliances, joint ventures, and other forms of cross-boundary working such as global teams, global sourcing, mass migration and so on.

The resulting degree of competition for jobs as a result of globalization has meant that the sophisticated 'commitment model' of HRM with its integrated package of high performance fuelled by high pay and benefits, excellent training, careful selection and the like has not been the only response from employers. Some employers using global sourcing have outsourced key jobs in a search for low cost labour. This and related dilemmas are explored throughout B827.

The Ten Selected Chapters

The ten chapters in this volume have been chosen because they provide complementary supports to the units and the on-line-assets of B827. Here's how:

Chapter 1: 'Beyond HR: Extending the paradigm through a talent decision science' by John Boudreau and Peter M. Ramstad. This chapter is a cutting edge piece which argues and seeks to demonstrate how HR considerations can be utilized when they are framed as part of a decision science. This chapter is based on an award winning Harvard Business School book and there is an accompanying video of John Boudreau explaining his thesis on the B827 Course website. It can be used to add further depth to Units 1 and 3. It is at times a challenging piece and may require more than one read.

Chapter 2: 'Changing Labour Markets and the Future of Work' by David Coats is selected because it puts people management decisions within the wider context of changing labour markets. It fits alongside Unit 2 on organisational forms.

Chapter 3: 'The Pursuit of HR's Core Purpose: The practical doing of strategic HRM' by Anthony J. Rucci is selected because it firmly locates the kinds of decisions which Boudreau and Ramstad are talking about within the 'core purpose' of making organizations more effective. Its starting assumption is similar to that adopted within B827 – namely that the perspective adopted is that of the senior strategic team which is required to weigh competing priorities. It complements Units 1 and 3.

Chapter 4: 'Managing Strategic Change' by David A. Buchanan is selected because it complements Unit 4 on 'Shaping Organisational Culture'. It is not specifically about culture change but it does address the practical issues of *how* to manage a change of that nature.

Chapter 5: 'HR Competencies that Make a Difference' by Wayne Brockbank and Dave Ulrich is a useful accompaniment to Units 3 (using HR specialists) and 7 (on capability building). It disaggregates and analyses the skills which constitute a competent HR strategist.

Chapter 6: 'Compensation' by Barry Gerhart is selected in order to provide a sound briefing on the various types of reward. It supports Unit 6 on performance management.

Chapter 7: 'Strategic Performance Management: Issues and Trends' by Manuel London and Edward M. Mone is selected because it explains the nature of performance management from a strategic perspective. It too supports Unit 6 of B827.

Chapter 8: 'Employee Engagement' by John Storey, Dave Ulrich, Theresa M. Welbourne and Patrick M. Wright gets to the heart of the issues explored in Unit 5. It attends to the four key questions in this area: what does engagement entail, what are the outcomes, what are the methods and what are the challenges?

Chapter 9: 'Human Resources, Organizational Resources, and Capabilities' by Patrick M. Wright and Scott A. Snell. This chapter supports Unit 7 on Building Capability. It explains human capital and social capital as underpinning the capabilities of organisations. It links capabilities to the idea of a value chain and it also introduces the idea of dynamic capabilities.

Chapter 10: 'Linking Human Resource Management and Customer Outcomes' by David E. Bowen and Douglas S. Pugh. This chapter supports Unit 8 on Evaluation. At its heart is the model which links HRM practices and customer outcomes – a model which we first introduce in Unit 1 of your course. This chapter thus serves to link the initial ideas and frameworks of the course with the final unit which is concerned with how we can know what policies and practices make a difference.

We hope as a course team that you will find the resources in this Companion to be a useful and enjoyable complement to your study of B827 Strategic Human Resource Management.

1

Beyond HR

Extending the paradigm through a talent decision science

John W. Boudreau and Peter M. Ramstad

Introduction

Why are professional disciplines such as Finance and Marketing so powerful in the minds of organization leaders, yet the discipline of HR remains stubbornly associated with personnel administration or human resource practices and programs? In this chapter, we propose that the hallmark of strategic disciplines such as Marketing and Finance is the foundational "decision science" on which they are based. We argue that such a decision science is about to emerge in the arena of the talent market. This evolution echoes the way Finance emerged in the early twentieth century to guide decisions about how organizations compete for and with the resource of money, and as Marketing emerged around the 1950s to guide decisions about how organizations compete for and with the resources of customers and offerings. We have called this the "essential evolution."

History shows that as a resource becomes more pivotal to strategic success, more scarce, and more analytically tractable, a decision science for that resource emerges to redefine its market. These are precisely the conditions that characterize the talent market today, and that characterized the markets for money and customers/offerings in early eras.

This chapter will describe the foundational elements of a talent decision science, and illustrates how those elements will evolve, by comparing the talent market to examples of more mature markets. We will also describe how the decision science principles that support this essential evolution will redefine the future of talent management, HR strategy, and indeed organizational strategic success.

Why a "decision science?"

We began using the term *decision science* around 1999/2000 to capture the essence of the way the underlying paradigm for HR was evolving. Since then, its use has become increasingly common among HR executives, thought leaders, and academics. The 2005 book of essays by thought leaders on the future of HR co-published by the Society for Human Resource Management contains an entire section entitled "See HR as a Decision Science and Bring Discipline to It" (Lossey et al., 2005). This section includes not only a chapter from us that applies talentship concepts to the sustainable enterprise (Boudreau and Ramstad, 2005b), but also other chapters such as "Science Explodes Human Capital Mythology"; "Human Resource Accounting, Human Capital Management, and the Bottom Line"; "Improving Human Resources' Analytical Literacy"; and "The Dual Theory of Human Resource Management and Business Performance."

Yet there is no widely accepted definition of, or a methodology for, a talent decision science. For decades there has been a general science of decisions and decision making, producing insights about how decision makers behave and the factors that enhance and reduce their rationality and accuracy. Our concept of a decision science for talent draws on this research. As we shall see, the components of a decision science help define the necessary elements for improving talent decisions and the relevance of the HR profession.

Stubborn traditionalism in HR management

In 2005 an article appeared in *Fast Company* entitled "Why We Hate HR" (Hammonds, 2005). It chronicled many of the all-too-common symptoms of a profession that focuses on administrative activities, requires compliance with rules, demonstrates little logical connection to strategic value, and works diligently on functional programs and practices that have no clear connection to business goals. The article has received a lot of attention. In 2006 a Web search on the title produced over twelve thousand hits, and its author asserts that it got more response than any *Fast Company* article in the prior two years (compensation.blr.com, 2006).

What many people don't remember is that in 1981 there was a similar article in the *Harvard Business Review* entitled "Big Hat, No Cattle" (Skinner, 1981). The title referred to a "tall, well-dressed businessman" in the Dallas, Texas, airport "wearing a large and immaculate Stetson hat." Nearby, two middle-aged, sunburned men in faded jeans looked him up and down and said to each other, "Big hat, no cattle." The businessman dressed like a cattleman but really had no herd. The sunburned men were the real cattle ranchers, and they didn't need to prove it with a big hat. In 1981 HR had the executive title and the executive offices, and looked and dressed like other business leaders, but the article asserted that all too often there was no evidence of real contribution to business success.

It's the same story twenty-five years apart. As we'll see, this doesn't mean that the HR profession hasn't progressed. It has. It doesn't mean that business leaders don't want to compete better for and with talent and how it is organized. They do. It *does* suggest that after twenty-five years of admonishments that HR professionals become strategic business partners, and calls for business leaders to tap the potential in their people, organizations still have not produced the kind of change we would expect. There is an answer to this problem, but it is not to continue doing the same thing better, and it is not achieved by the HR function alone.

Evidence from many sources confirms that the HR profession has made many technical advances, but in many ways it has changed little. Perhaps the most vivid evidence comes from a unique survey done by the Center for Effective Organizations. Beginning in 1995, HR professionals were asked how much time they spent on strategic pursuits compared to administrative pursuits. They noted the time they remembered spending on various activities five to seven years ago, and then they noted the time they currently spend. Every year the responses suggested that HR professionals perceived a statistically significant shift toward more strategic activities. Yet, when we examine what HR leaders said were their actual activities, then in every survey since 1995 virtually the same percentages have been reproduced each time (Lawler et al., 2006).

Obviously, today's arsenal of HR activities is very different and more sophisticated than it was in the mid-1990s, and of course, HR professionals are doing different things and doing many things better. There are improved information systems, scorecards, benchmarks, outsourcing contracts, and competency models. Workforce plans can now track the headcount moving between jobs using computerized databases and forecasting algorithms. Selection testing is done through kiosks or online surveys. These are better versions of the same tools that HR has been using for decades, and they have made important differences in the efficiency and effectiveness of the HR function. Yet by their own reports, HR professionals' focus is still largely on administrative and service-related goals, not on strategic decisions. The Center for Effective Organizations data vividly reveal a profession that is getting better at the traditional paradigm— but as we shall see, the opportunities for breakthrough strategic successes lie in a new, extended paradigm.

Talentship: the new decision science

As we will see below, the lessons from marketing and finance tell us that the goal of a talent decision science would be to increase the organization's success by improving decisions that impact or depend on talent resources. We have coined the term *talentship* to describe the new decision science and to reflect the notion of stewardship of employee talent resources. Talentship is to "human resource management," as finance is to accounting, and as marketing is to sales. The talentship decision science provides a logic that connects human capital, organizational design, organizational effectiveness, and ultimately, strategic success.

We considered for some time what to call the resource that is the focus of the talentship decision science. Finance deals with the resource of money, marketing deals with the resources of customers and offerings. We will use the word *talent* to mean *the potential and realized capacities of individuals and groups and how they are organized, including those within the organization and those who might join the organization.*

The talent resource as we define it includes not just the talents that an organization currently tracks and manages, but all those talents that are potentially available and valuable, if only you knew about them. It includes not just the people you have and how they are organized but the people you could potentially engage and the organizing decisions you could make about them. In the future, this may even go well beyond traditional employment. For example, a trend called "crowdsourcing" involves tapping customers and outside experts who are not employees, to contribute to organizational objectives. News organizations tap viewers to send in photos or videos of breaking news. Consumer products organizations tap their customers to create imaginative video ads they can post to the company website. Online search companies send mapping kits to local residents of remote regions to create more detailed maps. This is not traditional employment, yet it is certainly competing for and with talent in creative ways. Thus, the talent resource must transcend even traditional ideas about employment.

Improving the decisions about this talent resource is the domain of talentship. The talent resource includes not only the abilities of individuals; it also includes their motivations and the opportunities they encounter. It includes concepts such as human capital and knowledge. The decision science of talentship includes a structure for improving decisions about how to enhance individual contributions, and also how to enhance the way individuals interact in formal and informal groups, organizational designs, structures, and so on. Talentship is concerned with improving decisions about the talents of people and how they organize and interact.

Distinctions between markets, decision sciences, and professional practices

If we want to understand how a profession becomes strategic, we can't do it by looking within the profession or by asking internal customers whether it is strategic. Neither the HR profession nor the training of HR's constituents has prepared them to define the necessary strategic requirements. History shows that we must begin where strategy is formed and enacted, in the *markets* where organizations compete and thrive.

Consider three markets vital to organizational success: the financial market, the customer/ offering market, and the talent market. In the financial and customer/offering markets, there is a clear distinction between the professional practice that defines how organizations operate in the market and the decision science used to analyze and deploy the resources there. For example, there is a clear distinction between accounting (the professional practice) and finance (the decision science). Accounting is vital for management reporting and external requirements, while finance develops tools used to make decisions about appropriate debt structure, internal rate-of-return thresholds, and so forth. There is an equally clear distinction between the professional practice of sales and the decision science of marketing. Excellent sales practices and measures are vital, but they're very different from the tools used to make decisions about customer segmentation, market position, and the product portfolio.

Today the differences between accounting and finance are so clear that we seldom even consider them. The competencies to be a successful accountant are related to but are clearly distinct from those needed to make a successful financial executive (CFO, treasurer, etc.), and professional curricula reflect this. The industry itself has segmented this way—large accounting firms are very different from investment banking firms that focus on finance. Similarly, the competencies and activities of sales are clearly distinct from those of marketing.

This does not mean that the professional practice is merely administrative or less important. The decision science cannot exist without the professional practice; the professional practice must, in fact, precede the decision science. Few organizations survive with great marketing and ineffective sales, or with great finance and unprofessional accounting. Today the synergy between accounting and finance, or between sales and marketing, is so strong that it is easy to overlook how the decision sciences evolved from the professional practices and how they are both inextricably related yet distinct. Taking a closer look at this symbiotic relationship between the professional practice and the decision science reveals insights about the evolution of HR and the talent decision science that will change it.

Like finance and marketing, HR helps the firm operate within a critical market—in this case, the market for talent. Organizations cannot succeed in the financial and customer markets without both effective decisions and effective professional practices, but they are two very distinct elements. In the talent market, organizations will also increasingly compete through the synergy of effective decisions aligned with professional practices. When we see this distinction applied to HR and talent, we see that decision processes for competing in the talent market are less mature and refined than those used in the markets for money and customers/offerings. Yet, HR *professional practices* are often as mature as accounting and sales. Today the distinction between professional practices and effective decision systems is less clear in the talent market. Yet a clear understanding of this difference reveals the path for the coming evolution. Next, let us consider the power of combining *decisions* and *science*.

Decisions

Why focus on decisions? Service excellence alone cannot achieve strategic success through resources like money, talent and customers, because such decisions are integral and ongoing in the organization, not isolated within a single function or a particular yearly cycle. The majority of decisions that depend on or impact financial capital or customers are made by leaders and employees *outside the finance and marketing functions*. This is also true for talent decisions.

When we ask leaders inside or outside of HR to think of a decision that depended on or affected talent resources but in retrospect was not made well, even companies with best-in-class HR functions can describe numerous examples. The lessons from these examples are remarkably consistent. The talent decisions are *not* typically made by HR professionals. Poor talent decisions seldom have poor HR programs as the root cause. Rather, they were made by well-intentioned leaders outside of the HR profession, trying very diligently to be logical and strategic, but using poor talent decision models. So, they create unintended and unanticipated negative talent implications.

For example, one highly specialized high-tech firm made a decision to relocate to be closer to its key customer, one that accounted for well over 50 percent of revenues. The decision logic was that the organization could more efficiently and quickly serve this large customer by locating its operations closer. This is a talent decision being made with an operational efficiency logic. What was overlooked was that the key services required certain talent—several sophisticated and highly specialized experts. When the relocation requirement was announced, many of these essential experts left the organization, creating a disruption that was far more damaging to client relationships and the company's reputation than any possible benefits of proximity. The decision required integrating perspectives from finance, marketing, operations and talent. The financial, marketing and operational elements were logically considered, but the failure to accurately consider the talent implications undermined the intended benefits.

Several senior executives we have worked with have noted that HR strategies often reflect traditionally critical industry needs, such as "avoid employee strikes" in companies where unionized manufacturing is vital and where leaders often worked in labor relations before advancing to top HR roles. In many sales organizations the rallying cry is "reduce turnover" because turnover costs among top salespeople are so apparent. HR leaders point out that without a logical decision framework, such goals can become so prominent that they mask other significant organizational needs. It is not appropriate to do absolutely anything required to avoid a union strike, nor to spend indiscriminately to reduce turnover.

The greatest opportunity to improve decisions about talent and how it is organized is by improving those decisions that are made outside the HR function. Just as with decisions about financial and customer resources, talent decisions reside with executives, managers, supervisors, and employees. They make decisions that affect the talent over whom they are responsible, the talent they interact with, and their own personal human capital. Even in functional HR processes—such as succession planning, performance management, selection, and leadership development—potential improvements in effectiveness rely far more heavily on improving the competency and engagement of non-HR leaders than on anything that HR typically controls directly.

The relocation example is typical in that most significant business decisions impact multiple resources, so the objective should be to equip leaders with more comprehensive decision frameworks. It's not a matter of choosing between people versus profits, with the organization's financial controller arguing for profits and the HR leader acting as the employee advocate. Instead, the goal is a decision science that enables leaders to integrate talent resources with other vital resources. To be sure, this improves talent and organization decisions, but its ultimate goal is to improve strategic decisions more broadly.

Science

Why use the term *science*? Because the most successful professions have decision systems that follow scientific principles and that have a strong capacity to quickly incorporate new scientific knowledge into practical applications. Disciplines such as finance, marketing, and operations not only provide leaders with frameworks and concepts that describe how those resources affect strategic success; they also reflect the findings from universities, research centers, and scholarly journals. Their decision models are compatible with the language and structure of the scholarly science that supports them.

For example, in operations research there is often a very close connection between the technical tools used in industry and the scholarly research that informs them. In the arena of total quality management (TQM), the decision frameworks used by managers reflect fundamental logical elements—such as plan, do, check, and act—that translate into logical connections with such processes as inspection, maintenance, adjustment, and equipment replacement. This logic allows managers' decision models to be quickly informed by research on topics like statistical process control, control charts, and time-series statistical analysis. It also provides a context for researchers, who frame their research questions consistently with the logic and practical issues facing leaders who apply TQM (Schroeder et al., 2005).

With talent, the logical frameworks used by leaders often bear distressingly little similarity to the scholarly research in HR and human behavior at work (Colbert et al., 2005). This is regrettable because there is much that leaders can learn from scholarly findings and much that scholars can learn by better incorporating business leaders' insights into their research (Boudreau, 2003). Consider the contrast between the scientific approach to bond ratings in finance versus employee assessment practices in HR. Both strive to provide a valid and reliable measure of the future performance of an asset with some risk. A treasury department is expected to purchase information on scientifically rigorous bond ratings in its investment decisions. HR functions often cannot generate support for more scientific employee assessment investments (valid tests, interviews, assessment centers, surveys, etc.) because their constituents don't see the value. In fact, frameworks for comparing the costs of employment testing to their benefits have existed since the 1940s, but they are not widely used, in part because organizations' decision frameworks have few connections to the logical principles of these models (Cascio and Boudreau, 2008).

A decision science also approaches decisions through a scientific method, which means that questions are framed so that they are testable and falsifiable with data-based results. It means that the logic supporting the decision science is modified when new findings make old ideas obsolete. It means that the decision framework clearly translates new scientific findings into practical implications. This scientific method includes, but goes well beyond, a fact-based approach to HR. Many articles that carry the label of "decision science" are about improved analytics, measurement, or scorecards. Deeper measures and data are certainly an element of a decision science, as we will describe later, but much of the data being used by HR lack a logical framework required to advance either decisions or science.

A true decision science does more than just incorporate facts and measures. A decision science draws on and informs scientific study related to the resource. There is a vast array of research about human behavior at work, labor markets, and how organizations can better compete with and for talent and organization resources. Such disciplines as psychology, economics, sociology, organization theory, game theory, and even operations management and human physiology all contain potent research frameworks and findings. Unfortunately, the transfer of such findings into actual decisions is often woefully slow or nonexistent. Indeed, studies suggest that even HR professionals are often surprisingly unaware of findings that are routinely accepted by the HR academic research community (Colbert et al., 2005). A decision science connects research to the practical dilemmas facing decision makers in organizations. It also provides a means to apply research on talent and organization to other fields and to bring insights from other scientific fields (such as operations, strategy, marketing, etc.) to bear on talent decisions within organizations.

Components of a talent decision science

There are five important elements in a mature decision science:

- decision framework;
- management systems integration;
- shared mental model;
- data, measurement, and analysis;
- focus on optimization.

We will describe each component in detail below, but it is important to understand how they fit together. The decision framework is the logic that connects decisions about a resource and their ultimate effects on organizational success. It defines how decision makers should logically think about these connections. Without this logic, even the most elegant systems and measures can fail because decision makers simply do not know how to interpret the information they provide. The second element is the logic integrated into management systems. When a valid and consistent logic is embedded in management systems, they become powerful tools. Consider how powerfully the finance and accounting systems incorporate principles such as net present value or internal rate of return. The third element flows naturally from the first two. Valid and useful logic that is embedded in the management systems that decision makers use will cause decision makers to better understand and value the logical frameworks. They begin to develop shared mental models that define the vital connection points in their decisions about the resource. Organization leaders understand market segmentation so well, in part because the principles of market segmentation are seamlessly embedded in virtually every customer relationship management system. The fourth element of data, measurement and analysis is often the only way that HR leaders try to enhance decisions—giving leaders more numbers. Yet, as we can see, more data is hardly helpful without a shared and logical framework to understand it. In marketing and finance, the data and measures flow naturally from the shared logical models and thus are more easily understood and used. Finally, the fifth element, a focus on optimization, means that when the logic, systems and measures are well developed, it is not sufficient merely to maximize outcomes or describe activities. Organizations do not strive merely to maximize the capacity of every machine on an assembly line. Rather, they optimize capacity by balancing between machines, and focusing on bottlenecks. Organizations do not strive to maximize customer service for every market segment. Rather, they optimize customer service to reflect the strategic value of different market segments, providing greater service where it has the largest payoff.

Too often today, HR and talent systems focus either on describing the activities of the function, or on attempting to maximize outcomes everywhere. Typical examples are setting goals that every manager increase employee engagement, that every employee increase their learning, or that every position be populated with the best performers. None of these goals is likely to optimize. As we shall see below, one of the most important implications of a decision science for talent is that it will lead to frameworks that help organizations differentially increase learning, engagement, performance and other talent outcomes according to where they have the greatest strategic effect.

Decision framework

The decision framework defines the logical connection between the decisions about a resource and the organization's ultimate goals. It defines how the organization should think about the talent and organizational implications of business decisions in a common and consistent way. It provides the basis for evaluating and improving the decisions that involve the resource.

An effective decision framework provides a consistent logical model of the chain of causal connections divided into independent elements. The DuPont return on equity (ROE) model is a good illustration (Johnson, 1975). There is a goal—ROE—segmented into three elements (margin, asset productivity, and leverage), as shown in Figure 1.1.

ROE is a consistent and logical model that can be expressed as an algebraic formula. It also depicts the causal chain of capital:

$$\text{Equity} \rightarrow \text{Assets} \rightarrow \text{Sales} \rightarrow \text{Profits}$$

Starting at the denominator in the right corner of the model, the causal chain may be described as follows:

- Equity (investment) is used to acquire assets (the ratio of assets to equity is leverage).
- Assets are used to generate sales (the ratio of sales to assets is the asset productivity).
- Sales generate profits (the ratio of profits to sales is the margin).

There is a significant amount of independence between margin, asset productivity, and leverage. While there is almost never complete independence between the elements, a good decision framework will achieve as much as possible. Within the DuPont model, lowering the cost of goods sold could increase margins without affecting asset productivity or leverage. Increasing the accounts receivable could improve asset productivity without affecting margin or leverage. Finally, reducing equity by increasing debt could increase leverage without affecting asset productivity or operating margin. The same chain of causal connections can also be seen in the decision frameworks from marketing. While there can be many variations, a typical decision framework for marketing is:

Figure 1.1 DuPont return on equity model

Reprinted by permission of Harvard Business School Press, from *Beyond HR: The New Science of Human Capital* by John W. Boudreau and Peter M. Ramstad, Boston, 2007: 30.

The decision framework for talentship

The causal chain for talent and organization decisions may be described as:

Figure 1.2 illustrates the causal logic of finance, marketing, and talentship that we have described. While the analogy is not perfectly precise, you can see that the underlying logic is similar. The point is not that the talentship logic maps perfectly against marketing and finance,

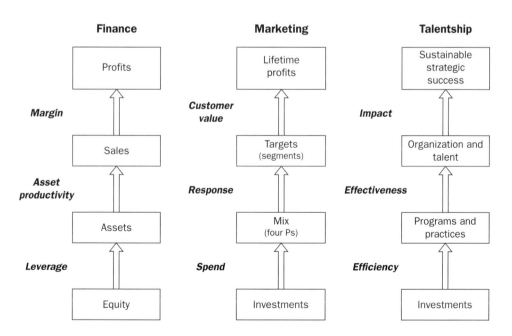

Figure 1.2 Finance, marketing and talentship decision frameworks

Source: Reprinted by permission of Harvard Business School Press from *Beyond HR: The New Science of Human Capital* by John W. Boudreau and Peter M. Ramstad, Boston, 2007: 31.

but rather that it is logically consistent with them. Resources are expended on activities or assets; those activities or assets produce changes in targets, such as sales, customers, and talent pools; those targets produce changes in financial outcomes or other sustainable strategic success factors.

The segments are also independent. You can spend the same amount to produce training activities (efficiency) and get far different results from the training programs and practices (effectiveness). Likewise, you can enhance skills to the same degree in different talent pools (effectiveness), but the outcomes achieved through the new skills can vary significantly. The same level of efficiency can produce different levels of effectiveness. The same level of effectiveness can produce significantly different impact. As we shall see, when organizations lack such a framework, they mistakenly consider only one part of the logical chain (such as squeezing HR budgets to produce more efficiency without considering effectiveness or impact), or they mistakenly assume that improving effectiveness improves impact (such as assuming that if employees have more training, the organization will compete better on its unique knowledge). This framework for organization and talent is called the "HC Bridge" framework, and refers to impact, effectiveness, and efficiency as "anchor points."

Traditional HR decision frameworks are often control systems

HR leaders' common first reaction to talentship and the need for a decision framework for HR is, "We already have many systems designed to help leaders outside HR make decisions, like salary structures and competency systems." Consider salary structures. Virtually everyone knows their salary grade, and employees and managers routinely use salary structures in their decisions about budgeting, headcount planning, merit pay, and other rewards. Because salary grades are often the only available framework for mapping the organization's talent resources, they can become the default framework for things such as signature authority, participation in leadership programs, parking space allocation, and many other decisions unrelated to the original purpose. The salary grade system certainly affects decisions, but it is not a decision framework in the way that we have defined it. It is an organizing framework for the delivery of an HR system, not a decision framework for the resource.

Competency systems that span an enterprise serve a similar purpose. When done well, they provide a common architecture for defining, measuring, and developing capabilities within an organization, including not only the requirements for a job but also the logical progression and important transition points between jobs. Such systems may be used to align key talent management systems, and individual measurement to help develop both individuals and the talent pool overall. Like salary grade structures, they are very important and useful, supporting both decisions and data analysis. Even well-developed versions of competency systems, however, do not provide necessary insight into important business questions such as the talent implications of alternative business models, organizational structures and design, competing talent market value propositions, and the value of HR investments.

Salary structures and competency systems are very similar to the organizing frameworks such as the "chart of accounts" in accounting that existed before the decision science of finance emerged.[1] The chart of accounts provides a classification system to organize large amounts of data, and it certainly improves the consistency of decisions. Like the chart of accounts, the salary grade system provides its primary value through systematic management control. It often creates more value in restraining excessive investment than in identifying areas where increased compensation would optimize organizational value. Competency models emerged more recently, to integrate and align HR services. When compensation and competency systems are integrated within a decision science framework, they become even more powerful and offer potentially greater impact on the organization, because they can be deployed in a more strategically relevant and integrated perspective.

Management systems integration

The next component of a decision science is the integration of its decision framework and key principles into the general management systems. When this is done well, decisions about different resources seamlessly support the overall organization and business processes. Decisions consider all the key resources, including talent, rather than focusing on resources in isolation. This integration also requires more alignment between the general business planning processes and functional planning processes, such as finance, marketing, information technology and talent. For example, planning for the finance and marketing functions is closely tied to planning for the overall organization.

A second important purpose of integrating a consistent and valid logic into management systems is that the logic is then routinely used and understood by leaders outside the functional area. Financial reporting and analysis systems reflect principles such as net present value and return on investment. Customer relationship management systems reflect principles such as market segmentation and lifetime customer profitability. Decision makers using these systems receive consistent reinforcement and encouragement to better understand the logical frameworks that underpin the decision sciences.

For example, financial frameworks are well integrated into general management systems in most organizations. In fact, one challenge to improving talent and organization decisions is that organizations often rely solely on financial management systems and lack well-developed decision systems for other important resources. For example, many organizations have strategic planning processes that focus on preparing the long-range financial plan, rather than on optimizing the overall strategic position across all resources, including talent. It is not so much that the finance function intentionally dominates but rather that its processes and frameworks are much more mature and integrated. The same integration is rarely apparent when it comes to the leadership capabilities that support the financial plan. Yet, those leadership capabilities may be far more pivotal to strategic success.

Which management systems must integrate the decision science?

Two types of management systems must be integrated with a mature decision science for organization and talent:

- Management systems outside the HR function, where talent issues should be considered and addressed, which include strategic planning, product line management, corporate development (e.g. mergers and acquisitions), operational budgeting, and capital budgeting.
- Talent management systems (often within the HR function) that must consider the strategic context of the organization, including workforce planning, staffing, development, performance management, compensation, and succession planning.

It is extremely difficult to change organizations merely by imposing new decision frameworks that compete with the familiar and useful management processes already in place. Too often, HR leaders roll out their new talent planning and decision systems as distinct and separate additions to existing processes. In our experience we've encountered workforce planning systems that have little commonality and integration with the long-range planning processes. HR leaders would often better serve the organization by improving the business planning process by integrating logical principles about talent decisions into existing systems, in partnership with other leaders, rather than deploying new and separate HR processes. When HR and talent planning processes are separate and distinct from the existing core management processes, they risk being less strategically effective.

Illustrating talent decision integration with capital budgeting

Let us illustrate how talent decision frameworks can integrate with management systems using the capital budgeting system, which is well refined in most organizations. A basic financial assumption is that higher returns carry higher risk. Yet, many of the potential risk factors in capital investments are linked to talent resources. One way that capital budgeting could be more integrated with talent decisions is to specifically identify the talent and organization risk factors associated with capital investments (availability and quality of leadership, degree of organizational change required, experience in the organization with the technology, etc.) and then set a higher required minimum return for investments that are higher risk due to organizational factors. Notice how this type of integration does not require leaders to learn a new leadership or talent system, but rather that it exploits the familiarity that leaders already have with the concept of risk, and embeds logical talent resource issues within that risk.

Integration requires aligning the timing of planning processes

Integration of talent and organization systems with management systems must also consider the sequence of planning processes. It is not unusual to encounter organizations where the talent planning process occurs long after the organizational planning process has concluded, and where the HR budget basically distributes the allotted budget for headcount or training. In some organizations HR planning couldn't possibly affect organizational strategic decisions because the HR planning process occurs *after* all the key strategic decisions are made. Even something as simple as adjusting the timing of the HR planning process so its results are available to the broader budgeting and planning process can significantly enhance integration and the resulting decision quality.

Leaders at Pepsi in the 1980s referred to decisions about hiring and training levels as the "human capex," meaning the human capital expenditure plan. They believed that organizations should treat the human capex process as equally important as the financial capex. As John Bronson, former senior vice president at Pepsi, recalls:

> One of the legacies of Andrall [Andy] Pearson at PepsiCo was the MRPA, the management resources planning audit. It was his audit of the talent of the organization. He was unabashed that it was his process, not HR's process, and not even the division presidents' process. He expected leaders to treat their human capex with the same importance as the more traditional financial capex. Andy believed that blue-chip companies required blue-chip players. He was relentless in driving the process through the PepsiCo organization. He was like a merchant banker reviewing a financing plan. If the business—unit CEO couldn't explain how the talent plan supported the growth, budget, and financial capex, not only would his plan be in jeopardy; he might lose his job. To Andy, if you didn't have a solid plan for how talent supported both superior business performance and growth, you weren't a serious contender for larger jobs.
>
> (Boudreau, 2006)

Integration requires professional consistency

A fundamental requirement for the kind of business leader accountability that PepsiCo achieved is a consistent decision framework that is aligned with functional and general management systems. HR is a less mature profession, so there is often less consistency in the decision models used within the profession when compared to more mature fields like finance. Here is one of our favorite discussion questions for business and HR leaders: suppose you asked ten controllers to address a specific financial challenge, and you asked ten HR professionals to address a specific organizational or talent challenge. Where would the responses be more consistent and aligned, among the controllers or among the HR professionals?

The answer is nearly always that there will be less consistency and alignment on the people issues than the financial ones. In addition, HR leaders' different backgrounds, experiences, and perspectives create wide variation in their responses. Often, there is significant misalignment between the guiding logic used by HR professionals at headquarters and those in the business units. Important areas such as performance management, motivation, rewards, learning, and the pipeline of talent are often presented through vastly different theories and logical frameworks. For example, when it comes to employee motivation, some may subscribe to the logic that emphasizes linking rewards to behaviors. Others may subscribe to a perspective that emphasizes creating systems that are perceived as fair. Still others may subscribe to an approach that emphasizes setting appropriately difficult and specific goals. Indeed, all of these approaches are valid, but none of them is valid by itself.

This is a symptom of HR functions operating without a common point of view. Without a consistent decision framework connecting the various elements of the talent management systems and decisions, HR professionals lack a consistent message to integrate their core systems, much less to affect the broader management systems outside the HR function. Thus, aligning internal HR systems, such as talent planning and HR functional planning, with a shared logical framework, is just as important as aligning systems outside of the HR profession with principles of talent markets.

Shared mental models

A successful decision science is used by organizational leaders as a natural part of their work. Its logic elements are a part of the mental models and mind-set of key decision makers inside and outside the profession. A very important obligation of professions with more mature decision sciences is to hold leaders *outside the profession* accountable for the quality of their decision models when it comes to the resource that is the domain of that profession. In a mature profession, all organizational leaders are expected to be conversationally competent in the basic principles of the decision framework. They are required to have the necessary skills and support from the profession to use the systems that require their direct involvement in decisions about the resource.

Shared financial mental models

For example, every organization leader must be conversant with principles from finance decision science, such as net present value and assets and liabilities. Likewise, they must be familiar with marketing decision science concepts, such as customer segments and product life cycles. The marketing and finance functions provide the minimum standards for leader competency, and they provide support and deeper professional capabilities when necessary, but all leaders know that they cannot abdicate the basic knowledge of finance and marketing principles to others. Leaders do not get to say, "I don't understand net present value, but that's just a finance concept that only accountants need to know."

As we noted above, these shared mental models are encouraged by the consistent use of professional logical frameworks within the systems that are routinely used by leaders outside the profession. For example, financial principles operate in management systems like budgeting, so leaders not only understand why they are important, but routinely use financial decision science concepts. When finance wants to improve leader competency, there is less resistance and more opportunity to improve decision making using those existing systems. It doesn't seem strange if marketing or finance suggest enhancements to the decision systems for general managers because those managers are already accustomed to systems that work with marketing and finance principles.

The importance of shared talent mental models

Today, individual leaders too often approach talent and organization decisions with vastly different mental models, divergent logical principles, and a focus on very different factors. Organizational leaders would never presume to adopt financial or marketing principles merely because they heard a compelling presentation, but their sources of talent principles are often adopted from sources as varied as the latest motivational speakers and high-profile executives to successful athletes and an occasional college professor. Such sources may well have valid information to offer, but in more mature professions the information is expected to be evaluated by the professional decision science, and incorporated into management systems before it earns widespread use. When leaders fail to see or understand a common set of principles, talent and organization management systems lack context and are seen as administrative or bureaucratic. As the talent and organization decision science matures, its principles will become more consistent and a more natural part of the mind-set of both line leaders and HR leaders, with the appropriate level of sophistication.

To achieve this goal, HR leaders will need to focus more on teaching than telling, a significant change. Finance and marketing are effective in part because their principles have been taught to business leaders in business school, followed up with executive development, and reinforced with real-world practice and career experiences in which leaders are usually coached by functional specialists. Even with very mature and strong staff functions within finance and marketing, the need for senior leaders with well-developed competencies in finance and marketing is seen as important. The emergence of the talentship decision science will very likely be supported by decision frameworks for talent and how it is organized, that will be consistently taught to organization leaders, becoming a natural part of their work and decisions.

Illustration of a motivation decision framework

When leaders are confronted with an issue involving operating cash flow, they do not attempt to invent a new measure of operating cash flow, nor do they insist that the accounting profession change their cash flow measures, so that the leader's results are stronger. It is well understand that a manager's approach to operating cash flow must be consistent with the professional standards of finance decision science.

Yet, when it comes to employee motivation, leaders often have vastly different guiding frameworks, and it is not unusual for leaders to ask HR professionals to adopt their particular motivation framework. Leaders will often say, "The employees in my unit are not performing well, so please create a new bonus incentive." Or, "I find the requirement that I rate employees on several facets of performance difficult, so let's just use one overall rating." Is cash flow really so much more important that leaders should be held to stringent standards for cash but be allowed to adopt vastly different standards for motivation?

In a mature decision science, the HR profession will be far more skilled at providing well-grounded logical frameworks for talent-related elements such as motivation. Moreover, the profession will require leaders outside of HR to become facile with these frameworks. Consider the required sophistication when it comes to motivation, for example. There are several prominent theories that describe well-supported elements of a complete solution to motivation issues (Pinder, 1998). Examples include:

- goals, that are appropriately challenging and clear;
- equity, that the motivation systems provide outcomes, processes and relationships that are perceived as fair and legitimate;
- needs, that rewards take the form of things that individuals value;
- valence-instrumentality-expectancy, that rewards are valued, seen as related to performance measures, and that individuals have confidence their efforts will produce performance outcomes;
- social influence, that group norms and perceptions affect how performance and rewards are valued and interpreted.

One can envision a future in which organization leaders are as routinely and carefully assessed for their ability to understand and apply these principles, as they would be for understanding and applying principles of operating cash flow, net present value, or customer segmentation.

Talentship decision frameworks are important within HR as well as outside HR

The need for a talentship mind-set is also vital for HR functional leaders. In our experience there are almost always some HR professionals in any organization who effectively understand, teach, and enhance decisions based on how talent connects to strategic success. These HR professionals typically admit that they learned to provide this kind of support in their own way, with little systematic instruction or development. One HR professional put it well: "This capability is critical to our future, but it doesn't scale because everyone does it and learns it differently."

A decision framework contributes to decision scale by developing, using, and teaching a consistent, logical point of view about how to connect talent resources to strategic success. A logical point of view provides a consistent script for an ongoing dialogue about talent and strategy, allowing more reliable and consistent diagnosis, analysis, and action on talent issues throughout the organization.

Data, measurement, and analysis

A mature decision science has data, measurement, and analysis aligned with its decision framework principles. These are refined and deployed throughout management systems, used by leaders who understand the principles, and supported by professionals who add insight and expertise. Today finance reflects this level of maturity almost everywhere. Marketing approaches this level of maturity, particularly in industries such as packaged consumer products and multilocation retail, where competitive dynamics hinge on marketing sophistication. For example, every leader at PepsiCo receives a daily report via email on their PDA (personal digital assistant) on product sales, broken down into very specific brands and customer segments.

These systems have evolved over decades, and today we hardly notice how well integrated financial measurement and analysis processes are with decision models. It seems to have always been that way. Today the ratios commonly measured in financial decisions and the structure of accounting statements link directly to the DuPont decision framework. Similarly, marketing decision frameworks provide the logical structure for customer relationship management and customer analysis systems, which use vast amounts of data mining and advanced analytics to produce competitive insights.[2]

In stark contrast, HR data, information, and measurement face a paradox today. Although there is increasing sophistication in technology, data availability, and the capacity to report and disseminate HR information, frustration increases when investments in HR data systems, scorecards, and integrated enterprise resource systems fail to create the strategic insights needed to drive organizational effectiveness. One reason for this paradox is that the technological advances have outpaced the fundamental logic connecting talent and organization decisions to strategic success (Boudreau and Ramstad, 2006; Boudreau and Ramstad, 2007, Chapter 9; Lawler et al., 2004). Major elements of marketing and finance are well over fifty years old, so those decision sciences were far more mature by the time technology advanced. The computer-enhanced systems could build on well-developed decision frameworks, integrated management systems, and shared mental models, making information technology much more valuable.

HR has not yet developed such a decision science and thus has no such decision framework to organize data and information technology. Thus, in HR, technology has found its greatest value in automating areas with more established organizing frameworks, such as payroll, but has not reached the level of impact in supporting more strategic decisions. For example, lacking a common logic regarding employee turnover, specific HR functions often create their own unique employee turnover classifications when installing a new software system. It's not surprising that even after years of using such systems, there remains too little insight into the factors that affect employee turnover, how it affects the organization, and what to do about it (Cascio and Boudreau, 2008). In contrast, operations management approaches inventory turnover with enterprise resource systems that adopt definitions and reporting protocols built on specific decision principles regarding inventory optimization.

As we have discussed before, HR measures exist mostly in areas where the accounting systems require information to control labor costs or monitor functional activity (Boudreau and Ramstad, 2003). Efficiency gets a lot of attention, but effectiveness and impact are often unmeasured. While there have been significant advances in applying analytics to the field of HR management—including high-level data analysis approaches like social network analysis and multivariate regression—such methods often suffer from the lack of a more comprehensive decision framework. For example, a statistical method from marketing, called "conjoint analysis," has been applied to employee survey data to see which work elements most significantly associate with employee engagement or turnover.[3] This provides insights into how HR programs might enhance those work elements, but it often fails to identify where engagement and retention matter most and why. Advanced analytics hold great promise for enhancing talent decisions, but it is often the logic, not the analytics, that creates the big breakthroughs.

A decision framework provides the logical structure to organizational data, measures, and analytics, and identifies gaps in existing measurement systems. Armed with such a decision science and framework, organizations can avoid investing in sophisticated data and analysis that fails to achieve its potential because the tools don't address the important questions.

Focus on optimization

The final pillar of a mature decision science is that its logic reveals how decisions can optimize the returns from a resource, rather than simply describing them or only partially maximizing them. A mature decision science reveals how to optimize results by balancing trade-offs instead of always assuming that more is better.

Optimization in finance: Focusing on investment returns not just profits

Finance provides a good illustration. Before the DuPont model (which marks the beginning of the decision science of finance), the goal was simply to maximize profits. Disproportionate amounts of capital were directed to businesses with large profits, often resulting in high margins but low return on capital. Instead of maximizing profits in isolation, the DuPont model strove to optimize profits by recognizing the constraints on financial capital resources (Johnson, 1975). As finance decision science matured, other factors were integrated. Financial decision models now not only maximize returns but use decision frameworks, such as portfolio theory, to optimize return in the context of risk and liquidity. Further refinements revealed how to balance liquidity in the broader strategy, by investing in ways that consider the range of future strategic options that investment might enable.

Optimization versus maximization in talent decisions

By contrast, many HR decisions often try to increase learning, engagement, or retention without limit or context. This is very different from optimizing a portfolio of HR practices against the organization's unique resource opportunity costs and constraints (Boudreau and Ramstad, 1999). For example, if more sales training increases product knowledge, which increases selling success, a less mature decision framework might apply training more broadly. Having proved the value of training by linking it to increased sales, the right decision seems to be to acquire more training. Several executives we have worked with have termed this the "peanut-butter" approach, because it spreads something equally across the entire organization.

In fact, considering the necessary investments (time, money, etc.) to achieve increased selling success through training, enhancing product knowledge from an already high level may be very expensive. The optimal solution might involve less product knowledge and more motivation, and thus less training and more incentives. The key point is that a mature decision science frames the question in terms of optimal solutions rather than just describing relationships or increasing one desired outcome out of context. Even when optimal decisions cannot be precisely defined, the logic that a focus on optimization provides will often lead to insights that are missed by a less comprehensive approach.

Distinguish average from marginal value

A core principle in optimization is the difference between average and marginal (or incremental) impact. Although something can be highly valuable, increasing or decreasing the amount of it may not have a big effect. For example, suppose an organization has a hundred sales representatives and total revenue of $50 million, making the average sales per sales representative $500,000. What is the optimal number of sales representatives? You can't tell from the average. Optimizing requires that you know the potential effects of increasing or decreasing the sales force. If the same $50 million in revenue could be generated by ninety representatives, then the marginal value of the last ten representatives would actually be zero. On the other hand, if these sales representatives were working to their capacity and there were available sales territories without adequate sales coverage, additional reps would create significant incremental sales.

A mature decision science clearly articulates the difference between resources or activities that provide high average value and those that provide high marginal value. We use the word *pivotal* to describe the marginal effect of resources, activities, and decisions. *Pivotal* captures the idea of a lever, where a small change at the fulcrum causes very large changes on the other end. Highly pivotal areas are those where a small change makes a big difference to strategy and value. A resource, decision, or activity can be highly valuable and important, even if it is not pivotal. For example, every machine on an assembly line is important because each machine contributes something unique to the production process. However, increasing the capacity of every machine is not pivotal. The marginal value of increased capacity is much higher in the machine that represents the bottleneck, or constraint. Some resources, decisions, or activities are both important (highly valuable on average) and pivotal (changes make a big difference).

Pivotal versus important in product design

Consider how two components of a car relate to a consumer's purchase decision: tires and interior design. Which adds more value on average? The tires. They are essential to the car's ability to move, and they impact both safety and performance. Yet tires generally do not influence purchase decisions, because safety standards guarantee that all tires will be very safe and reliable. Differences in interior features—impressive sound system, elegant upholstery, portable technology docks, number and location of cup holders—likely have far more effect on the consumer's buying decision. In terms of the overall value of an automobile, it cannot move without tires, but it can function without cup holders and an iPod dock. Interior features, however, clearly have a greater impact on the purchase decision. In our language, the tires are important, but the interior design is *pivotal*.

Figure 1.3 shows this example in the form of what we call a "performance yield curve." The performance yield curve for tires is much higher than for interior features, which reflects tires' importance. The yield curve for tires is relatively flat across a large range of performance levels, and it drops quickly on the left if tire performance falls below a certain level. Tires create tremendous value and are very important, but once they reach a certain level, increasing their performance does not add value to the consumer's purchasing decision. Yet, if they fall below the minimum standard (as happened with the Firestone tires on Ford SUVs, resulting in a massive recall in 2000), the result is very bad indeed. The key to optimizing tires against their effect on the initial purchase decision is to get them to standard, not significantly higher. Beyond this point the incremental cost of increasing tire performance exceeds the incremental value in customer purchases.

The marketing and finance decision sciences have sophisticated systems to exploit the distinction between marginal and average value. As marketing decision science evolved, the concept of segmentation was applied at multiple levels, including markets, customers within markets, products, and as we just discussed, product features within products. Conjoint analysis and other statistical tools use data from extensive consumer research to produce deep insights about the incremental value of features, which informs decisions about product designs. They carefully isolate those attributes (such as safe tires) that are core or expected (sometimes referred to as "table stakes") from those where differences drive perceptions of value (such as the interior design of a new car). Optimization requires investing based on the incremental contribution, not the average contribution. To do this, features must be segmented on their marginal value

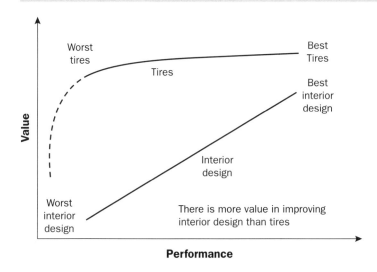

Figure 1.3 Yield curves for automobile features: tires vs. interior design

Source: Reprinted by permission of Harvard Business School Press from *Beyond HR: The New Science of Human Capital* by John W. Boudreau and Peter M. Ramstad, Boston, 2007: 41.

(pivotalness), not their average value (or importance). Failing to segment based on pivotalness often results in equal investments, even when the potential marginal return is significantly different.

Distinguishing what is pivotal from what is important in talent decisions

This seems fundamental, but it is frequently misapplied in organization and talent decisions. What we have called "talent segmentation" is still very rudimentary (Boudreau and Ramstad, 2005a). We see this in the frequent tendency of organizations to apply the same investments and activities across a wide range of jobs or talent pools. Examples include: "If stock options are good for executives, then they should be expanded to all employees" and "If it's important to increase attention given to our customers, then everyone should have thirty hours of training in customer awareness" and "If weeding out the bottom 10 percent of performers makes sense in our sales force, let's weed out the bottom 10 percent in every job."

Effective segmentation based on marginal value in talent and organization decisions helps answer questions such as "Where does my strategy require increasing the performance of our talent, or our organization?" The answer cannot be "everywhere," because that is cost prohibitive. The answer also cannot be "nowhere," because competitive advantage must have some source—one or more multi-incumbent roles, or talent pools, where superior talent quality makes a significant strategic difference. Lacking a decision science that guides this kind of talent segmentation, organizations typically invest too little in talent pools that are most pivotal and too much in talent pools that are important but far less pivotal. The idea that talent and organization decisions are vital to competitive advantage is a virtual truism today, as we noted earlier, yet the very essence of competitive advantage is finding unique and different ways to advance a particular value proposition, seize specific market opportunities, or leverage distinctive strategic resources. We have described how organizations including Boeing, Corning, Disney and Williams-Sonoma that have achieved this with talent, in ways that are consistent with the principles described here (Boudreau and Ramstad, 2007). Still, today's decisions about organization and talent are often made with an eye toward duplicating the practices of other successful companies, rather than in-depth internal analysis to find the appropriate investments for specific contexts. The absence of a decision science that distinguishes marginal from average value is a significant cause.

Segmentation in auto insurance

Segmentation based on marginal impact produced a competitive advantage for Allstate Insurance Company. Allstate (then a division of Sears) was one of the first companies to adjust rates based on age, auto usage, and claims history—a revolution at the time (Allstate, 2006). This easily described idea had massive implications for virtually all aspects of the auto insurance business. Allstate was able to extract much more value from the insurance market and provide much greater value to its customers by adjusting what it charged according to customer characteristics related to the probability of accidents and other factors. Allstate has continued its tradition of innovative differentiation in its pricing models by bringing in a variety of new factors that it now markets under the brand "Your Choice Auto Insurance," which is based on sophisticated pricing models. This changed the game from a product definition perspective by providing customers with a much wider variety of choices. Before, customers could choose their level of coverage and size of deductibles. Now they can customize policies on features such as accident forgiveness and what types of rewards they would like associated with good driving records.

Allstate's research revealed interesting and surprising patterns in auto safety among different consumer groups. A *BusinessWeek* item noted:

> For decades, Allstate had lumped customers into three main pricing categories, based on basic details such as a customer's age and place of residence. It now has more than 1,500 price levels. Agents used to simply refer to a manual to give customers a price; now they log on to a computer that uses complex algorithms to analyze 16 credit report variables, such as late payments and card balances, as well as data such as claims history for specific car models. Thus, [drivers who are safe bets] are rewarded, saving up to 20% over the old system, and high-risk drivers are penalized, paying up to 20% more. It has worked well enough that Allstate now applies it to other lines, such as homeowners' insurance.
>
> (Carter, 2005)

What are the implications for talent? Financial services organizations such as insurance, mortgage and credit-card companies have vastly increased the number of variations in their offerings. This has often meant that the traditional jobs of pricing products simply did not capture the new requirements of sophisticated statistical analysis of customers and markets, and actuarial savvy in setting and adjusting prices to fit demand and supply. One implication was the need to segment the talent market for insurance pricers. Traditionally, employees in the pricing jobs were facing only a few products that did not change very much. With the emergence of such highly segmented insurance products, it was necessary to distinguish traditional pricing capability from the capability to apply very deep mathematical, statistical and actuarial methods to continually adjust pricing based on customer and market data. Allstate now needed to create a new talent segment—pricers who could apply sophisticated mathematical algorithms. Indeed, this talent segment was so new that traditional job descriptions did not even describe it (Boudreau, forthcoming).

Thinking differently using decision science principles

A decision is an invitation to think differently. Historically, as decision sciences become embedded within organizations, natural synergies emerge across the five decision science elements. This creates tangible but very organic changes in the way business and HR leaders, employees, investors, and potential employees converse about a strategic resource. Consider the power of just three changes in the way your organization approaches its talent and organization decisions.

First, clearly distinguish between pivotalness and importance. This motivates a focus on the marginal value of talent decisions. It is as important to talent decisions as the distinction between the marginal and average value of advertising. It helps decision makers avoid getting lost in a sea of important initiatives and set priorities correctly.

Second, consistently use performance yield curves, to identify the nature of pivot-point slopes and shapes. Not only does this kind of discipline help identify where decisions should focus on achieving a standard versus improving performance, it also provides a way to think about the risks and returns to performance at different levels. It helps people avoid making decisions based on well-meaning but rudimentary rules such as "get the best person in every job."

Third, focus on optimization, not just maximization. This creates an environment in which trade-offs can be discussed with less of the emotion that usually prevents good decisions and often leads to decisions like "Let's just do the same thing for everyone to be fair." Optimization presumes that talent investments will be unequal but also creates a high standard for analyzing and communicating good reasons for such unequal investments.

Thus, even in the early stages of implementing a decision science, tangible changes occur in how talent and organizations are understood and made. History shows that it is from these small tangible steps that significant untapped strategic success flows.

Conclusion

When new decision sciences emerge, they typically present difficult changes in social, organizational, and personal traditions. Before the new logic is used by competitors, a failure to make decisions more optimally doesn't create any relative disadvantage, so less sophisticated decision systems still allow organizations to stay competitive. Before Allstate applied the decision science principle of customer segmentation and optimization, no one did any worse by following the old model. Yet first movers who apply a new decision science often create formidable competitive advantages. Once Allstate generated value by adopting a more sophisticated decision science, its competitors were at a disadvantage. Soon everyone began to realize the power of the new decision framework and tried to catch up.

We believe that HR, and the larger domain of organization and talent decisions, is at precisely this historical point. A few organizations are beginning to develop some elements of a more mature decision science. For example, at Corning, HR leaders who support key divisions use talent-focused strategy analysis during their annual strategy sessions. At the Hartford Financial Services Group, Inc., investments in HR programs are allocated in part based on where they will have the most pivotal effect (Farrell, 2004).

Still, because the effects are so isolated, there is not yet an urgent need to evolve. The vast majority of organizations can compete effectively, even while making more traditional talent and organization decisions. A new decision science, however, will emerge for talent, just as surely as it emerged for other resources. The first organizations to apply the new decision framework will achieve significant first-mover advantages, forcing others to react. In time we envision the talent decision science becoming as natural a part of management thinking as finance and marketing are today, but before that happens there are opportunities for game-changing strategic decisions by organizations that apply it first.

Acknowledgment

This chapter has been adapted by the authors with permission of Harvard Business School Press from *Beyond HR: The New Science of Human Capital* by John W. Boudreau and Peter M. Ramstad, Copyright © 2007 by the Harvard Business School Publishing Corporation; all rights reserved.

Notes

1 In accounting the *chart of accounts* is a listing of all the accounts in the general ledger, with each account accompanied by a reference number. Examples might include assigning numbers 1000–1999 to asset accounts, 2000–2999 to liability accounts, and 3000–3999 to equity accounts. Source: "Chart of Accounts," NetMBA, http://www.netmba.com/accounting/fin/accounts/chart/.
2 Customer relationship management (CRM) is a corporate-level strategy that focuses on creating and maintaining lasting relationships with customers. CRM enables organizations to better manage their customers through the introduction of reliable systems, processes, and procedures. Source: "Customer Relationship Management," *Wikipedia*, http://en.wikipedia.org/wiki/Customer_Relationship_Management.
3 Conjoint analysis is a tool that allows a subset of the possible combinations of product features to determine the relative importance of each feature in the purchasing decision. Source: "Conjoint Analysis," QuickMBA, http://www.quickmba.com/marketing/research/conjoint.

References

Allstate Corporation (2006) "Press Kit: History & Timeline 1930s," Allstate, http://www.allstate.com/Media/PressKit/PageRender.asp?page=1930s.htm.
Boudreau, J.W. (2003) "Strategic Knowledge Measurement and Management." In Susan E. Jackson, Michael A. Hitt, and Angelo S. DeNisi, eds, *Managing Knowledge for Sustained Competitive Advantage* (San Francisco: Jossey-Bass/Pfeiffer): 360–96.
Boudreau, J.W. (2006) *Interview of J.S. Bronson, former senior vice president of HR*, Pepsi, August.
Boudreau, J.W. (forthcoming) "Allstate's 'Good Hands' Approach to Talent Management." In Robert Silzer and Ben Dowell, eds, *Exceptional Leadership Talent Management* (New York: Jossey-Bass), Chapter 16.
Boudreau, J.W. and Peter M. Ramstad (1999) "Human Resource Metrics: Can Measures be Strategic?" In Patrick Wright et al., eds, *Research in Personnel and Human Resources Management*, Supplement 4, *Strategic Human Resources Management in the Twenty-First Century* (Stamford, CT: JAI Press): 75–98.
Boudreau, J.W. and Peter M. Ramstad (2003) "Tapping the Full Potential of HRIS: Shifting the HR Paradigm from Service Delivery to a Talent Decision Science." In PeopleSoft, *Heads Count: An Anthology for the Competitive Enterprise* (Pleasanton, CA: PeopleSoft): 69–88.
Boudreau, J.W. and Peter M. Ramstad (2005a) "Where's Your Pivotal Talent?" *Harvard Business Review*, April: 23–4.
Boudreau, J.W. and Peter M. Ramstad (2005b) "Talentship, Talent Segmentation, and Sustainability: A New HR Decision Science Paradigm for A New Strategy Definition." In Mike Lossey, Dave Ulrich, and

Sue Meisinger, eds, *The Future of Human Resource Management: 64 Thought Leaders Explore the Critical HR Issues of Today and Tomorrow* (New York: Wiley).

Boudreau, J.W. and Peter M. Ramstad (2006) "Talentship and Human Resource Measurement and Analysis: From ROI to Strategic Organizational Change," *Human Resource Planning Journal* 29, 1: 25–33.

Boudreau, J.W. and Peter M. Ramstad (2007) *Beyond HR: The New Science of Human Capital* (Boston: Harvard Business School Publishing).

Carter, A. (2005) "Telling the Risky from the Reliable," *BusinessWeek*, August 1, http://www.businessweek.com/magazine/content/05_31/b3945085_mz017.htm.

Cascio, Wayne F. and John W. Boudreau (2008) *Investing in People* (Upper Saddle River, NJ: Prentice-Hall).

Colbert, Amy E., Sara L. Rynes, and Kenneth G. Brown (2005) "Who Believes Us? Understanding Managers' Agreement with Human Resource Research Findings," *Journal of Applied Behavioral Science* 41, 3: 304–325.

Compensation.blr.com (2005) "Writer Defends 'Why We Hate HR' Article," November 29, http://compensation.blr.com/display.cfm/id/154876.

Farrell, L. (2004) "Turning HR Cost Reduction Into Opportunity at The Hartford." Presentation in *Beyond the Bottom Line* executive program. Center for Effective Organizations. April.

Hammonds, Keith H. (2005) "Why We Hate HR," *Fast Company*, August: 40–8.

Johnson, H.T. (1975) "Management Accounting in an Early Integrated Industrial: E. I. DuPont de Nemours Powder Company, 1903–1912," *Business History Review* 49, 2: 184–204.

Lawler III, Edward E., John W. Boudreau, and Susan Mohrman (2006) *Achieving Strategic Excellence* (Palo Alto, CA: Stanford University Press).

Lawler III, Edward E., Alec Levenson, and John W. Boudreau (2004) "HR Metrics and Analytics: Uses and Impacts," *Human Resource Planning Journal* 27, 4: 27–35.

Lossey, Mike, Dave Ulrich, and Sue Meisinger, eds. (2005) *The Future of Human Resource Management: 64 Thought Leaders Explore the Critical HR Issues of Today and Tomorrow* (New York: Wiley).

Pinder, Charles C. (1998) *Work Motivation in Organizational Behavior* (Upper Saddle River, NJ: Prentice-Hall).

Schroeder, Roger G., Kevin Linderman, and Dongli Zhang (2005) "Evolution of Quality: First Fifty Issues of *Production and Operations Management*," *Production and Operations Management* 14, 4: 468–81.

Skinner, Wickham (1981) "Big Hat, No Cattle: Managing Human Resources," *Harvard Business Review* 5: 106–14.

2

Changing labour markets and the future of work

David Coats

Introduction

The purpose of this chapter is not to describe the world as it might look to an HR practitioner in twenty years' time but to map the terrain of "what we know" and make a modest assessment of the challenges that we face. It explores the changes that have taken place in the labour market, identifies the forces influencing these developments, looks at the shifting structure of organisations and at the reshaping of work – with some discussion of the question of job quality. Inevitably, the account given here reflects the author's experience in the UK, but evidence is drawn from other countries too.

Futurist speculation is the curse of any discussion about the changing world of work. In the early 1990s popular commentators predicted with great confidence that the permanent full-time job was a thing of the past, that we would all have to get used to a world of persistent employment insecurity, that increases in contingent work were inevitable and that employees would need to become footloose, opportunistic and flexible (Handy 1994). It was never explained how this vision of the future could be squared with the high-volume protestations that "our employees are our greatest asset", or with the other "inevitability" that comparative advantage, productivity and performance would increasingly depend on the skills, knowledge and talents of motivated, committed employees.

Other analysts speculated that we were about to witness "the end of work", as information technology unleashed a wave of job destruction across the developed world (Rifkin 1996). It was asserted that this could explain the inexorable rise in US unemployment from the 1960s (average 4.8%) to the late 1980s (average 7.3%). One might attribute this line of thought to an almost pathological technophobia, but it is much better understood as an effort to construct an alarmist argument on rather shaky economic foundations.

Those with slightly longer memories might recall that a similar prospectus was offered in the UK in the late 1970s (Jenkins and Sherman 1979, 1981), with the suggestion that technology would lead to an "excess" of leisure time rather than unemployment. Both hypotheses have proved wanting when tested against events. "The end of work" cannot explain the return of something close to full employment in the liberal market (and Nordic) economies and the rapid pace of technological development has not led to a significant reduction in working hours

(Coats 2006). The selective use of evidence has proved to be no more reliable than gazing directly into a crystal ball.

For our purposes the lesson is clear. We should all tread a little warily before we start making overconfident predictions about the likely direction of change; although that does not mean that we must abandon all efforts to assess the likely challenges. Perhaps there is more to be gained by eschewing futurism in favour of an accurate description of the world today, reflecting the scale and pace of change since the 1980s. Once we can see how much (or how little) is different we might be rather better positioned to make a judgment about the course of developments over the next twenty years. But even this more modest approach raises some difficulties. Apparently "new" "trends" tend to be exaggerated and then projected forward – hence the suggestion that we are witnessing the exponential growth of short-term and temporary contracts.

So even though the past can never be a guide to the future, it should be possible, exercising a judicious degree of caution, to detect trends in the present that were also observable in the recent past. Some constructive thinking about the likely shape of the future is unavoidable if government and employers want to be well positioned to anticipate change. Of course, we should recognise that sometimes predicted events will fail to materialise, that the unexpected will happen and that governments, employers and other stakeholders will continue to be surprised by Rumsfeldian "unknown unknowns".

Perhaps the most important part of the story is that national policies still matter – the level of unemployment, the extent of income inequality, the impact of minimum wages, the perception of workplace justice and even the general health and life expectancy of workers all remain within the purview of domestic policy influence (Layard 2005, Marmot 2004). This is a rather positive story, offering a direct response to that of "global pessimism", which tells us that there are unstoppable economic forces sweeping across the world and that we must all adapt to these new realities or suffer the consequences.

Structural changes and the labour market

A useful place to start our discussion is the basic structure of the labour market. How much change have we really witnessed over the last two decades? Certainly so far as the UK is concerned some of the changes have been profound – a big fall in employment in manufacturing, a continued feminisation of the workforce, rising skill levels and a burgeoning of employment in business services, particularly knowledge-intensive services. Yet an observer from the mid-1980s would also find much that is familiar (see Figure 2.1). Most jobs are permanent and full-time. Part-time work has grown slightly over the last two decades, but most of the growth took place in earlier periods. Temporary and contingent employment as a share of total employment has remained stable for much of the last twenty years. In short, on these dimensions, today looks much like yesterday.

A swift glance at the data reinforces the judgment that the guru-driven narratives of the early 1990s have proved to be rather unreliable guides. There is no significant evidence to endorse the view that we will all be flexible, self-employed portfolio workers in the future; most second job holders are low-paid and work part-time. Nor has Rifkin's "end of work" prediction been vindicated. The UK has a high employment rate (74.6% in 2006), relatively low unemployment and a lower rate of labour market inactivity (people who say they would like to work if they could find a job, but have abandoned active job search) than was the case in 1971 (Brinkley et al. 2007). A dispassionate observer might conclude that this is a rather remarkable achievement, given the high rates of unemployment that were experienced in the 1980s and 1990s.

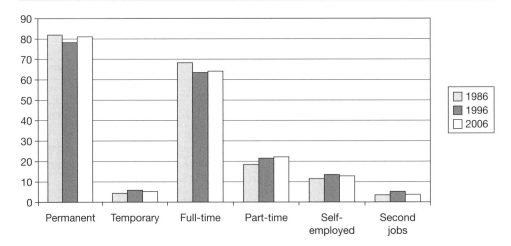

Figure 2.1 Employment change in the UK labour market 1996–2006 (% share of total employment)

Source: Labor Force Survey, Social Trends No 30.

Of course, it is important to understand that these experiences are not universal. Indeed, the labour markets of the OECD countries display a wide range of diverse characteristics – experiences have been as different as one could imagine. For example, France and Germany have experienced high unemployment at the same time as the UK and the USA have seen unemployment fall and long-term unemployment virtually disappear. The Nordic countries have retained the essence of their social model – strong welfare states, limited income inequality, high unemployment benefits, strong trade unions and widespread coverage of collective bargaining – at a time when welfare states elsewhere have been under pressure, trade unions have seen membership decline and income inequality has grown (especially in the "liberal market economies" of the Anglo-Saxon world).

The extent of contingent employment reflects this diversity too. Around a third of jobs in Spain are classified as temporary but, despite the rhetoric of "labour market flexibility", the Anglo-Saxon economies have the lowest levels of temporary work (EU Labour Force Survey, 2006). Indeed, we might conclude that there seems to be an inverse relationship between the level of labour market regulation and the extent of contingent work – although we might observe too that the flexibility of liberal market economies means that regular work at the bottom of the labour market looks much like contingent work elsewhere.

In the early part of the 1990s, many reputable commentators were suggesting that there was only "one right way" to achieve low unemployment and stable non-inflationary growth. For want of a better phrase we might describe this as the "orthodox" or "neo-liberal" view that there was simply no alternative to weak welfare states, low taxation, and a low level of labour market regulation, weak trade unions, low unemployment benefits and coercive welfare to work regimes for the unemployed. The OECD offered the following definitive advice to developed countries in their 1994 Jobs Strategy: follow our prescription or suffer the consequences. Now, thirteen years on, the position looks a little more complex. Indeed, in their recent review of the Jobs Strategy the OECD have abandoned the "one right way" thesis and have accepted that there is something positive to be said for the Nordic model too, particularly the Danish notion of "flexicurity".

This is a particularly important development because it suggests that a labour market characterised by a strong welfare state, moderately strict employment protection legislation, strong trade unions, high unemployment benefits (albeit with strong job search conditions attached) and active labour market programmes (rather than passive support for the unemployed) are, according to the OECD, all compatible with non-inflationary growth and good employment performance (OECD 2004, 2005). Indeed, the developing discussion about social policy in the EU draws inspiration from these findings and may offer a useful framework for a revival of the social dimension of the EU.

It might be an overstatement to say that the OECD have performed an abrupt U-turn, but there can be no doubt that their position has changed. Even the strongest enthusiast for the neo-liberal model must concede the point.

There are two self-evident conclusions to be drawn from this very rapid review. First, national policies really do matter. Second, there are no *irresistible* forces constraining national policy choices. Countries can choose to have more or less income inequality, they can choose to offer a high or low level of workplace justice and they can choose more or less coercive regimes for the unemployed — sometimes a carrot can be more effective than a stick (Coats 2006). In other words, the impact of global trends is highly differentiated across countries.

Returning to our earlier theme, it would be wrong to give the impression that *nothing* has changed in the labour markets of developed countries. Perhaps a better characterisation is that we have seen both continuity *and* change. Certainly the most significant development, in the UK at least, is not in the structure of the labour market but in the "rise and fall of industries". It is this phenomenon which explains why the labour market of 2007 looks very different from the labour market of 1977. At that time slightly more than one in four workers were employed in manufacturing, whereas today the figure is close to one in ten; employment in services has grown apace, rising from 69% of total employment in 1986 to 75% in 1996 and 81% in 2006.

Looking to the future, the big story is the growing importance of employment in high-value *knowledge-intensive* services. The phenomenon can be observed across Europe, with the biggest increases in employment to be found in knowledge services, as widely defined, including business services, financial services, communications, education and health. Indeed, recent research suggests that the UK has a significant advantage in these sectors, which are contributing an increasing share of the country's international trade and in which the UK has a large trade surplus, valued at around 3.4% of GDP (Brinkley 2007).

Moreover, the best projections of occupational change in the UK suggest that by 2014 more than 45% of all employees will be in the top three occupational groups (managers, professionals and associate professionals), which might be contrasted with the position in 1984, when the same groups accounted for around 30% of employees (see Figure 2.2). To some extent the changing occupational structure is a consequence of the rise and fall of industries too, with fewer manual workers in manufacturing and more white-collar employees elsewhere.

This change in the structure of the economy can be observed across the developed world, with technology as the principal driver – the number of units produced by UK's car industry is at roughly the same level as in the 1970s although the workforce is much smaller; and the same might be said of the UK's steel industry, which has levels of output similar to the 1970s (albeit in more specialised products) but with a much smaller workforce. A simple way of describing the process is to say that we are moving from an economy where a worker could make a decent living by using their physical capabilities, to an economy where a premium is placed on intellectual or cognitive qualities. The most striking phenomenon described by Figure 2.2 is the dramatic fall in employment in elementary occupations – there will be relatively few jobs that require brawn alone; workers will need to live by their wits. It is this phenomenon which explains why policy makers place so much emphasis on the importance of the "knowledge economy" and devote relentless attention to skills policy.

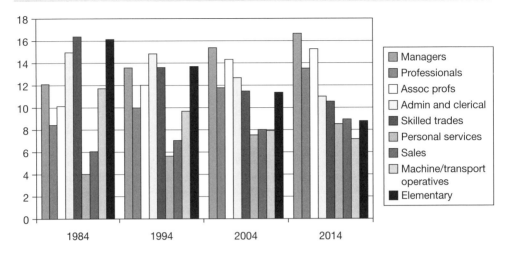

Figure 2.2 Occupational change in the UK 1984–2014 (% of all in employment)

Source: SSDA (2006).

Of course the experience has not been painless and some communities have been severely disadvantaged as a result. But the important point to note is that the phenomenon is ubiquitous. Indeed, one might even say that it reflects no more than the process of "creative destruction" that has always been the fundamental dynamic of capitalism (Schumpeter 1943). For policy makers the most important question is to find instruments that can manage the adverse consequences equitably without losing the self-evident benefits of competitive markets. How this outcome can be achieved is the issue to which we now turn.

Explaining the changing world of work

Some commentators have suggested that all these "trends" are best explained by "globalisation", but that term is so loaded with both positive and negative associations that it is of limited analytical use. While some NGOs call for "global resistance", market fundamentalists argue that "resistance is useless". Both fall into the trap of believing that "globalisation" can account for almost anything good or bad in the global economy and both believe that nation states are powerless. As we shall see, the truth is slightly more complex than either side will allow.

Three preliminary points may help to clarify our discussion. First, structural change has been a constant in economic history – often with devastating consequences for the workers affected. Handloom weavers were legitimately worried that steam-powered looms and the factory system were threats to a well-established way of life. Their response (machine breaking) may have looked rational in the short term, but there can be little doubt that industrialisation laid the foundations on which our modern democratic welfare states have been built. The process may have been messy, unpleasant and a cause of social conflict, but few would contest the argument that in the long run the sacrifices of previous generations made today's prosperity possible.

Second, disruptive change was taking place before anybody coined the term "globalisation"; indeed, it has been suggested that the world was just as globalised in 1900 as it is today (Hirst and Thompson 1996, Wolf 2004). Capital was free to move across borders, real-time financial information could be transmitted across continents, tariff barriers were relatively low (market liberalisation had been an instrument of British policy since the repeal of the Corn Laws), there was a regime of fixed exchange rates and a single global currency (gold) and huge movements of populations across national borders. In that sense the world in which we live today contains many features that were observable a century ago and, taking account of some likely perplexity about modern technology, a time traveller from 1900 with an analytical cast of mind would not find the structure of today's global economy either particularly novel or astonishing.[1]

Third, managing restructuring has always posed a problem for policy makers and other stakeholders. Public agencies can either anticipate change or adopt a "wait-and-see" approach, dealing with negative consequences after they have materialised. Employers can either anticipate the likely impact on their business of emerging technologies, new competitors and new markets or find themselves the victims of economic transformation. Trade unions can either recognise change as a constant and equip their members for a very different world of work or play a rather negative role by campaigning to "save all the existing jobs".

Referring explicitly to globalisation, the development economist and philosopher Amartya Sen makes the case for public policy to observe the following principles:

> The appropriate response has to include concerted efforts to make the form of globalisation less destructive of employment and traditional livelihood, and to achieve gradual transition. For smoothing the process of transition there have to be opportunities for retraining and acquiring new skills . . . in addition to providing social safety nets for those whose interests are harmed – at least in the short run – by globalising changes.
>
> (Sen 1999)

This is both an intelligent and humane response, but other commentators have suggested that there *is* something new and historically unprecedented about our situation that requires a more radical reaction. The argument can be expressed in two words – India and China. It is said that both countries are so huge, with a growing human capital stock (millions of scientists and engineers) that the West will struggle to compete. It is argued further that skills upgrading may have been an appropriate answer when competition was intensifying between *developed* countries, but it is an inadequate response to the integration of China and India into the world trading system.

Alan Blinder, an eminent US economist and former adviser to President Bill Clinton, has suggested that millions of American service jobs will be potentially "offshoreable" in the near future (Blinder 2007). Low labour costs and the availability of technology will make it much cheaper and therefore more profitable to locate in the emerging markets of the new global superpowers. And these jobs will not necessarily be low-skill jobs. Blinder is quite explicit: the middle classes are about to experience a degree of insecurity fuelled by international competition that hitherto has been confined to relatively low-skill groups. And the process could lead to some reduction in living standards: "In addition to job losses, it is quite likely that, by stripping away their previous immunity to foreign competition, offshoring will depress the real wages of many service workers who do not lose their jobs" (Blinder 2007, p. 9).

Richard Freeman, an equally renowned labour economist, has talked of the "great doubling" of the global workforce following the collapse of the Soviet Union and the ready availability of labour in India, China and Russia (Freeman 2005). Joseph Stiglitz, another former Clinton adviser and former chief economist at the World Bank, has been equally explicit: the wages of low-skilled workers in developed countries are *already* being adversely affected by globalisation (Stiglitz 2006). Thomas Friedman, the *New York Times* columnist, has told us that "the world is flat" and all developed countries are now in direct competition with lower cost and highly skilled workers elsewhere in the world (Friedman 2005).

And Lord Digby Jones, former director general of the CBI (the UK's principal employers' organisation) and now a trade minister in Gordon Brown's government, has suggested that China and India will "eat our lunch" unless the UK becomes a lean, mean knowledge economy with a relentless focus on the reduction of costs, low levels of business taxation, weak trade unions and a small welfare state. Those of a nervous disposition will already be terrified by these predictions, but even the most imperturbable citizen might be rather discomfited by forecasts that amount to little more than "be afraid, be very afraid".

The risk with this kind of rhetoric is that some people might be persuaded to embrace a protectionist response. Anxiety about change leads people to demand that government act to "save all the jobs", increase tariff barriers and insulate national economies from international competition. It is something of a paradox that Alan Blinder, who is now perhaps quite wrongly associated with the "be afraid" camp, is also an enthusiastic free trader and an advocate of liberalisation on the grounds that trade openness leads to higher global prosperity. Unfortunately, by talking about a "new industrial revolution" and "great dislocation" he adds fuel to the protectionist fire, even as he concludes that in the long run global prosperity will be higher.

How might we answer these influential voices? What possible arguments might we use? To begin with, we could quite reasonably observe that the process of economic development has never, in the past, led to the immiseration of the already affluent. In other words, a rising tide can lift all boats. The emergence of Germany as an industrial power did not make the UK poorer; the same might be said of the United States or the countries of Southern Europe that have become much more prosperous since joining the EU, or the newly industrialised Asian countries that joined the world trading system in the 1990s.

Enabling India and China to grow their economies and join the world trading system is a route to higher overall global prosperity and higher incomes in both those countries. Developing countries may benefit from an element of "infant industry" protection at the early stage of development (as was the case for now prosperous Western economies in the early phase of industrialisation) but the objective must be eventually to achieve full integration into the world trading system (Chang 2002). Competition between *developed countries* leads to the more effective exploitation of comparative advantage and a more efficient allocation of capital. Allowing China and India to continue on this path would be the greatest anti-poverty programme the world has seen.

There is also a serious question whether Richard Freeman's "great doubling" is a real phenomenon anyway. For example, much of the labour force in India and China remains rural rather than urban, even though rapid urbanisation is taking place. India suffers from widespread illiteracy and China may be reaching the limits of its current growth model (Hutton 2006). Skilled workers in the West have little to fear from the theoretical possibility that agricultural workers in Asia are now part of the global labour force.

We might also ask whether the prediction of widespread offshoring is consistent with recent experience. Applying a crude version of Alan Blinder's argument leads to the inevitable conclusion that the economies of developed countries in the future will be wholly constituted by non-tradable services, simply because nobody believes that it makes any economic sense to travel to Bangalore for a cheaper haircut or a manicure. Yet contrary to all the arguments advanced above, some developed countries with high labour costs are continuing to perform well in industries that are exposed to intense international competition. Germany may have relatively high unemployment, but it remains the world's largest exporter and has doubled its exports to China over the past five years. The Nordic countries have high labour costs and high taxes but have continued to experience moderately strong non-inflationary growth and low unemployment. Common sense suggests that there are only weak reasons to be "afraid" of the emerging economic strength of India and China.

Empirical data support this conclusion. The USA creates and destroys around 500,000 jobs every week. As Will Hutton has pointed out, in any one year around one-fifth of the nation's jobs have been eliminated and another one-fifth have been created (Hutton 2006). By way of comparison, even the most hawkish commentators have only attributed around 100,000 jobs per year in lost job opportunities to trade with China in the period 1989–2005, which equates to about 2.24 million in total. This could be said to be a relatively small number in the context of the US economy overall during this same period (Palley 2005).

So far as offshoring is concerned (where jobs are directly transferred from the developed to the developing world), on one measure the numbers are smaller still in both the UK and the USA. According to the Bureau of Labour Statistics only 16,000 workers in the USA were affected by offshoring in 2005 (1.7% of mass layoffs) and the European Restructuring Monitor identified 19,000 jobs offshored from the UK in the same period (Hutton 2006, Palley 2005). However, we should note that these figures are contested and that other commentators have suggested that up to 406,000 US jobs were offshored in 2004 (Bronfenbrenner and Luce 2004). However, while almost half a million jobs sounds like a big number, it is still relatively modest in the context of the whole US economy.

It should be obvious that not all these figures can be right. So is the fear of globalisation more myth than reality? There can be no doubt that the level of anxiety is rising and that reputable commentators are worried, particularly in the USA. But it would be wrong to view this discussion only through an American lens. Experiences elsewhere offer a more positive outlook; the debate about offshoring in the UK and in Northern Europe seems to be following a slightly different trajectory.

One possibility of course is that the USA is being affected by an openness to trade which other countries have experienced for some considerable time. According to the OECD, the Nordic countries are *more* open to trade than the USA, have opened their markets with more enthusiasm over the last decade *and* still have employment rates that are amongst the highest in the developed world (OECD 2007). Perhaps the real cause of the problem is that the USA remains one of the *least open* economies in the OECD, despite all the rhetoric of liberalisation. In other words, while the UK and some other European economies have got used to dealing with the "creative destruction" that comes with openness, the USA is still learning how to manage these processes; a conclusion that returns us directly to Amartya Sen's injunction about how "globalisation" should be handled.

Indeed, despite the rather crude interpretation of some of his recent public statements, Alan Blinder would not necessarily disagree. The important conclusion is to recognise that there can be losers as well as winners from these economic processes (although open trade benefits global prosperity in the long run). Governments must act to compensate the losers – or more accurately, equip them with the wherewithal to succeed in a knowledge economy. His most recent work offers a policy prospectus that would look familiar to policy makers in the Nordic countries: higher unemployment benefits and a stronger welfare state, high-quality active labour market programmes and investment in education and skills (particularly communication and problem-solving skills).

In other words, the critical challenge for policy makers is to manage difficult economic transitions with sensitivity. A degree of labour market flexibility may help and there are already models in operation in Scandinavia that offer real promise for the rest of the developed world. Indeed, from a more parochial perspective, much of the policy mix in the UK is already consistent with Blinder's proposals and the emerging discussion about "flexicurity" at EU level offers real promise for the future (European Commission 2007). There is no reason therefore why "globalisation" should necessarily have either an adverse impact on employment or lead to increasing income inequality (OECD 2007).

This latter consideration is particularly important because there is a widespread view that increases in income inequality are in large measure attributable to "globalisation". It is undeniable of course that income inequality grew in many countries over the course of the 1980s and has continued to accelerate in the USA since that time (Esping-Anderson 2005). The position in the UK is a little more complex, with the trend towards greater inequality halting in the early part of this decade and some evidence of a small reduction in the period 2001–05 (Jones 2006).

A particular concern has arisen around the incomes of the group best classified as the super-rich, the top 0.1% of the income distribution or, in Robert Frank's words, the inhabitants of Richistan (Frank 2007). Yet even here experiences across the developed world are not uniform. Certainly, those in the top 0.1% of the income distribution have got significantly richer in the UK, the USA and Canada over the last thirty years. But the same cannot be said for the same group in either France or Japan, which leads the OECD to conclude that: "differences in national policies and institutions also play an important role in determining the income share going to the top 0.1% and how it is affected by economic integration" (OECD 2007, p.117).

How might we describe these national variations? Self-evidently, there will be differences in tax systems, in the remuneration strategies of large corporations, in the extent of social norms of "acceptability" that place limits on executive pay, in the structure of capital markets, in the ease of merger and acquisition and in corporate governance arrangements. And the fact that these differences exist at all shows us that nations continue to have real social, economic and political choices available to them.

Andrew Glyn makes a similar point in noting that the extent of the growth in inequality has varied significantly between countries operating at a similar level of economic development and with similar exposure to international trade (Glyn 2000). And the OECD's analysis confirms that the USA and Japan, with similar degrees of trade openness, have had very different experiences of income inequality. Whatever is happening here, it cannot be attributed exclusively to globalisation.

We would therefore be wrong to conclude that the continued growth of India and China will lead to the impoverishment of the West or that rising income inequality is an inevitable consequence of these developments. Our experience shows us that the developed world can remain affluent if productivity continues to grow and wages rise broadly in line with productivity. Certainly, there is an irresistible case for investing in training and skills, but that has more to do with being able to respond to the changing nature of consumer demand in developed countries combined with the impact of technology than it does with supposed trade effects. Indeed, having suggested that globalisation is to blame for falling wages, Joseph Stiglitz contradicts himself and concedes our point by accepting that technology is the proximate cause of the deteriorating position of the unskilled (Stiglitz 2006, p. 273).

This is a useful step forward, but there may be other factors that are equally important in the US context. For example, the USA has witnessed rapid inward migration from Central and South America and, at the same time, has seen trade union influence decline and the federal minimum wage fall from what was, in international terms, an already low level. The basic laws of economics suggest that when the supply of a commodity increases significantly the price can be expected to fall if demand rises somewhat more slowly. This is a reasonably accurate description of the US labour market over the last decade and it helps to explain why the incomes of workers below the median have been under pressure. Experience in the UK offers a lively counter-example. Inward migration has been relatively high, but the National Minimum

Wage has continued to rise rapidly over the 2001–06 period. Low-paid workers have done well and there is no evidence of downward pressure on average earnings as a result of migration, trade or any other external factor (Coats 2007). Our previous conclusion still holds: national policies matter.

If we really want to understand how labour markets are changing then we would be better advised to look at the domestic institutional factors that reflect national policy choices and cultural preferences. Capital markets are of great importance, particularly because they shape the market for corporate control; and regulatory requirements can affect the extent of mergers and acquisitions, the role of private equity and the extent to which transactions are highly leveraged. A debt-laden company controlled by a private equity house may be highly sensitive to interest rate changes and may, as a result, have a relentless focus on reducing labour costs. As Martin Wolf has pointed out, the financial architecture of the so-called "new capitalism" is a much more important influence on the nature of work than the supposed effect of international trade (Wolf 2007).

Changing organisations

Alongside all these changes attributed to trade and technology are changes that have taken place in the nature of corporate organisation and the design of jobs. Richard Sennett has suggested that there has been a significant shift in the strategies adopted by multi-national companies in highly competitive international markets (Sennett 1998, 2006). These are the organisations that have downsized and delayered, moved from networks to hierarchies, instituted new forms of corporate organisation and now look more like an archipelago than a conventional "command-and-control" pyramid.

Virtual teams, flat hierarchies and porous departmental boundaries are all fundamental features of what Sennett also calls the "new capitalism". Whether these are widespread developments remains an open question, and Sennett is very careful to restrict his account to multi-nationals operating in global markets. Nonetheless, the story that he tells has some resonance in popular consciousness and, even though his work is almost entirely qualitative, the argument is supported by quantitative research which finds some evidence of similar phenomena (Gallie et al. 2004, White and Hill 2004).

Even if we accept the critique that Sennett is talking about a narrow rather than a widespread experience, we are still left with a profound question about the implications for organisations engaged in permanent structural change:

> How can we decide what is of lasting value in ourselves in a society which is impatient, which focuses on the immediate moment? How can mutual loyalties and commitments be sustained in institutions that are constantly breaking apart or continually being redesigned?
>
> (Sennett 1998, p. 10)

Sennett argues further that there is something to be said for hierarchy in a traditional "command-and-control" model, principally because employees know where they stand and they know who to blame when things go wrong. We might say that a traditional "Fordist" organisation is characterised by predictability and stability – things may change but they will not change fast, partly because of the complexity of the products being produced and the relative inflexibility of traditional mass production systems. Second, tasks are clearly delineated, workers know what they have to do and have the opportunity to build strong relationships with colleagues over time. Third, in the past, workers in a mass production environment would probably have been trade union members with access to effective voice institutions. Simply put, in a Fordist organisation workers are secure about their own position, they know who to go to if they have a problem, they know they can make themselves heard and they know that they will be dealt with fairly.

Whatever one makes of this argument, companies must be adopting new strategies for a reason; it cannot be the case, for example, that some persuasive management consultants have convinced firms to behave quite irrationally and adopt practices that are ineffective. An obvious answer is that new organisational forms enable companies to be nimbler in reacting to consumer demand in an economy where the tastes of an affluent population are becoming increasingly differentiated.

HR and high-performance working

Much of the management rhetoric suggests that these developments are an unqualified good for both employers and employees; "flexibility" is definitionally benign because it offers workers more autonomy and guarantees higher productivity for employers. A more determined application of "high-performance" management practices will lead us to the sunlit uplands where "work is more fun than fun". Continuous change is a fact of life and workers must learn to embrace uncertainty with enthusiasm; anything less is a retreat from an increasingly complex world and little more than wishful thinking.

This characterisation may seem a little extreme, but a swift glance at the smorgasbord of HR conferences shows that organisations are always in search of a magic bullet. Better employee engagement, higher effort levels and increased commitment are all supposed to follow the application of "enlightened" HR practices in redesigned and re-engineered organisations. Individual employee involvement is said to be a necessary condition for engagement. Relating pay more closely to individual effort is said to generate higher individual productivity. Yet what is perhaps most striking is the relatively weak evidence supporting the supposed superiority of new organisational models, new forms of work organisation and the bundle of "high-performance" HR practices. Put crudely, management gurus may claim to know "what works" and even "what works best" in our "globalised" world, but their models rarely reach the exacting standards of social science and as we have seen are sometimes founded on rather weak evidence.

An array of studies purport to demonstrate that people management has a direct and beneficial impact on productivity. However, as Toby Wall and Stephen Wood have pointed out, most of the efforts to prove causal relationships have so far produced little more than persuasive associations (Wall and Wood 2005). Much of the research is cross-sectional rather than longitudinal and the performance measures are often not robust enough to withstand rigorous stress testing. Moreover, there may be some "contamination" between measures of HRM and measures of performance, making it difficult to disentangle the direction of causation. Wall and Wood conclude that the evidence is "encouraging but ambiguous", even though there are "strong theoretical grounds for believing an HRM system centred on enhancing employee involvement should be beneficial for organisational performance" (Wall and Wood 2005, p. 454). In other words, we probably know less than we think about the importance (or otherwise) of HR as a strategic function that is supposed to ensure the alignment of individual aspiration with organisational mission and the delivery of strong organisational performance.

One can also find more critical commentaries, suggesting that applying the full bundle of "high-performance" practices can be self-defeating (Godard 2004). It is said that "high-performance" practices lead to an increase in labour costs and employers respond to these rising costs through an intensification of work. As a result employees lose faith in the practices, withhold discretionary effort and any further effort to apply the practices is abandoned because employers have become convinced that the business benefits are small or non–existent. This may be a rather harsh assessment, but it might explain why practices that are widely believed to improve performance have been applied so sparingly – or, in the words of the most comprehensive account of these developments, why the "diffusion of so-called 'high involvement management' practices has been rather muted in recent years" (Kersley et al. 2006, p. 107).

A consequence of the critical line of thinking promoted by Wood and Wall is that HR practitioners should begin to question some of their most cherished assumptions. Is it true, for example, that relating pay to individual performance is such an unqualified good that we can reasonably anticipate a world where every organisation has a system of individual performance pay? On one view the answer might be taken to be a slightly qualified "yes". After all, there is ample evidence to show that the adoption of performance pay proceeds apace – especially in the UK's public sector. But the evidence supporting PRP is at best ambiguous and at worst suggests that employers would be well advised to abandon the individualisation of reward at the earliest possible opportunity.

Perhaps the biggest surprise here is that individual performance pay continues to be so popular when the weight of the evidence suggests that there are serious difficulties associated with the practice. One leading commentator has suggested that "much of the conventional wisdom about pay today is misleading, incorrect and sometimes both" (Pfeffer 1998, p. 110). It is said that individual performance pay has been shown to undermine teamwork, encourage employees to focus on the short term and lead people to "link compensation to political skills and ingratiating personalities rather than to performance". Sometimes half-truths and total nonsense can get in the way of the hard facts that are needed for effective evidence-based management (Pfeffer and Sutton 2006).

We might take the view that this amounts to little more than a plea for better data, but practitioners may be a little too impatient to wait for a robust longitudinal study and have to make immediate decisions using the best research available. What might we say to them about new organisational forms, new forms of work organisation and new HR practices? How might these phenomena shape developments over our twenty-year time horizon?

Perhaps we should start with research findings that are at least moderately persuasive. So far as the pay question is concerned, this would suggest that organisations would be well advised to consider collective forms or remuneration (team-based pay) and abandon the focus on individualisation and intrusive performance management – of which more later.

Similarly and despite the critical assessment that we have already explored, there is evidence to show that "high-performance" practices can have a beneficial impact on performance when they are allied to effective arrangements for both direct and indirect employee participation (OECD 1999, Sisson et al. 1997). Other studies have reached similar conclusions, suggesting that "high-trust" relationships with trade unions when combined with "high-performance practices" deliver better results than either no employee involvement or individual employee involvement alone (Black and Lynch 2000). There is also evidence to show that, in the UK at least, high-performance practices are more widespread in unionised workplaces (Cully et al. 1999, Kersley 2006). Furthermore, another study shows that the level of openness is lower in those enterprises that only used direct forms of voice (individual employee involvement) and that multiple channels for consulting the workforce (trade unions, consultative committees, works councils and individual involvement methods) have proved to be mutually reinforcing (Wood and Fenton O'Creevy 2005).

All of this may seem a little distant from Sennett's new capitalism, but a moment's reflection will show that there is a link to the problems that he has identified. The real criticism of the "archipelago" model of the organisation is that it leaves employees feeling rootless, disconnected and the victims of events, with little or no control over their circumstances. The studies looking at the application of "high-performance practices" suggest that these practices can be made to work most effectively where organisations have a high level of social capital. Most importantly, perhaps, the strength of interpersonal relationships is sustained by the effectiveness of both direct employee involvement and collective consultation. For example, teamworking demands more effective interactions between members of the team. Joint problem solving can only be successful if individuals know that they can trust each other and trust their managers. Looking to the future, we might say that organisations with a proven capability to create and sustain high-trust relationships are also most likely to demonstrate resilience in the face of an increasingly competitive business environment.

Robert Putnam has offered us the very helpful observation that:

> A society characterised by generalised reciprocity is more efficient than a distrustful society, for the same reason that money is more efficient than barter. If we don't have to balance every exchange instantly, we can get a lot more accomplished. Trustworthiness lubricates social life.

(Putnam 2000, p. 21)

Life at work is simply a variety of social life and what applies to society at large applies in microcosm to the workplace. There may be no escaping the "new capitalism", whether we use Martin Wolf's definition of a new financial architecture or Richard Sennett's definition of new organisational forms, but we now have some compelling research findings that are at least suggestive of an agenda that can enable employers to reconcile efficiency and productivity with workers' demands for justice in the workplace.

Job quality in a changing labour market

Of course, a sceptic may say that this is all far too positive, and that the sad reality is that the new capitalism has been associated with work intensification, declining job satisfaction and the more widespread use of intrusive performance management systems. The story is widespread, popular and comes from the same stable as the argument that "globalisation" is a threat to both decent wages and high-quality jobs. The evidence offers a somewhat more ambiguous picture which, in its essentials, suggests that we should be optimistic rather than pessimistic about the future.

For the avoidance of doubt, it has to be made clear that a wholly positive account is open to the accusation of Panglossian optimism. There is substantial evidence to suggest that the quality of work has deteriorated in the recent past. In a paper for the UK's Economic and Social Research Council, Robert Taylor identified declining satisfaction with work throughout the 1990s, particularly dissatisfaction with pay and working time (Taylor 2002). The UK's Workplace Employment Relations Survey confirmed this finding and also suggested that employees had less influence over key workplace decisions than they would like (Kersley 2006). We know from the epidemiological research that autonomy and control over the process of work can have a significant impact on health and life expectancy (Marmot 2004). But recent studies have shown a decline in autonomy and task discretion in British workplaces, with barely two in five workers reporting that they can choose or change the order of tasks, choose or change the method of work, choose the speed or rate of work, influence their choice of working partners or take breaks when they wish (DTI 2007, Gallie 2004). Using a composite measure of job content suggests that the UK has something of a problem, being ranked with countries that languished under Soviet-style command economies for forty years (Romania, Bulgaria, and Lithuania) rather than the Nordic social democracies (DTI 2007).[2]

Yet, once again, we might observe that these experiences are not universal and wide variation can be observed across the EU's twenty-seven member states. For example, workers in the Nordic countries and the Netherlands all report a high level of autonomy at work, workers agree that their jobs often involve learning new things and they report a high level of "functional flexibility" (autonomous teamworking and job rotation). In general the process of work in all these countries is more intense than in the UK. The critical question here is the extent to which workers have control over what they do. Working at high intensity need not necessarily have an adverse impact on employees as long as they possess appropriate skills and are offered a high level of task discretion. As Michael Marmot has pointed out, contrary to the widespread perception, the security guard on the front desk is a more likely victim of coronary heart disease than the "highly stressed" senior manager on the executive floor (Marmot 2004). Richard Layard has offered a slightly more polemical account:

> Perhaps the most important issue is the extent to which you have control over what you do. There is a creative spark in each of us, and if it finds no outlet then we feel half-dead. This can be literally true; among British civil servants of any given grade, those who do the most routine work experience the most rapid clogging of the arteries.
>
> (Layard 2005, p. 68)

Skills development is obviously part of the answer to the job-quality conundrum, but the quality of management matters too. Those studies that identified the phenomenon of work intensification in the 1990s also suggested that rising skill levels had not been matched by a consequent change in employer policies and practices (Green 2003). Simply put, skills were not being fully utilised by employers, leaving workers frustrated and dissatisfied. Employers' skills requirements may have been rising (see our earlier discussion) but workers' levels of formal qualification were rising faster, leaving an increasing proportion of employees overqualified for the jobs that they did.

Of course, this might be a temporary or transitional effect that will disappear as the labour market assumes a new shape, but employers would be wise to pay close attention to the phenomenon, simply because it could have a damaging impact on recruitment, retention and business performance.

Throughout the 1990s, authoritative surveys consistently showed that people believed they were working harder (Green 2003) – work intensification was a well-documented phenomenon. However, the process has either slowed or been halted in the current decade (Brown et al. 2006, Green 2003). In part this can be attributed to an increasing employee familiarity with information and communications technologies (ICT). For example, PCs, laptops and email had become ubiquitous by the end of the 1990s, but initially at least employees were uncertain how to handle these technologies. Devices that were supposed to be productivity enhancing came to be seen as instruments that demanded more effort from workers – handling a raging torrent of emails, for example – and allowed employers to monitor performance more closely (counting keystrokes as a measure of productivity is a particularly egregious example). As time passed employees, however, learned how to manage the new technologies at lower levels of effort, with the consequence that the work intensification phenomenon was brought to a halt. Of course, it might be that we are about to witness another wave of technology-induced work intensification (the Blackberry syndrome) but so far the evidence for such an effect is either patchy or anecdotal.

Once again, the best conclusion is that national policies can have a decisive effect on the relationship between organisational change and job quality – otherwise it would be impossible to explain the differences between the UK, the Nordic countries and the Netherlands. Workplace institutions seem to be particularly important. In each of the "high-performing" countries workers have some opportunity to influence the course of events, both as individuals and through representative institutions like works councils or trade unions. Employee voice and the quality of management are therefore critical factors in ensuring that an appropriate trade-off is achieved between business efficiency and workplace justice.

Some final reflections

We have seen that the world of work remains the proverbial curate's egg – good in parts – and that while the basic structure of the labour market today has some similarities with twenty years ago the big story is about the transformation of the occupational structure and the rise and fall of industries. Although this chapter has sought to avoid the pitfalls of predicting the future it is reasonable to assume that some of the trends we have witnessed in the recent past are likely to continue.

First, we might anticipate that competition will intensify, partly as a result of technological change and rising prosperity but also because of conscious public policy decisions like the completion of the EU single market and the liberalisation of the global trading regime.

Second, demographic trends (which have not been discussed in detail in this chapter) will continue to play an important role in reshaping the labour market, employer strategies and government policies. For example, falling fertility rates and the changing dependency ratio will lead to somewhat later retirement and longer working lives, with both employers and government needing to change policy as a result. Moreover, demographic change will also require employers and governments to make it easier for women in particular to reconcile work and their caring responsibilities. Unless action is taken on this front then skills shortages are likely to emerge and a huge amount of productive potential (women's skills) will be wasted. And finally on this point, if the economy is to continue to grow at its trend rate (around 2.5% per annum) then government will need to have a positive attitude to managed migration to ensure that employers have access to an adequate supply of skilled labour.[3]

Third, there will be some disruption to established patterns of employment. As we have seen, it would be wrong to attribute this phenomenon exclusively to "globalisation", largely because "creative destruction" is an unavoidable consequence of capitalism. There is some disagreement about the scale and pace of change but rather more agreement about the appropriate policy response that is designed to *anticipate* change – investment in skills, an enabling welfare state ("a hand up, not a hand-out"), high unemployment benefits, active job-search obligations, moderate employment protection legislation and a fairly high level of labour market flexibility. To use the European jargon, a "flexicurity" model will enable developed countries to manage the consequences of structural change with a degree of sensitivity and humanity.

Fourth, we have seen that organisations are changing too in response to changing technologies and changing markets. These developments have not necessarily been an unqualified good for workers and it is not entirely clear either that all the "new" organisational models have had a positive effect on business performance. Yet while some uncertainty remains, we can still be confident in saying that good management matters for high performance (Bloom et al. 2007) and that effective workplace institutions that lubricate workplace relationships and create or sustain trust are important ingredients in the overall mix.

This brief review of international experience demonstrates that national policies matter. We are not at the mercy of impersonal or unmanageable forces that have been unleashed by neo-liberalism. There is still ample room for social, economic and political choice. And the same might be said of business models too. Capitalism is protean, multi-faceted and diverse – with open market economies being entirely compatible with very different institutional patterns and wide variations in the extent of income inequality. There is no "one right way" to economic success and no inevitable convergence on a single business model. These are essential facts to bear in mind if we are to face the future with confidence and rise to the challenge posed by the rapid restructuring of developed economies.

Notes

1 Although they might, like most of us, struggle to understand the bewildering array of financial instruments traded in derivatives markets.
2 The composite measure of job content includes whether the job involves monotonous tasks, learning new things, resolving unforeseen problems on your own and handling complex tasks (DTI 2007).
3 The USA does not have quite the same problem as most countries of the EU. Fertility rates are somewhat higher and we have already observed that there has been a large influx of migrant labour over the last two decades.

References

Black, S. E. and Lynch, L. (2000), *What's Driving the New Economy: The Benefits of Workplace Innovation*, National Bureau of Economic Research Working Paper 7479.

Blinder, A. (2007), *Offshoring: Big Deal or Business as Usual?* CEPS Working Paper No 149, June.

Bloom, N. et al. (2007), *Management Practice and Productivity: Why They Matter*, Centre for Economic Performance LSE and McKinsey.

Brinkley, I. (2007), *Trading in Knowledge and Ideas*, The Work Foundation, London.

Brinkley, I., Coats, D. and Overell, S. (2007), *Seven out of Ten: Labour under Labour 1997–2007*, Work Foundation, London.

Bronfenbrenner, K. and Luce, S. (2004), *The Changing Nature of Corporate Global Restructuring*, report prepared for the US-China Economic and Security Review Commission.

Brown, A. et al. (2006), *Changing Job Quality in Britain 1998–2004*, Employment Relations Research Series No 70, Department of Trade and Industry, London.

Chang, H.-J. (2002), *Kicking Away the Ladder*, Anthem Press, London.

Coats, D. (2006), *Who's Afraid of Labour Market Flexibility?*, The Work Foundation, London.

—— (2007), *The National Minimum Wage: Retrospect and Prospect*, The Work Foundation, London

Cully, M. et al. (1999), *Britain at Work*, Routledge, London.

DTI (2007), *Job Quality in Europe and the UK*, Employment Relations Research Series No 71, Department of Trade and Industry, London.

Esping-Anderson, G. (2005), Inequalities of Incomes and Opportunities, in Giddens, A. and Diamond, P. (eds), *The New Egalitarianism*, Polity Press, Cambridge, UK.

European Commission (2007), *Towards Common Principles of Flexicurity: More and Better Jobs Through Flexibility and Security*, Communication from the Commission to the Council, the European Parliament, the Economic and Social Committee and the Committee of the Regions, June.

Frank, R. (2007), *Richistan*, Piatkus Books, London.

Freeman, R. B. (2005), What Really Ails Europe and America: The Doubling of the Global Workforce, *The Globalist*, 3 June.

Friedman, T. (2005), *The World is Flat*, Allen Lane, New York.

Gallie, D. et al. (2004), Changing Patterns of Task Discretion in Britain, *Work Employment and Society*, 18: 243–66.

Glyn, A. (2000), Unemployment and Inequality, in Jenkinson, T. (ed.), *Macroeconomics*, OUP, Oxford, UK.

Godard, J. (2004), A critical assessment of the high performance paradigm, *British Journal of Industrial Relations*, 42(2): 349–78.

Green, F. (2003), The Demands of Work, in Dickens, R. (ed.), *The Labour Market Under New Labour*, Palgrave, Basingstoke.

Handy, C. (1994), *The Empty Raincoat*, Hutchinson, London.

Hirst, P. and Thompson, G. (1996), *Globalization in Question*, Polity Press, Cambridge, UK.

Hutton, W. (2006), *The Writing on the Wall*, Little Brown, New York.

Jenkins, C. and Sherman, B. (1979), *Collapse of Work*, Eyre Methuen, London.

—— (1981), *Leisure Shock*, Methuen, London.

Jones, F. (2006), *The Effects of Taxes and Benefits on Household Incomes, 2004/05*, Office of National Statistics.

Kersley, B. et al. (2006), *Inside the Workplace*, Routledge, Abingdon, UK.

Layard, R. (2005), *Happiness: Lessons From a New Science*, Allen Lane, New York.

Marmot, M. (2004), *Status Syndrome*, Bloomsbury, London.

OECD (1999), *OECD Employment Outlook*, OECD.

—— (2004), *OECD Employment Outlook*, OECD.

—— (2005), *OECD Employment Outlook*, OECD.

—— (2007), *OECD Employment Outlook*, OECD.

Palley, T. (2005), Trade Employment and Outsourcing: Some Observations on US–China Economic Relations, in Auer et al. (eds), *Offshoring and the Internationalisation of Employment*, ILO.

Pfeffer, J. (1998), Six Dangerous Myths About Pay, *Harvard Business Review*, May–June: 109–19.

Pfeffer, J. and Sutton, R. (2006), *Hard Facts, Dangerous Half-truths and Total Nonsense*, Harvard Business School Press, Cambridge, MA.

Putnam, R. (2000), *Bowling Alone*, Touchstone, New York.

Rifkin, J. (1996), *The End of Work*, Warner Books, Clayton, Australia.

Schumpeter, J. (1943), *Capitalism Socialism and Democracy*, Unwin edition 1987.

Sen, A. (1999), *Development as Freedom*, Random House, New York.

Sennett, R. (1998), *The Corrosion of Character: Personal Consequences of Work in the New Capitalism*, WW Norton and Co., London.

—— (2006), *The Culture of the New Capitalism*, Yale University Press, New Haven, CT.

Sisson, K. *et al.* (1997), *New Forms of Work Organisation: Can Europe Realise its Potential?*, European Foundation for the Improvement of Living and Working Conditions.

Stiglitz, J. (2006), *Making Globalisation Work*, Allen Lane, New York.

Taylor, R. (2002), *Britain's World of Work: Myths and Realities*, Economic and Social Research Council.

Wall, T. and Wood, S. (2005), The Romance of Human Resource Management and Business Performance, and the Case for Big Science, *Human Relations*, 58(4): 429–62.

White, M. and Hill, S. (2004), *Managing to Change*, Palgrave, Basingstoke.

Wood, S. and Fenton-O'Creevy, M. (2005), Direct Involvement, Representation and Employee Voice in UK Multinationals in Europe, *European Journal of Industrial Relations*, 11(1): 27–50.

Wolf, M. (2004), *Why Globalisation Works*, Yale University Press, New Haven, CT.

—— (2007), Unfettered Finance is Fast Reshaping the Global Economy, *Financial Times*, 18 June.

3

The pursuit of HR's core purpose

The practical doing of strategic HRM

Anthony J. Rucci

HR management is about managing people. 'Strategic' HR management is about making people and organizations successful. It should be noted that these are two very different things.

The focus of this chapter will not be on making HR more strategic, but rather on making organizations more effective. I would suggest that no matter how inelegant or unsophisticated the strategic framework of the HR strategy in an organization may look or sound, any HR professional or function that helps align human and intellectual capital behind the successful achievement of an organization's goals is, by definition, 'strategic'. Over the past twenty years or so, the HR profession has been littered with conferences on 'becoming a strategic partner'. So much so, that in the search for the holy grail of a good HR strategy, the profession may actually have lost its focus on *why we exist*.

So, for the duration of this chapter, let me ask you to suspend disbelief. Let us forget about making the HR profession strategic. In doing so, we may find that our definition of 'strategic HR' has been misplaced and misguided for some time. The entire premise of this treatment is that it's *not* about making HR strategic, it's about making organizations strategically successful.

HR's core purpose

In 1996, Collins and Porras published a now classic article in the *Harvard Business Review* entitled "Building your company's vision". In particular, Collins and Porras describe an organization's 'core ideology', a combination of two factors which those authors take great pains to define operationally. They encourage organizations to be very deliberate about *discovering* these two factors. The two factors of core ideology are: core values and core purpose. It may surprise you to learn that we are going to skip over the core values discussion here in search of the strategic role of HR. We will do this not because core values are not vitally important, but because core purpose is so fundamentally related to strategy.

Collins and Porras describe core purpose as an organization's "reason for being". It goes beyond strategy, beyond goals and beyond business objectives. It gets to the deeper meaning for an organization's existence. A core purpose "reflects people's idealistic motivations for doing the company's work" (p. 68). Does Disney 'operate theme parks', or do they exist to make people happy? Does Fannie Mae 'grant mortgage loans', or do they democratize home ownership? The difference in those two examples illustrates the important affective and inspirational value of a core purpose.

So, what if we were presumptuous enough to attempt to articulate a core purpose statement for the entire HR profession around the world? And not just for HR in for-profit companies, but any variety of organizations . . . universities, philanthropies, governments, publicly traded companies, religions, military agencies, sports franchises and charities? What might that core purpose statement look like? *Why does HR exist?* Based on practicing, studying and observing for over thirty years, my admittedly subjective attempt at a statement of core purpose for the HR profession would look something like this: "To build organizational capabilities that help achieve sustained *value creation*, by *focusing* the *commitment* of people's energy, effort and *ideas* on a common *vision*."

There are four key themes evident in the italicized words in the above core purpose statement for HR. Each of the four themes – 1. *value creation*, 2. *focus and vision*, 3. *commitment* and 4. *ideas* – has profound implications for the practice of HR as a profession, and in judging when HR is strategic, and when it's not. These themes will create the architecture for the discussion and practical considerations treated here. We will come back at the very end of this discussion to focus on HR itself.

Value creation

This is *not* a financial reference. Any organization exists to create value, whether it be a for-profit, charitable, educational, military or religious organization. In fact, organizations *must* create value, for someone – customers, shareholders, employees, members, society – or they will cease to exist, period. Religions can create value spiritually for their members by enabling them to find meaning and order in their lives, and spiritual peace of mind. If a religious entity doesn't do that, it will cease to exist. Military and police organizations create value by protecting the domestic security of their citizens. If they fail to do that they will cease to exist. And for-profit companies create value by producing goods and services that consumers will purchase on financial terms that generate acceptable returns on invested capital for the owners of the firm. If a for-profit company fails to do that, it will cease to exist, because investors will not continue to channel capital into that entity.

Historically, the very term 'value creation' has been used to describe economic benefit generated, but in the proposed core purpose statement for the HR profession it is not meant to connote only economic value creation. In fact, we will come back to this topic later and argue that successful organizations define value creation much more broadly than economics in order to achieve sustained high performance.

Focus and vision

Focus is all about alignment behind the Vision. Value creation cannot be achieved without human energy, effort and ideas being channeled toward the achievement of a desired outcome. When human creativity and effort are focused on the accomplishment of a common, desirable goal the outcome can be powerful.

The key elements here are: (1) alignment of an organization's intellectual and human capital behind a goal; and (2) a 'clear line of sight' for every employee – from the CEO to the fork-lift operator – as to how each of their jobs contributes to the achievement of the value creation goal. In order for human beings to contribute their energy, effort and ideas to a goal *they must know what the goal is.* This seems like a stunningly simple statement, but it is disheartening how many organizations fail to explain their strategies and goals to their employees, volunteers, soldiers, ministers. In fact, many organizations tend to keep their goals and strategies a secret, for fear of giving away competitive information. It is possible to convey strategic focus without disclosing proprietary information.

Commitment

This is a pivotal concept in our statement of core purpose for the HR profession. It speaks to active *commitment* by people to the purpose and goals of the organization, rather than passive acceptance of what they are told to do. But be careful what you wish for. When you unleash people's energy and ideas and ask them to channel those toward a goal, they can become inspired but non-compliant if they see a better way.

The greatest gift you can be given by a member of your organization is a conversation that starts out with them saying something like this, "You know, I was thinking last night at home about our issue and . . .". In that simple statement you know you enjoy the commitment of that individual. They've given you the two most valuable things they have to contribute to your organization . . . their time and their ideas.

Ideas

We could easily have isolated energy and effort here as well, but the true value creator in any organization today is ideas . . . new, different and energizing ideas. How does an organization foster, encourage, acknowledge and reward ideas? Large organizations by their very size tend to suppress human innovation and creativity. As organizations get older, larger and more complex there's an unseen 'regression to the norm' effect. Unwittingly or not, organizations seek and reward uniformity and conventional behavior and thinking. How can a company's people practices provide a needed counter-balance to this inexorable regression to the norm?

We know that highly successful organizations are those that conceptualize how to *differentiate* themselves from competitors, not just replicate best practices (Porter, 1996). Ironically, much of HR's heritage in the latter half of the twentieth century was designed to create order in organizations as they became bigger and more diffused. In today's complex world of value creation, dependency on uniformity is not only non-strategic, it can actually be a value destroyer.

Those four key themes from our core purpose statement for HR – value creation, focus and vision, commitment and ideas – will frame our discussion of the strategic role of HR in organizations at both a conceptual and practical level. Let's broadly define the strategic implications for HR for each of those four right now, and then through the remainder of this chapter we will consider the practical implications of each one.

Table 3.1 HR's core purpose and strategic implications

Core purpose: To build organizational capabilities that help to achieve sustained value creation, by focusing the commitment of people's energy, effort and ideas on a common vision.
Strategic implications: 1. Define value creation broadly to include intangible factors. 2. Get people focused on the vision and their role in driving achievement of that vision. 3. Promote employee commitment by involving people in the strategy. 4. Generate ideas and innovation by selecting leaders who encourage open, enlightened debate.

Strategic implication #1: Define value creation broadly

HR must help organizations 'mature' into a broader definition of value creation than merely the historic, myopic, economic-viability definition. In other words, HR must help organizations build models that reflect the value generated by intangibles.

Strategic implication #2: Get people focused on the organization's vision

Help your organization to frame its purpose, goals and strategies in ways that capture the imagination of people, and which can be readily communicated and understood by people throughout the organization.

Strategic implication #3: Promote commitment

Work on gaining the discretionary energy, effort and ideas of people in your organization by focusing on people management practices that foster commitment.

Strategic implication #4: Select and promote leaders who generate ideas from people

Support and promote leaders, managers and supervisors who are not threatened by ideas that may end up being better than their own.

Strategic implication #1: Define value creation broadly

Traditionally, value creation was a concept viewed as pretty much the exclusive domain of economists and finance professionals: "Does an organization in the for-profit domain generate returns on invested capital greater than their average weighted cost of cumulative capital employed?" If so, then intrinsic economic value has been generated. Historically, in line with this economic definition of value creation, an organization's market value moved in direct ratio to its book value. In fact, going back to the mid-1960s through the late 1980s, the best predictor of an organization's market value was its book value.

Book value, in laymen's terms, is what the 'hard assets' of the firm would be worth if you threw a gigantic, global garage sale. Put all the plants, warehouses, equipment, raw inventories and real estate out at the curb – how much could you get for the hard assets? From the 1960s until 1990, the ratio of market value to book value was roughly 1:1 for the typical publicly traded company. Between 1990 and 1995 that increased to approximately 4:1. In the late 1990s the ratio climbed even spuriously higher in the 'irrationally exuberant' dot-com period. Post the 2000 market decline, the market-to-book ratio of companies recovered to about 3:1 in 2003, and in mid-2008 that ratio once again stands at about 4:1. What does that 4.1 ratio tell us? It means that only 20–25% of the market value of companies today can be explained by their hard assets. Conversely, it means that over 75% of the market value of companies can be attributed to 'soft' assets. Or to use the more common term, 'intangible' assets.

What are intangible assets? It could be a long list, but ultimately intangible value drivers boil down to two broad categories: customer equity as represented in brand reputation and customer service excellence, and intellectual and human capital. Much of the thought leadership on intangible asset valuation referenced here is based on the work of economist Baruch Lev (2001), who has been tracking company market values and performance indicators for nearly forty years, first at Berkeley and later at New York University. Lev and other insightful economists have challenged the 'tangible assets' model of value generation in favor of a more balanced model that also considers the value-added contribution of intangible assets. In fact, Lev has argued that intangible assets can be economically valued, in what he calls the 'Value Chain Scoreboard', and he has provided algorithms for estimating the actual economic value of a company's intangible assets.

So why is Lev's work so relevant here? It illustrates what other non-economists have been researching and hinting at for a number of years. Authors such as Heskett, Sasser and Schlesinger's (1997) work on the 'service-profit chain'; Rucci, Kirn and Quinn's (1998) work on the 'employee-customer-profit chain'; and Ulrich, Zenger and Smallwood's (1999) work on results-based leadership clearly show that 'soft' (read *intangible*) factors like customer service, customer loyalty, leadership effectiveness and employee commitment are significant leading indicators of economic value creation. In fact, some of these authors have developed mathematical algorithms that quantify what a 5% improvement in employee or customer satisfaction will translate into in increased revenues at a later point in time. More recently, Ulrich and Smallwood (2003) have extended the concept of intangibles to organizational capability and leadership effectiveness.

The strategic implication for HR professionals for this work on intangibles is that it is possible to build a model for your organization that quantifies the economic value of intangibles. Measure what matters. Instead of wasting your time and energy on secondary or intermediary factors related to human capital, build models that show how customer satisfaction and employee commitment directly drive economic value growth like revenue, earnings and cash flow. Such models have been built and demonstrated at Sears Roebuck and Co., Cardinal Health and the Ohio State University Medical Center, and many other organizations are working toward such models, including Starbucks, Home Depot and others. Kaplan and Norton's fine work on the Balanced Scorecard (1996) was an important early conceptual model that considered employee, customer and operational factors as leading indicators of value creation. More recently, David Norton and the Balanced Scorecard Collaborative have been working with a number of global organizations on quantifying intangible value creators and building predictive models (Kaplan and Norton 2004a, b).

In order to do this, however, HR executives and professionals need to understand the competitive strategy of their organizations, understand how their organizations create value, be economically literate and then figure out how people management practices map directly back onto value creation. In short, strive to be a business *person*, not just a business *partner*. You can no longer expect your organization's leadership to accept the platitude that 'people are our most important assets' as an article of faith. You need to demonstrate that fact in economically viable terms. It is possible to do this. Broaden your organization's definition and frame of reference regarding value creation to include intangible value creation for customers and employees as leading indicators of economic value growth.

Strategic implication #2: Get people focused on the organization's vision

Before beginning to read this section, ask yourself three questions:

1. Does my organization currently have a simple statement of vision – *a clear, elevating goal*?
2. Has this clear, simple statement been widely communicated at all levels of the organization?
3. Do people's individual performance objectives reflect how they will personally support the vision? In short, does the vision translate to individual employee behavior?

49

If you answered no to any one of the above questions, you now have a golden opportunity to help accelerate value creation in your organization.

Vision and strategy are important. And it's important to get it right. People like Porter (1996) and Hamel and Prahalad (1994) have done a very effective job over the past fifteen or twenty years of impressing on organizations how critical good strategy is to their success at value creation. Organizations have taken it to heart and have improved their discipline in the area of strategy, often introducing comprehensive planning efforts throughout their organizations. This has presumably led to better strategies within organizations. But increasingly, leaders are discovering that the most elegant and well-thought-out strategies will under-deliver on the promise unless that strategy, (a) can be stated simply to any level of employee in their organization, and (b) people's efforts are aligned behind the successful achievement of the strategic goals. In fact, in a 2007 survey by the Conference Board of CEOs from global companies with over $5 billion in sales, 'consistent execution of strategy' was the number one area of greatest concern for those CEOs, with 42% agreeing with that issue. That concern ranked ahead of 'sustained top line growth' (39%), and 'profit growth' (33%)!

More recently, Bossidy, Charan and Burck (2002) and Kaplan and Norton (2004a, 2006) have begun to address the issue of strategy *execution*, rather than strategy *formulation*, as the 'missing ingredient' to translating good strategy into value creation outcomes. Through the application of the Balanced Scorecard methodology, Kaplan and Norton (2006) have focused organizational attention on how to operationalize a strategy to achieve performance results. What is particularly encouraging about Kaplan and Norton's work is that they are increasingly focused on the 'intangible' dimensions of strategy execution like human capital and customer equity. In fact, much of Kaplan and Norton's work (2004b) has outlined three intangible areas of necessity in order to drive strategy to value creation: human capital, information capital and organization capital.

In short, the opportunity to identify a simple statement of strategy, communicate it effectively and then align human capital behind the strategy is a big value creation opportunity for organizations today, and for HR. So, as an HR professional how can you make a strategic intervention into your company's value creation efforts? If your answer to any or all of the opening three questions was 'no', try the following (Warning: this section has nothing to do with HR, per se, and may even get you looked at a little askance the first time you talk to your CEO, CFO or head of corporate development about it):

- Offer to lead an effort to capture your organization's vision and articulate it in a clear, simple phrase.
- Once armed with that simple statement of strategy, communicate it broadly to every individual in your organization in a personal way.
- Once they understand the simple statement of strategy, require people at all levels to translate the strategy into what it means in their job – in practical terms – in their day-to-day behaviors.

People cannot support the strategy unless they know it and understand it. A blinding flash of the obvious, perhaps, but many organizations don't take the time to articulate the strategy in simple terms and then communicate it to their employees. So, how can you accomplish the three steps outlined above?

Get three or four of your senior managers together in a room for about ninety minutes and ask them each to describe the current vision of your organization. They'll have a difficult time doing this. They'll ask questions about whether you mean vision, mission, goal or strategy, because they think those four things are different. That will be a stall tactic, because they're just feeling awkward about not being able to accomplish the simple task you requested. Don't let them off the hook. Keep pressing. If you want to help them, ask them to tell you what they'd say to their brother-in-law across the Thanksgiving dinner table the next time he asks, "Hey, what does your organization actually do?". If you can get your senior managers to answer that simple question in twenty-five words or less . . . no, fifteen words or less, you are well on your way to adding real strategic value.

Next, get someone who's got the creative 'right brain' thing going to give you a hand in making whatever your senior managers came up with even simpler. The goal here is to be as brief and concise as possible, and not to have this sound like something a Harvard B-School MBA team dreamed up. It has to be a simple, credible statement that can be communicated to anyone, at any level and have them nod their head. Pressure test that simple statement with your senior managers one more time. Now begin to communicate this simple statement throughout your company. Whatever your intuition tells you is the right amount of communication, triple that amount and you'll start to reach the level of communication needed. Use a variety of ways to communicate it: town hall meetings, group presentations, videos, websites, newsletters. Do *not* rely exclusively on wall plaques and laminated wallet cards. Those can be used, but they are not sufficient. Leadership needs to take this message out to people face-to-face in order to be effective.

Once people know what the simple strategy is, ask them to consider how their job can directly support the achievement of that vision. Ask them to write it down. In fact, ask people at all levels to develop individual performance objectives in support of the vision as part of the performance management system of the organization, and get their manager to agree to those objectives.

There it is. In those three steps you have taken a major step toward focusing and aligning your organization behind the strategic vision. Don't over-complicate this process. Sacrifice some precision and wordsmithing in favor of engaging as many people as possible in knowing the direction in which you want them to head.

Strategic implication #3: Promote commitment

The premise for this third piece of HR being strategically relevant is based on a simple idea (see Figure 3.1). *Employee commitment* is a leading indicator of customer outcomes and value creation. In Figure 3.1, you see an employee-customer-profit value creation chain. Ultimately, we want to generate sustained value creation, however we define that (e.g. financially, socially, spiritually, militarily). This is the outcome we exist to create. The model in Figure 3.1 suggests that two critical, intangible factors can be a leading indicator of value creation: customer satisfaction and employee commitment. In fact, a number of practitioners and researchers across a wide spectrum of organizations have demonstrated this empirically (Buckingham and Coffman, 1999; Heskett et al., 1997; Rucci et al., 1998).

If employee commitment is such a powerful value creator, what is it and what factors contribute to strengthening it? Rucci, Ulrich and Gavino (1998) have defined 'employee commitment' as "*gaining discretionary energy, effort and ideas from people*". Commitment is not

| Employee commitment (leading indicator) | + | Customer satisfaction (leading indicator) | = | Value creation |

Figure 3.1 A simple idea about intangible value creation

'satisfaction', and is not 'loyalty', two terms that have been used historically as an explanation for the emotional attachment an employee feels toward an organization. The evidence to date is pretty clear. You can have satisfied employees; you can have loyal employees, but those factors are not leading indicators of customer satisfaction and other value creation outcomes. Commitment speaks to a much more active *involvement* by people in the achievement of strategic goals. Employees' answers to satisfaction questions like "I like my pay", "I like my benefits" are important to know, but those types of traditional employee survey questions do not measure commitment. How do you know if you enjoy 'commitment' that leads to better customer and value creation? Ask your employees how strongly they agree with the following kinds of statements:

> *My work gives me a sense of accomplishment.*
> *I am proud to say I work here.*
> *I have a good understanding of our business strategy.*
> *We are making changes necessary to compete effectively.*
> *We make customers a top priority.*
> *We are investing in innovative products and services for our customers.*
> *I see a direct connection between my job and the goals of the organization.*
> *I feel good about the future of the organization.*
> *We are driven to achieve high standards of performance.*
> *People take personal accountability for their actions here.*
> *I have a good understanding of our core values.*
> *I like the kind of work I do.*
> *Dignity of the individual is never compromised here.*

Questions like these are not an index of how 'happy' or satisfied employees are. They are an indicator of how much an employee understands the strategy of the organization, how confident they feel in helping to drive strategic outcomes, and finally how they feel they are treated as individuals by their leaders. In fact, LaFasto and Larson (2002) talk about a virtuous cycle that summarizes the two themes here of *focus and vision* and *commitment*. Their simple algorithm is:

> *Clarity* → *Confidence* → *Commitment*

Employees who are *clear* about the goals of the organization will have a greater degree of *confidence* in their ability to contribute effectively to that goal, and will therefore be more *committed* to the goal, and to the organization. Driving employee commitment is a major determinant of successful strategic execution, and we've already discussed that execution of strategy is a critical value creator.

So, what organizational factors and practices lead to greater employee commitment? The list is pretty concise, pretty clear and pretty simple. People remain committed to three things in organizations:

- an inspiring vision that they relate to;
- teams they value being part of;
- leaders they choose to follow.

As an HR professional, if you want to make a meaningful strategic contribution to your organization's success, focus on efforts in these three areas. We've already discussed how important it is to help the organization frame and communicate its vision in an earlier section, and we will leave team effectiveness for a later day. But now, let's focus on the final strategic implication theme: ideas, and the crucial role of leaders who drive employee commitment and ideas.

Strategic implication #4: Select and promote leaders who generate ideas from people

Earlier we suggested that it is ideas which drive value creation in organizations today. Market valuations and market multiple premiums go to organizations that take hard assets and add incremental value in the form of innovation, design and customer awareness (Hamel 2000). The earlier discussion of Lev's (2001) work on market-to-book-value ratios clearly illustrates that this intangible idea 'premium' is very real. Once again, the value creation potential of 'intangible' factors is increasingly recognized.

It is leaders who either promote idea generation from people, or suppress it. So, if your goal is to gain the discretionary energy, effort and *ideas* from people, then as an HR professional you should focus your efforts on helping the organization select leaders who will accelerate the idea generation capacity of your culture. First, have processes in place that facilitate the identification, selection and development of leaders. This includes things like: have a clear set of leadership competencies your organization looks for, have a leadership planning process in place, be serious about development efforts for future leaders, take selection of supervisors and managers very seriously, and use things like 360-degree survey information on leaders. We could review about fifty years of research literature here (see, for example, Bennis, 1989; Collins, 2004; Goleman, 1998; Rucci, 2001; Zaleznik, 1977) on what makes a good leader, but very simply, as an HR professional if you want to help your organization select leaders who drive idea generation, then help it to select leaders who do the following four things:

- create a vision and involve and inspire others;
- achieve results and hold people accountable;
- reinforce values and hold people accountable;
- treat people with dignity and build their confidence.

These four leadership capabilities are fairly self-descriptive, except perhaps for the theme of 'accountability' in both numbers two and three. Successful organizations and successful leaders are not about making people happy or creating a nice place to work. They are about achieving value creation, doing it the right way and holding people accountable for both 'what' they achieve, but also 'how' they achieve it. And really effective leaders do not tolerate employees who are not contributing and performing; they are equally intolerant of employees who are behaving in ways that are not consistent with the core values of the organization.

Leaders who demonstrate the above four capabilities are more likely to gain the discretionary ideas from those they lead. And ideas drive value creation. Put processes in place in an organization which cause it to focus on selecting these kinds of leaders.

Adding strategic value in HR

This chapter has attempted to focus on ways to make HR a meaningful contributor to an organization's success at sustained value creation. By focusing on HR's core purpose, more than an HR strategy, the profession can actually become strategically integrated. Ironically, the less we focus on being 'strategic in HR', and the more we focus on helping organizations create value the more relevant we become. In fact, I look to the day when we don't have to discuss the strategic role of HR. The debate only serves to beg the question and detracts from HR's core purpose: to help organizations achieve sustained value creation, by focusing the commitment of people's energy, effort and ideas on a common vision. And the way to realize that core purpose, as suggested here, is for HR professionals to focus not on strategy in HR, but rather on value creation in four ways, as discussed and summarized in Table 9.1.

What does this mean for HR?

So what conditions need to exist within an HR organization that will enable it to make the contribution required in each of the four areas above? There are any number of things that could be considered to answer that question, including: Does HR have a plan for itself? Has HR translated the strategic goals of the organization into its people implications? Does HR have the resources needed to carry out the mission? But I would like to conclude this chapter on the strategic relevance of HR by focusing on the one question that I believe will ensure that the HR profession is making a meaningful contribution to value creation in organizations: Do we have the right people in HR in our organizations?

What do the very best HR professionals look like?

They have personal credibility

The most successful HR professionals are also those who enjoy a personal reputation for trust and credibility. That doesn't merely mean that they are nice people. It means that they honour commitments they make. They follow through on promises. They personally achieve results and have high performance standards. They hold themselves accountable for their performance, and don't make excuses when they or the function fail to perform. They maintain confidences and they operate confidently based on a clear sense of purpose, both about the profession and themselves and what they stand for.

They are business people

Notice this didn't say 'they have business acumen', or 'they are a business partner'. Rather, the very best HR professionals are those who not only understand business, but actually enjoy it. This is the biggest liability among the profession and its professionals today (see Hammonds, 2005). We should expect HR professionals and executives to be no less a business person and leader than we expect from a CFO, a general manager or a CEO. In order to accomplish that, HR professionals must understand their organization's business. They must not just be able to understand financial numbers, but know the business of the organization. They should be able to answer three simple questions: Who is the customer? Who is the competition? Who are we? This should reflect a realistic assessment of their own organization. An HR professional should be able to conduct a credible twenty-minute business discussion about their organization with a customer, a supplier, an investment manager, an investment analyst, a community leader.

They are change agents

More than ever, organizations need an internal catalyst for change in order to remain competitive. HR professionals are in a unique position to be drivers of change, rather than merely be asked to help manage change. But that requires some real assertiveness and personal risk taking. It means being willing to put yourself on an operating leaders' calendar and discussing issues of concern well beyond HR issues, raising issues that you see anywhere in the organization and having credible recommendations about how to address those issues. In order to be taken seriously in your efforts to command the attention of non-HR leaders in your organization, you can see why personal credibility and business understanding discussed above are so critical. You will not be able to create change, or even be taken seriously, if you cannot exhibit those two capabilities.

They have excellent professional skills

It should go without saying that in order to be effective in a professional HR role you need to have excellent professional skills. Understand the professional areas of importance: employee relations, labour law, compensation, benefits, development, organization development, information technology and systems, etc. However, the critical concept here may be a bit surprising to you. Have good professional skills and knowledge, just don't strive to be known for that. Keep your professional knowledge and skills low-key, particularly among non-HR leaders in your organization. They assume you know what you're doing professionally, and want to be assured that you are focusing on their business and strategic issues, not any parochial professional issues.

They are employee advocates

Despite all of the prior rhetoric in this chapter, this is the final (seemingly inconsistent?) requirement for effective HR professionals. Beyond helping organizations create value, beyond being strategic, beyond being business relevant, have real courage of conviction about your 'ultimate' role as an advocate for employees. Nothing about the importance of business relevance or the strategic relevance of what HR does in any way excuses or absolves an HR professional from the professional obligation of protecting the dignity of people in organizations. If we believe that the commitment of people's energy, effort and ideas are what create value in organizations, then this final requirement is not only consistent with that core purpose, but is the foundation of that purpose. The very best HR professionals and executives, the very best business people and the very best leaders will put their own personal interests at risk to protect the dignity of the people they lead. It is the foundation of value creation in organizations where 'intangibles' drive sustained strategic success.

References

Bennis, W. and Bennis, W.G. (1989) *On Becoming a Leader*. Perseus Publishing, New York.
Bossidy, L., Charan, R. and Burck, C. (2002) *Execution: the discipline of getting things done*. Crown Business, New York.
Buckingham, M. and Coffman, C. (1999) *First, Break all the Rules*. Simon & Schuster, New York.
Collins, J. (2004) Level V leadership. *Harvard Business Review*, 79(1): 66–76.
Collins, J. and Porras, J. (1996) Building your company's vision. *Harvard Business Review*, 74(5): 65–77.

Goleman, D. (1998) What makes a leader. *Harvard Business Review*, 76(6): 92–102.

Hamel, G. (2000) *Leading the Revolution: How to thrive in turbulent times by making innovation a way of life.* Harvard Business School Press, Boston.

Hamel, G. and Prahalad, C. (1994) *Competing for the Future.* Harvard Business School Press, Boston.

Hammonds, K. (2005) Why we hate HR. *Fast Company*, 97: 42–47.

Heskett, J., Sasser, W. and Schlesinger, L. (1997) *The Service Profit Chain.* The Free Press, New York.

Kaplan, R. and Norton, D. (1996) *The Balanced Scorecard: translating strategy into action.* Harvard Business School Press, Boston.

Kaplan, R. and Norton, D. (2004a) Measuring the strategic readiness of intangible assets. *Harvard Business Review*, 82(2): 52–63.

Kaplan, R. and Norton, D. (2004b) *Strategy Maps: converting intangible assets into tangible outcomes.* Harvard Business School Publishing, Boston.

Kaplan, R. and Norton, D. (2006) *Alignment: using the balanced scorecard to create corporate synergies.* Harvard Business School Publishing, Boston.

LaFasto, F. and Larson, C. (2002) *When Teams Work Best.* Sage Publications, London.

Lev, B. (2001) *Intangibles: management, measurement and reporting.* Brookings Institution, Washington DC.

Losey, M., Ulrich, D. and Meisinger, S. (2005) *The Future of Human Resource Management: 64 thought leaders explore the critical issues of today and tomorrow.* John Wiley & Sons, New York.

Porter, M. (1996) What is Strategy? *Harvard Business Review*, 74(6): 61–78.

Rucci, A. (2001) What the best business leaders do best. In R. Silzer (Ed.), *The 21st century executive.* Jossey-Bass, San Francisco.

Rucci, A., Kirn, S. and Quinn, R. (1998) The employee-customer-profit chain at Sears. *Harvard Business Review*, 76(1): 82–97.

Rucci, A., Ulrich, D. and Gavino, M. (1998) Unpublished work. *The VOICE Model of Leadership*.

Ulrich, D. and Smallwood, N. (2003) *Why the Bottom Line Isn't!: How to build value through people and organization.* John Wiley & Sons, New York.

Ulrich, D., Zenger, J. and Smallwood, N. (1999) *Results Based Leadership.* Harvard Business School Press, Boston.

Zaleznik, A. (1977) Managers and leaders: Are they different? *Harvard Business Review*, May–June: 67–73.

Managing strategic change

David A. Buchanan

Objectives and context

This chapter has three objectives. First, we will examine potential roles for the human resource management function in relation to strategic organizational change. Second, key aspects of the nature and processes of organizational change are outlined. Third, following that analysis, the implications for practice are considered. With compelling evidence for the impact of human resource policy on organizational performance, the function is positioned to contribute in significant ways to corporate strategy. However, this chapter argues that, curiously, the function is often under-represented in the change process, and 'punches below its weight' in this regard. Consequently, in order to be more effective players in the strategic change game, human resource practitioners need to be able to compete more effectively with change agents in other management functions. This in turn means that human resource professionals must be able and willing to use more sophisticated political skills.

Given the pattern of change that most organizations now experience, the role of the human resource function should be pivotal, but this contribution is rarely recognized in the change management and organization development literature. Tracking the top 50 companies in Britain through the 1990s, Whittington and Mayer (2002) observe that, by the beginning of the twenty-first century, large businesses were implementing major reorganizations every three years, on average. In addition, most businesses were also regularly conducting many minor reorganizations. This pattern of repeat change, they argue, is driven by three factors:

1. intensified competition and stockmarket turbulence in the private sector, and consumerism and government pressures in the public sector;
2. the pace of technological innovation;
3. increasing knowledge-intensity, placing a premium on good organization design to reduce barriers to information flows.

This study also observed that change outcomes are often poor, in terms of financial returns and damaged morale. One of the main reasons for these results lies with the focus on technical and structural issues (such as expensive new accounting and information technology systems) in major change programmes, and the relative lack of attention to cultural and behavioural factors. And as Caldwell (2001) observes, major strategic investments will rarely be deferred on human resource management grounds, although such issues will almost always arise. Whittington and Mayer (2002) thus argue that, as 'the soft stuff' becomes more important, so does the role of the human resource management function, which is central to the success of repeat change through the knock-on effects this has on organization culture, leadership styles, and senior management succession, along with staff recruitment, retention, careers, rewards, training, and skills. One of the main conclusions from this study is that repeat change puts a premium on the skills of *adaptive reorganization*, constantly redesigning in response to trends and opportunities. Managing change is no longer a one-off task with clear start and end points, but an ongoing, and critical, responsibility. A more important conclusion, perhaps, is that the ability to redesign the organization frequently contributes more significantly to competitive advantage than one particular structure.

The necessary organizational capabilities for repeat reorganization include clear formal structures and reporting relationships, standardized performance metrics, consistent organization-wide compensation policies, propensity to organize in small performance-oriented units, and culture of change (Whittington and Mayer, 2002, p. 26). They conclude that the attributes of those leading repeat organizational change should include:

- action- and results-oriented;
- able to play many roles, from visionary to organizer to lobbyist;
- self-critical and restless in seeking improvements;
- involvement in collegial interactions across boundaries;
- politically sensitive but not politically motivated.

Despite these findings, the human resource management function had a leading role in organizational change in only one in five of the organizations involved in this research. In exploring how the function's influence and contribution can be strengthened in this respect, we will consider in this chapter the significance of political skill in particular, accepting the need for sensitivity in this domain. However, it will be necessary to challenge as unhelpful the advice that the human resource manager should not be politically motivated.

Typologies of typologies

With respect to the role, or roles, of the personnel or human resource management function, a major concern over the past two decades has been the development of appropriate typologies. Definitions of the concept of strategic human resource management, contrasted with that of the traditional personnel function, consistently emphasize the function's role in organizational change. Storey (1992) characterizes the strategic, interventionist orientation of human resource 'changemakers', in sharp contrast to the personnel function's stereotypical roles as 'regulators', 'advisors', and 'handmaidens'. Revisiting his earlier typology of personnel roles, including 'clerk of works', 'contracts manager', and 'architect', Tyson (1995) argues that the pace of change creates opportunities for the human resource management function to contribute to major change initiatives. Ulrich (1998) argues that the function needs a 'new agenda' with four components, noting that competency in change management in particular is vital to the career success of the human resource professional. These four components are:

1. strategic partners, working with line managers in strategy execution;
2. administrative experts, offering expertise to reduce costs and improve quality;

3. employee champions, representing staff concerns and working to increase employees' contribution to performance;
4. agents of continuous transformation, developing capacity for change.

Schuler, Jackson and Storey (2001, p. 127) similarly argue that human resources has four roles, as 'strategic partner', 'innovator', 'collaborator', and 'change facilitator'. But is the function's change role itself open to further clarification? Considering in particular Storey's changemakers and Ulrich's change agents, Caldwell (2001) sought to establish in more detail the nature of the various roles that human resource professionals play in organizational change. From his survey of 98 British companies, followed by 12 interviews, the typology in Figure 4.1 was developed, based on the distinction between transformative and incremental change, and between providing a vision in contrast to providing expertise. Almost 70 per cent of respondents, in personnel and human resource jobs, identified change agency as one of their roles, and the model identifies four types of change agent:

- **champions**: senior executives who lead major human resource initiatives and policy changes;
- **adapters**: middle managers who build support for change, translating visions into action;
- **consultants**: specialists and external consultants who implement discrete projects;
- **synergists**: senior managers and external consultants who co-ordinate and integrate multiple large-scale change initiatives.

Caldwell (2001) supports the view that current trends allow the human resource management function to move beyond the traditional personnel role and to make decisive contributions to organizational effectiveness by leading significant changes to employment policies and practices.

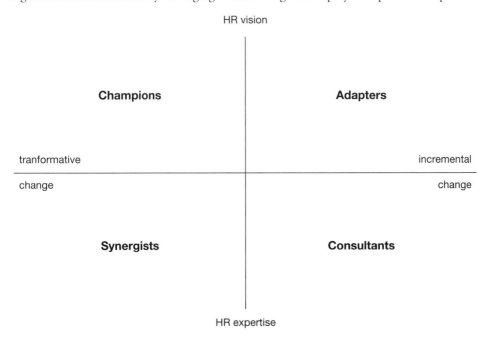

Figure 4.1 HR change agent roles

However, Caldwell also argues that any neat typology, including his own, cannot adequately capture the overlaps, ambiguities, confusions, conflicts, and tensions of the human resources role, and of these various contributions in practice. Some of his human resource interviewees, for instance, felt that the role of 'change champion' was an unrealistic one for their profession, as this involved the risks that accompany the sponsorship of strategic change, in contrast with the safer ground of providing advice. However, that view was not shared by all of his respondents. The function, he concludes, will always have multiple roles and role combinations, shifting over time with circumstances. These typologies perhaps reflect an unrealizable set of ideal stereotypes, but they also characterize the aspirations of many members of the function with regard to a strategic change champion role.

With the exception of Caldwell (2001), most commentators advocating a change-orientated role for the human resource management function have not then asked, 'What kind of change agent?'. The generic literature of change agency, or change leadership as this is now often styled, is itself dominated by role types and typologies. Schön (1963) highlights the importance of the 'change champion'. Stjernberg and Philips (1993) refer to 'souls of fire', from the Swedish 'eldsjälar' meaning 'driven by burning enthusiasm'. Change, of course, is rarely implemented by one person: Hutton (1994) talks of a 'cast of characters'. Ottaway (1983) thus identifies ten roles in three categories, of change generators, implementers, and adopters. Beatty and Gordon (1991) distinguish patriarchs who originate ideas, from evangelists who implement them. Buchanan and Storey (1997) identify the eight change-related roles summarized in Table 4.1. Accompanying these typologies, typically, is discussion of the skills, knowledge, and other attributes required in those roles.

In the second half of the 1990s, the iconic agent of strategic change was the transformational leader (Bass and Avolio, 1994; Burns, 1978). However, the charismatic, visionary, heroic transformational leader has recently attracted widespread criticism. Denis *et al.* (2001) describe instead the role of 'leadership constellations' in driving major change. Various commentators have been critical of transformational figures, describing them as 'a dangerous curse' (Khurana, 2002), and emphasizing the role of middle managers who implement 'quiet change' by 'stealth', working 'below the radar' (Badaracco, 2002; Huy, 2001; Meyerson, 2001). The human resource management role is absent from these perspectives, although the consequences of repeat organizational transformation can include stress, initiative fatigue, and burnout, which potentially damage individual and organizational effectiveness. These observations led Abrahamson (2000) to advocate 'painless change' that is more sensitively timed and paced to allow individuals and social systems to make appropriate adjustments.

The generic literature of change agency is too broad to summarize here, but two observations are particularly significant. First, the analysis of change agent (or change leader) roles and competencies does not appear to have informed analysis of the change-related role, or roles, of the human resource management function. Second, the potentially controversial political

Table 4.1 Change agency roles

initiator	the ideas person, the heatseeker, the project or process 'champion'
sponsor	the main beneficiary, the focal person, the project or process 'guardian'
agent or driver	promotes, implements, delivers – often the process or 'project manager'
subversive	strives to divert, block, interfere, resist, disrupt
passenger	is carried along by the change
spectator	watches while others change
victim	suffers from changes introduced by others
paramedic	helps others through the traumas of change

skills of change agency, in influencing, persuading, negotiating, and manipulating others into accepting, if not welcoming, change proposals, do not appear to have been recognized as significant to the change-oriented strategic human resource management function. The relevance of political skills will be examined after we have considered current thinking with regard to the nature of organizational change processes.

Recipes and processes

The literature of organizational change is large and fragmented, and is difficult to summarize for several reasons (Iles and Sutherland, 2001). First, it contains work from different theoretical and practical perspectives; there are several *literatures*. Second, while valuable contributions have been made over the past five or six decades, recent work has not necessarily reduced the relevance, interest, or value of earlier work. Third, the evidence draws from a range of organizational settings, using a range of methodologies with varying degrees of rigour, and it is difficult to reach sound generalizable conclusions. In addition, there are major problems in establishing clear cause and effect relationships across complex, iterative change processes that unfold over extended periods of time. This causality problem is exacerbated by two other sets of issues. First, even straightforward changes are often multidimensional, both in their nature and outcomes, and causality is always difficult to establish in such settings. Second, organizational change usually implicates numerous stakeholders, who may have quite different views of the nature of the problem, appropriate solutions, and desirable outcomes; this generates the problem of whose criteria to use.

Two strikingly different perspectives on organizational change are currently influential. One is described by Collins (1998) as offering 'n-step guides' to change implementation which, as this label suggests, provides a plethora of numbered checklists. One of the most widely cited of these guides is that developed by Kotter (1995), whose 'recipe' has eight ingredients: establish a sense of urgency, form a powerful guiding coalition, create a vision, communicate the vision, empower others to act on the vision, plan for and create short-term wins, consolidate improvements and produce still more change, and finally institutionalize new approaches. In Britain, the professional body for human resource management, the Chartered Institute for Personnel and Development (2006), has developed a similar change recipe, identifying 'the seven Cs of change': choosing a team, crafting the vision, connecting organization-wide change, consulting stakeholders, communicating, coping with the stress of change, and capturing the learning. Gustafson *et al.* (2003) develop a recipe for predicting the success of organizational change, identifying 18 ingredients under six headings: the solution, the adoption decision, external links, structural support, organizational and people readiness, and change agency. These recipes all claim, broadly, that if their respective ingredients are present, then change is more likely to be successful. None of these guidelines makes explicit mention of the role of the human resource management function.

A second influential perspective concerns the processual-contextual theories of change developed by, for example, Pettigrew (1985), Van de Ven and Poole (1995), and Dawson (2003). Critical of the neat and tidy 'rational linear' assumptions on which n-step guides are based, this approach argues that the outcomes of change are influenced instead by the interaction between change nature or substance, the organizational context (inner and outer), and the implementation process. Change here is seen as messy, iterative, and highly politicized, as different individuals and groups jostle and manoeuvre to establish the legitimacy of their own proposals, and weaken the credibility of others. This untidiness renders inappropriate any universal solution or 'best practice' recipe for implementing change. In addition, a theory that tries to link independent variables (changes) to dependent variables (outcomes) is inappropriate. Instead of variance theory, process theory sees change as an event sequence unfolding over time, as a narrative with many authors (Buchanan and Dawson, 2007), where the human resource function is one of a number of stakeholder groups seeking to influence the nature, direction, pace, and outcomes of change.

One implication of this brief overview is that, if human resource managers are to play a more proactive role in strategic organizational change, the nature of this task is not immediately apparent. Will this involve the routine implementation of a series of preplanned steps? Will this instead involve a more contingent and iterative process in which political skill matters as much as conventional change management technique? It is almost certainly the case that, the more significant the changes in terms of their impact on the organization, its working practices, and its employees, the more politicized the change process is likely to be (Buchanan and Badham, 2008; Frost and Egri, 1991). Any manager, and not just human resource managers, lacking political skills when engaging this kind of process is likely to struggle.

A further implication is that, if there is no one best approach to change, it is difficult to specify one perspective with regard to change agency (or leadership), which in turn is contingent and fluid. And where the outcomes are open to the competing assessments of different stakeholders, this creates opportunities for results to be represented as successful, on carefully selected criteria, even where results have been less than impressive in other respects. While it is important to be able to establish the legitimacy of one's proposals for change, it is equally significant to be able to present the consequences in a positive manner, especially where negative outcomes attract accusations of error or failure, and can damage the reputation of those responsible for advocating those initiatives in the first place.

Something to sell

The function's contribution to strategic change has been reinforced by welcome evidence that links human resource policies and practices demonstrably to organizational performance. Put crudely, treat your staff properly, and your profits will rise. Proof of returns on investment in human resource initiatives is clearly important to the adoption of those initiatives, and those returns also have implications for the status and influence of human resource practitioners. At the core of this argument lies the concept of *high performance work practices*. In order to measure their use, Huselid (1995) identifies 13 such practices, in two categories, concerning skills and structures, and motivation, respectively:

Employee skills and organizational structures
1. information-sharing programmes;
2. job analysis;
3. internal appointments for promoted posts;
4. workforce attitude surveys;
5. quality of work life programmes, quality circles and participative teams;
6. company incentive and profit-sharing plans;
7. training hours per employee;
8. formal grievance procedures and complaint resolution systems;
9. employment testing for new recruits;

Employee motivation
10. performance appraisals to determine financial reward;

11. formal performance appraisals;
12. promotion based on merit or performance rating, not seniority;
13. the number of qualified applicants for the five most often recruited posts.

Huselid (1995) surveyed around 3,500 organizations to measure the use of high performance work practices in American organizations, predicting that these would reduce labour turnover, and increase productivity and profitability. His main findings were that:

- organizations using high performance work practices had higher levels of productivity and financial performance;
- organizations using high performance practices in the employee skills and organization structure category had lower employee turnover;
- a significant proportion of the impact of high performance practices on financial performance was due to lower labour turnover, or higher productivity, or both;
- high performance practices contributed US$18,500 per employee in shareholder value, and almost $4,000 per employee in additional profits (1995 prices).

Investment in human resource policies can thus bring demonstrable financial returns in the form of reduced employee turnover, improved productivity, and profitability. These findings support the argument that high performance work practices improve financial performance regardless of the organization's strategy. Huselid's findings were among the first to present a major challenge to those who would dismiss human resource management (in its new or traditional personnel management guise) as commercially irrelevant.

Pfeffer (1998) similarly argues that human resource practices can raise an organization's stock market value by US$20,000 to $40,000 per employee. He claims that 'profits through people' are produced by seven people management policies:

1. emphasis on job security;
2. recruiting the right people in the first place;
3. decentralization and self-managed teamworking;
4. high wages linked to organizational performance;
5. high investment in employee training;
6. reducing status differentials;
7. sharing information across the organization.

In Britain, research by the Sheffield Group (Patterson et al., 1997) has also revealed a measurable impact of human resource management on productivity and profitability. This work involved a ten-year study of over 100 manufacturing companies, using 'human resource management variables' similar to Huselid's (1995) high performance practices. This study also assessed the contributions to organizational performance of other management strategies and tactics, finding that none had the same positive impact on business performance as human resource management. The findings showed that two clusters of high performance practices were significantly related to productivity and profitability. These clusters are similar to the main factors in Huselid's perspective:

1. skills development: the acquisition and development of employee skills, through selection, induction, training and the use of performance appraisal systems;
2. job design: the design of jobs, including skill flexibility, job responsibility, variety, and the use of teams.

63

The main findings from this study were that:

- high overall job satisfaction and organizational commitment are positively linked to high company profitability;
- an organization culture that demonstrates concern for employee skill development and well-being is linked to high productivity and profitability;
- skills development and job design practices such as teamworking are positively linked to increased productivity and profitability;
- human resource management practice is a good predictor of performance: quality emphasis, corporate strategy, technological sophistication and investment in research and development contribute only weakly to productivity and profitability.

Comparative research by this team showed that British manufacturing companies place less emphasis on empowering and capturing the ideas of employees, and on adopting high performance practices than Australia, Japan, and Switzerland. Problems of poor comparative productivity and innovation may thus lie with work organization and management processes.

One of the most intriguing findings in this line of research is that human resource practices reduce hospital mortality rates. West *et al.* (2002) surveyed 61 hospitals in England and carried out ten case studies, asking chief executives and human resource directors about human resource practices covering all clinical, administrative, support and managerial staff. Data were then collected on the numbers of deaths following emergency and non-emergency surgery, admission for hip fractures and heart attacks, and readmission. Care was taken to account for variations in mortality due to region, local population, hospital size, and doctor–patient ratios. Analysis showed that mortality rates were significantly lower in hospitals with human resource practices related to appraisal (with extensive and sophisticated systems), training (with well-developed policies and budgets), and teamwork (with high staff numbers working in teams, and trained to do so). These relationships were even stronger where the human resources director was a full voting member of the hospital management board.

Surely it is the skills and knowledge of nurses, doctors, and surgeons which affect patient care and survival, and medical staff were suspicious of these research findings. How can human resource practices applied to staff who are not involved in patient diagnosis and treatment affect mortality rates? West and Johnson (2002, p. 35) reply:

> Our answer is simple, though it may seem strange to those who deal with individuals rather than organizations. If you have HR practices that focus on effort and skill; develop people's skills; encourage co-operation, collaboration, innovation and synergy in teams for most, if not all, employees, the whole system functions and performs better. If the receptionists, porters, ancillary staff, secretaries, nurses, managers and, yes, the doctors are working effectively, the system as a whole will function effectively.

A hospital is a community which depends on the interaction of all its members. Although clearly important, the skills and performance of doctors is not the only factor which affects the quality of patient care. The impact of human resource practices, therefore, is *systemic*. It is unlikely that this conclusion is limited to healthcare organizations.

From those research findings, the human resource manager seeking to influence organization strategy not only has a clear agenda concerning the kinds of changes that are likely to contribute significantly to performance (with appropriate adaptation to local circumstances), but can also point to proof demonstrating that these methods work. Scepticism concerning 'the soft stuff' can now be confronted with hard evidence. The empirical research supporting the positive, quantifiable impact of human resource policies and high performance practices is difficult for other senior managers to ignore. In short, the function has something valuable to sell. Why, then, do so few human resource functions play leading 'change champion' roles in their organizations (Guest and King, 2004), why are most organizations struggling with the concept of the human resource function as 'strategic partner' (Arkin, 2007), and why do most organizations employ so few of those high performance practices? The answers seem to lie with the observation that good ideas and compelling evidence, on their own, are rarely sufficient to promote a new idea, a new product, or a change initiative.

Making things happen, getting things done

Organizational change is a politicized process because it typically generates conflict, over the definition of problems, and over the nature and timing of the solutions that are required to address them. Conflict is often regarded in negative terms, as an undesirable condition that must be resolved, if not avoided. Organization politics are typically seen as a damaging waste of time, as 'dirty tricks', as behaviours to be shunned. However, not all new ideas are good ideas, and conflict can be desirable, in order to stimulate appropriate debate and to sharpen the quality of decisions. Mangham (1979, p. 16) observes that reasonable people often disagree, with regard both to ends and means, and can thus be expected 'to fight for what they are convinced is right and, perhaps more significantly, against that which they are convinced is wrong'. Butcher and Clarke (1999) thus describe politics as 'battles over just causes'. Hardy (1996) argues that political forces generate the energy for organizational change. To shut down political behaviour is to turn off this source of energy.

Change agents who are not able and willing to engage with the politics of the organization are thus likely to fail in their enterprise. Pfeffer (1992, p. 30) argues that, 'unless we are willing to come to terms with organizational power and influence, and admit that the skills of getting things done are as important as the skills of figuring out what to do, our organizations will fall further and further behind'. This means abandoning the notion, popular in the field of organization development, that change agents are 'neutral facilitators' using appropriate techniques to encourage information-sharing, joint problem-solving and collaborative action planning among the organization's willing members. Zanko *et al.* (2008) explain the absence of attention to the evident human resource management issues in the implementation of an innovative approach to product development in a military electronics manufacturing company with reference to power and political structures in the organization, and to the political positions and tactics of the various key management players.

At any given time in an organization, there are likely to be in circulation several innovative ideas, proposals, projects, or initiatives, competing for management attention and resources. This is especially the case in the current context of repeat organizational redesign. The process through which ideas attract support is based in part on a reasoned business case. But good ideas do not sell themselves. As ideas compete, the selection process is a political one, and the human resource manager, like any other manager wishing to facilitate or drive change, has to play the politics game. The manager who is politically aware, but who is not politically motivated, as Whittington and Mayer (2002) advise, will thus find it difficult to engage effectively with the organization's change agenda.

Organization politics is also usually defined in terms of getting one's own way despite resistance. It is important to note that 'one's own way' can often involve organizational as well as individual benefits, and potentially both at the same time. While political behaviour is typically equated with self-interest, there is no reason why personal and corporate gain cannot both be pursued through the same actions. Indeed, maintaining or enhancing one's interests, to no corporate gain, may be appropriate and desirable in order to protect personal credibility for use on future occasions. The successful implementation of clusters of high performance work practices, for instance, may thus improve corporate profitability while simultaneously enhancing the reputation, and continuing influence, of the human resource manager responsible for the design of this initiative. It is significant, however, that Ferris *et al.* (2000, p. 30) define political skill as:

> an interpersonal style construct that combines social astuteness with the ability to relate well, and otherwise demonstrate situationally appropriate behaviour in a disarmingly charming and engaging manner that inspires confidence, trust, sincerity, and genuineness.

Skilled organization politicians may thus have to disguise their self-serving intentions to avoid being labelled as 'political', even where their proposals will deliver corporate gain. Traditionally, the human resource function has not only lacked organizational power, but has also been suspected of being unwilling to engage with organization politics (Legge, 1978, 2005; Watson, 1977). Lack of influence may be explained in part by structural conditions, but also by the willingness of the function's members to engage with their organization's political system, for a blend of personal and professional reasons.

Organization politics is a particularly rich and creative aspect of management activity. In an attempt to capture this variety, Buchanan and Badham (2008) identify the ten categories of tactics summarized in Table 4.2. Those category labels stand for a variety of tactics wider than the indicative examples. There is a range of image-building or impression management methods beyond dress and appearance (Singh *et al.*, 2002). Managers create and use different kinds of networks in different ways (Ibarra and Hunter, 2007). In advocating and driving strategic organizational change, two of these sets of tactics are particularly significant to the human resource management function: positioning, and issue-selling.

Table 4.2 Political tactics

image building	we all know people who didn't get the job because they didn't look the part – appearance is a credibility issue
information games	withholding information to make others look foolish, bending the truth, white lies, massaging information, timed release
scapegoating	this is the fault of another department, external factors, my predecessor, a particular individual
alliances	doing secret deals with influential others to form a critical mass, a cabal, to win support for and to progress your proposals
networking	lunches, coffees, dinners, sporting events, to get your initiatives onto senior management agendas, to improve visibility
compromise	all right, you win this time, I won't put up a fight and embarrass you in public – if you will back me next time
rule games	I'm sorry, but you have used the wrong form, at the wrong time, with the wrong arguments; we can't set inconsistent precedents
issue-selling	packaging, presenting, and promoting plans and ideas in ways that make them more appealing to target audiences
positioning	switching and choosing roles where one is successful and visible; avoiding failing projects; position in the building, in the room
dirty tricks	keeping dirt files for blackmail, spying on others, discrediting and undermining, spreading false rumours, corridor whispers

Positioning

Earlier in this chapter, Table 4.1 summarized eight typical roles that actors play in relation to organizational change: initiators, sponsors, drivers, subversives, passengers, spectators, victims, and paramedics. One individual may play several roles with regard to one particular change initiative, while simultaneously holding different positions in relation to other concurrent projects. That role typology is a useful analytical tool, as different skills and behaviours are required in different roles (even though they may be held by the same person). So, for example, the role of the initiator is to stimulate enthusiasm for change in others; that is quite different, in terms of behaviours and timescales, from the role of delivering change.

That role typology is also a political tool, with interesting practical consequences, in prompting the obvious question, 'which position, or positions, do you want to play?' Assuming that one has a choice, the pattern of positions that one adopts has significant implications, not merely for current workload, but also for skills development, personal reputation, career prospects, and the ability to continue to influence the organization in ways that one believes to be desirable. Thus, the human resource manager (indeed any manager) who consistently plays the roles of passenger and paramedic in relation to the organization's major changes is unlikely to develop an influential voice with regard to shaping future initiatives, and will develop few skills in change management. In contrast, the initiators, sponsors, and drivers of successful strategic initiatives are more likely to grow their reputational capital, develop their expertise (actual and perceived), and maintain their credibility and voice in the organization. Change roles may sometimes be vacant ('we need a sponsor for this initiative') and can be occupied opportunistically, when appropriate. But as indicated earlier, initiating or sponsoring major change programmes can entail risk, and if it is likely that an initiative will stumble, or fail, with consequent reputational damage, it may be more appropriate to revert to a spectator or passenger role, while avoiding becoming a victim.

The pattern of roles that the human resource manager decides to play at any one time is highly contingent on organizational circumstances and personal aspirations. Nevertheless, to be an effective strategic change agent, careful and considered positioning with regard to current and future initiatives is a vital element of political skill, which commentary on the evolving change roles of the function appears to have neglected.

Issue-selling

If the human resource management function has something to sell, this is not going to happen just because there is good supporting evidence. Good marketing is also necessary. The role of evidence in the diffusion of innovation, and in organizational change, is problematic. Products and ideas are rarely accepted just because they have research evidence to back them. For example, the American diplomat, Henry Kissinger, once said that,

> Before I served as a consultant to Kennedy, I had believed, like most academics, that the process of decision-making was largely intellectual and all one had to do was walk into the President's office and convince him of the correctness of one's view. This perspective I soon realized is as dangerously immature as it is widely held.
>
> (Pfeffer, 1992, p. 31)

To initiate and successfully deliver strategic changes, human resource managers thus need to be aware of the concept and techniques of issue-selling.

How do change proposals get off the ground? Problems have to be recognized as such, and be interpreted as significant, before they attract attention and get onto the senior management agenda. The factors influencing problem interpretation include the attributions of those involved, organization design and culture, the availability of resources, external pressures, and the promise of irresistible opportunities. A problem gets little or no attention when those in positions of influence do not recognize the issue as important, or where the causes of the problem are attributed to other factors, which may be beyond their control. Issues can be side-lined when the solution is perceived to benefit only some other (competing) group or function, or where key decision-makers have already decided that resources need to be deployed to higher priority tasks, or believe that the opportunities in this case are minimal. Change proposals which are perceived to benefit only employees, which will drain resources from other strategic issues, and which promise only vague or uncertain financial returns, are thus less likely to find senior management backing.

How, then, should the available evidence be presented and communicated? How can human resource managers ensure that what they regard as priorities for improvement are also regarded by the organization as a whole as priorities? For those who wish to initiate major change, therefore, a key political task is to ensure that their proposals figure prominently on a management agenda which is likely to be crowded with other competing initiatives. March and Olsen (1983, p. 292) refer to this as the 'organization of attention'. Dutton et al. (2001) refer to this as marketing ideas, as orchestrating impressions, and as 'issue-selling', observing that an organization is 'a market-place for ideas', each competing for decision and resources. Ideas do not appear on the management agenda because they are 'obvious' or even where they are supported by evidence. Ideas rise to prominence by the efforts of their advocates to market or to sell those issues to colleagues. This helps to explain why some lousy ideas are often imple-mented, and why some great ideas stay on the shelf. While some issue-selling methods are public and visible, others occur backstage, and while those may be less easy to identify, they involve methods that are just as common and easy to use.

Dutton describes three categories of techniques for manipulating senior management perceptions, agendas, decisions, and actions. *Packaging moves* concern ways in which ideas can be 'wrapped' to make them more appealing, more urgent, more acceptable, and include presentation tactics and bundling tactics. *Involvement moves* concern ways in which relationships and structures can be exploited to build support for ideas. *Process moves* concern preparation, timing, and degree of formality in issue-selling.

Packaging moves

Presenting

- using the logic of the business plan, 'running the numbers', using lots of figures and charts, conveying a logical and coherent structure, emphasizing bottom-line impacts;
- continuous proposal-making, raising issues many times over a period, prepare the target to better 'hear' a full proposal;
- making changes appear incremental, by 'chunking' ideas into components to make them more palatable to potential targets.

Bundling

- tying issues to profitability, market share, organizational image;
- tying issues to the concerns of key constituents.

Involvement moves

- targets of involvement; knowing who to involve and when;
- involving senior management in supporting ideas;
- clearing the idea with your immediate superior;
- involving colleagues and other departments in supporting ideas;
- involving outsiders, like consultants, to gain credibility;
- customizing issue-selling to stakeholders;
- using formal committees and task forces to legitimize issues;
- creating a task force with a diverse membership.

Process moves

Formality

- deciding appropriate degree of formality in issue-selling.

Preparation

- collecting background information on context before selling, preparing people to support an idea when the time comes;
- understanding social relationships, organizational networks, and strategic goals and priorities.

Timing

- being persistent through a lengthy issue-selling process;
- sensing when to hold back and when to move forward, based on level of support;
- involving relevant others at an early stage.

Sonenshein (2006) develops a similar approach to 'issue-crafting', which involves the manipulation of public language to make issues appear to be more legitimate, urgent, and trustworthy for the audience. Issues are crafted through embellishing (emphasizing particular features), subtracting (playing down parts of the argument) and through consistency (we all share the same values and goals). These tactics can rely either on a normative perspective (fairness, obligation, values, do the right thing) or on an economic perspective (objective, rational, commercial, business-oriented). In Sonenshein's study, the most common issue-crafting tactics involved economic embellishing and normative subtracting, in other words emphasizing commercial gain and paying less attention to values. It is tempting to observe that human resource management initiatives may often do the opposite, emphasizing welfare, health and safety, skills development, while advocating the values of a 'good employer'. These are not complex techniques that require extensive skills training, but routine everyday behaviours that require awareness and informed judgement for their effective use.

If you don't play, you can't win

In conclusion, despite the human resource implications of adaptive reorganization, and the accumulation of evidence concerning the impact of human resource policies, the function rarely appears to be at the forefront of strategic organizational change. This chapter has argued that one explanation for this lack of involvement concerns the need for human resource professionals to work with the political dimensions of change agency, to play a more sophisticated game. While the term 'manipulation' is often used in a negative sense, suggesting devious, disreputable behaviour, many commentators argue that managers who are not prepared to use such methods are likely to find that their good ideas do not attract attention, and are not pursued, while competing initiatives find support and resources.

It is not enough to categorize the function as strategic partner or change champion, in the hope that a fresh label will generate new actions. Commentary on the role of human resource management in strategic change has focused on role typologies, idealized models of implementation, and unrealistic assumptions concerning the power of evidence to persuade. The failure of change initiatives is variously attributed to lack of coherence across multifaceted agendas, to lack of project management skills, to inadequate training in new technologies, to poor communication, to resistance to the content and process of change, and to ineffective leadership. These explanations overlook the politics of change, and do not address the need to act politically to progress proposals. The failure of change to deliver is rarely attributed in public to lack of political skill (but see Buchanan and Badham, 2008).

For Whittington and Molloy (2005), the competencies relevant to the human resource manager as change champion include the ability to make a strategic business case, to align change initiatives with overall corporate functioning, and to use sound project management techniques. This chapter has sought to demonstrate that, while those skills and capabilities may be necessary, they are not sufficient. The human resource professional, like any other change agent, is unlikely to succeed without the political skills required to sell, initiate, drive, and deliver strategic organizational change. Equipped with that combination of conventional and political expertise, is the function's problem solved? No. The acquisition of political skill merely gives the function a ticket to the game. Also significant is the manner and context in which such skills are deployed, and the nature and efficacy of the tactics used by the other players. But as Frankel (2004, p. 19) observes, 'if you don't play, you can't win'.

References

Abrahamson, E. (2000) 'Change without pain', *Harvard Business Review*, 78(4): 75–79.

Arkin, A. (2007) 'Street smart', *People Management*, 5 April: 24–28.

Badaracco, J.L. (2002) *Leading Quietly: An Unorthodox Guide to Doing the Right Thing*. Boston, MA: Harvard Business School Press.

Bass, B.M. and Avolio, B.J. (1994) *Improving Organizational Effectiveness through Transformational Leadership*. Thousand Oaks, CA: Sage Publications.

Beatty, C.A. and Gordon, J.R.M. (1991) 'Preaching the gospel: the evangelists of new technology', *California Management Review*, 33(3): 73–94.

Buchanan, D.A. and Badham, R. (2008) *Power, Politics, and Organizational Change: Winning the Turf Game*. London: Sage Publications (second edn).

Buchanan, D. and Dawson, P. (2007) 'Discourse and audience: organizational change as multi-story process', *Journal of Management Studies*, 44(5): 669–686.

Buchanan, D. and Storey, J. (1997) 'Role taking and role switching in organizational change: the four pluralities', in Ian McLoughlin and Martin Harris (eds), *Innovation, Organizational Change and Technology* (pp. 127–145). London: Thomson International.

Burns, J.M. (1978) *Leadership*. New York: Harper & Row.

Butcher, D. and Clarke, M. (1999) 'Organizational politics: the missing discipline of management?' *Industrial and Commercial Training*, 31(1): 9–12.

Caldwell, R. (2001) 'Champions, adapters, consultants and synergists: the new change agents in HRM', *Human Resource Management Journal*, 11(3): 39–52.

Chartered Institute for Personnel and Development (2006) *Approaches to Change: Key Issues and Challenges*. London: Chartered Institute for Personnel and Development.

Collins, D. (1998) *Organizational Change: Sociological Perspectives*. London: Routledge.

Dawson, P. (2003) *Reshaping Change: A Processual Approach*. London: Routledge.

Denis, J.-L., Lamothe, L. and Langley, A. (2001) 'The dynamics of collective leadership and strategic change in pluralistic organizations', *Academy of Management Journal*, 44(4): 809–837.

Dutton, J.E., Ashford, S.J., O'Neill, R.M. and Lawrence, K.A. (2001) 'Moves that matter: issue selling and organizational change', *Academy of Management Journal*, 44(4): 716–736.

Ferris, G.R., Perrewé, P.L., Anthony, W.P. and Gilmore, D.C. (2000) 'Political skill at work', *Organizational Dynamics*, 28(4): 25–37.

Frankel, L.P. (2004) *Nice Girls Don't Get The Corner Office: Unconscious Mistakes Women Make That Sabotage Their Careers*. New York: Warner Business Books.

Frost, P.J. and Egri, C.P. (1991) 'The political process of innovation', in L.L. Cummings and B.M. Staw (eds), *Research in Organizational Behaviour, Volume 13* (pp. 229–295). Greenwich, CT: JAI Press.

Guest, D. and King, Z. (2004) 'Power, innovation and problem-solving: the personnel managers' three steps to heaven?', *Journal of Management Studies*, 41(3): 401–423.

Gustafson, D.H., Sainfort, F., Eichler, M., Adams, L., Bisognano, M. and Steudel, H. (2003) 'Developing and testing a model to predict outcomes of organizational change', *Health Services Research*, 38(2): 751–776.

Hardy, C. (1996) 'Understanding power: bringing about strategic change', *British Journal of Management*, 7(special conference issue): 3–16.

Huselid, M.A. (1995) 'The impact of human resource management practices on turnover, productivity, and corporate financial performance', *Academy of Management Journal*, 38(3): 635–672.

Hutton, D.W. (1994) *The Change Agent's Handbook: A Survival Guide for Quality Improvement Champions*. Milwaukee, WI: ASQC Quality Press.

Huy, Q.N. (2001) 'In praise of middle managers', *Harvard Business Review*, 79(8): 72–79.

Ibarra, H. and Hunter, M. (2007) 'How leaders create and use networks', *Harvard Business Review*, 85(1): 40–47.

Iles, V. and Sutherland, K. (2001) *Organizational Change: A Review for Health Care Managers, Professionals and Researchers*. London: National Co-ordinating Centre for NHS Service Delivery and Organization Research and Development.

Khurana, R. (2002) 'The curse of the superstar CEO', *Harvard Business Review*, 80(9): 60–66.

Kotter, J.P. (1995) 'Leading change: why transformation efforts fail', *Harvard Business Review*, 73(2): 59–67.

Legge, K. (1978) *Power, Innovation, and Problem Solving in Personnel Management*. London: McGraw-Hill.

Legge, K. (2005) *Human Resource Management: Rhetorics and Realities (Anniversary Edition)*. Basingstoke: Macmillan Business.

Mangham, I. (1979) *The Politics of Organizational Change*. Westport, CT: Greenwood Press.

March, J.G. and Olsen, J.P. (1983) 'Organizing political life: what administrative reorganization tells us about government', *American Political Science Review*, 77(2): 281–296.

Meyerson, D.E. (2001) 'Radical change, the quiet way', *Harvard Business Review*, 79(9): 92–100.

Ottaway, R.N. (1983) 'The change agent: a taxonomy in relation to the change process', *Human Relations*, 36(4): 361–392.

Patterson, M.G., West, M.A., Lawthom, R. and Nickell, S. (1997) *Impact of People Management Practices on Business Performance*. London: Institute of Personnel and Development.

Pettigrew, A.M. (1985) *The Awakening Giant: Continuity and Change in ICI.* Oxford: Basil Blackwell.

Pfeffer, J. (1992) *Managing With Power: Politics and Influence in Organization.* Boston, MA: Harvard Business School Press.

Pfeffer, J. (1998) *The Human Equation: Building Profits by Putting People First.* Boston, MA: Harvard Business School Press.

Schön, D.A. (1963) 'Champions for radical new inventions', *Harvard Business Review*, 41(2): 77–86.

Schuler, R.S., Jackson, S.E. and Storey, J. (2001) 'HRM and its link with strategic management', in John Storey (ed.), *Human Resource Management: A Critical Text* (pp. 114–130). London: Thomson Learning (second edn).

Singh, V., Kumra, S. and Vinnicombe, S. (2002) 'Gender and impression management: playing the promotion game', *Journal of Business Ethics*, 37(1): 77–89.

Sonenshein, S. (2006) 'Crafting social issues at work', *Academy of Management Journal*, 49(6): 1158–1172.

Stjernberg, T. and Philips, A. (1993) 'Organizational innovations in a long-term perspective: legitimacy and souls-of-fire as critical factors of change and viability', *Human Relations*, 46(10): 1193–1221.

Storey, J. (1992) *Developments in the Management of Human Resources: An Analytical Review.* Oxford: Blackwell Business.

Tyson, S. (1995) *Human Resource Strategy: Towards a General Theory of HRM.* London: Pitman Publishing.

Ulrich, D. (1998) 'A new mandate for human resources', *Harvard Business Review*, 76(1): 124–134.

Van de Ven, A.H. and Poole, M.S. (1995) 'Explaining development and change in organizations', *Academy of Management Review*, 20(3): 510–540.

Watson, T.J. (1977) *The Personnel Managers.* London: Routledge & Kegan Paul.

West, M. and Johnson, R. (2002) 'A matter of life and death', *People Management*, 8(4): 30–36.

West, M.A., Borrill, C., Dawson, J., Scully, J., Carter, M., Anelay, S., Patterson, M. and Waring, J. (2002) 'The link between the management of employees and patient mortality in acute hospitals', *International Journal of Human Resource Management*, 13: 1299–1310.

Whittington, R. and Mayer, M. (2002) *Organizing for Success in the Twenty-First Century: A Starting Point for Change.* London: Chartered Institute of Personnel and Development.

Whittington, R. and Molloy, E. (2005) *HR's Role in Organizing: Shaping Change.* London: Chartered Institute for Personnel and Development.

Zanko, M., Badham, R., Couchman, P. and Schubert, M. (2008) 'Innovation and HRM: issues, absences and politics', *International Journal of Human Resource Management*, 19(4): 562–581.

HR competencies that make a difference[1]

Wayne Brockbank and Dave Ulrich

The competency approach has emerged from being a specialized and narrow application to being a leading logic for diagnosing, framing and improving virtually every aspect of human resource management. This chapter addresses the question: "What are the competencies that are required of HR professionals if they are to add substantial value to key stakeholders?"

The competency approach to HR management

The competency approach to human resource management has its origins in military staffing decisions during World War II. Over the ensuing years, the theory and application of competencies has become a central paradigm in HR practices (McClelland 1976; Boyatzis 1982a; McClelland & Boyatzis 1982; McLagan & Suhadolnik 1989; Spencer & Spencer 1993; Schoonover 1998). In 1982, Boyatzis (1982b, p. 221) defined a competency to be "a characteristic of a person that results in consistently effective performance in a job". These characteristics may be conceptualized to include values, knowledge, abilities and skills that are required for job performance.

Over the years the competency approach has been specifically applied to the following purposes:

1. to specify human characteristics that are required for job performance (McClelland 1973);
2. to communicate and train people to improve performance (McClelland 1973);
3. to monitor and measure performance (McClelland 1976);
4. to predict superior human performance (Spencer & Spencer 1993);
5. to match individuals with jobs (Kolb 1984);
6. to implement business strategy and create competitive advantage (Intagliata, Ulrich & Smallwood 2000);
7. to integrate and harmonize potentially fragmented management and HR practices (Intagliata, Ulrich & Smallwood 2000);
8. to develop high value adding HR departments (Ulrich 1987; Nadler & Nadler 1989; Schuler 1990; Morris 1996; Ulrich 1997; Losey 1999).

While it is difficult to trace the first application of the competency approach to the HR function, early studies include the work of the Ontario Society for Training and Development in 1976 (Kenny 1982) and an American Society of Training and Development sponsored study in 1967 (Lippitt & Nadler 1967; McCullough & McLagan 1983). These were followed by extensive studies of HR competencies by Patricia McLagan for the American Society for Training and Development in 1983 and 1987 (McLagan & Bedrick 1983). These important studies detailed the competencies for specialists in human resource development and documented the variety of possible roles for the human resource profession as a whole (see McLagan and Suhadolnik 1989).

In the late 1980s, Dave Ulrich and Wayne Brockbank from the Ross School of Business at the University of Michigan and The RBL Group initiated the longest and largest ongoing study of the competencies of HR professionals. This study has been conducted in four major waves over sixteen years.[2] The foundational work of this study began with the work of Dave Ulrich who surveyed 600 HR professionals (Ulrich 1987). From this data set, three categories of HR professional competencies were identified: knowledge of business, HR delivery and change management.

In 1988, Ulrich was joined by other colleagues at the University of Michigan including Wayne Brockbank, Dale Lake and Arthur Yeung. The 1988 Human Resource Competency Study was designed to include more elaborate questions and a larger number of participants. This survey was designed on the basis of 360° logic in which individual HR professional participants evaluated themselves and were, in turn, evaluated by HR and non-HR associates (who were familiar with the participant's functioning as an HR professional). Of the approximately 10,000 respondents from 91 firms in the survey, almost 9,000 were associates. Thus, their work avoided many of the problems inherent in self-evaluation. The study included HR professionals from every HR position and from virtually every industry. It also accounted for the strategic as well as the operational aspects of HR (Ulrich et al. 1989). The result of the study was a benchmark of effective HR competencies using rigorous quantitative statistical methods to analyze a large-scale survey population.

In the 1992 round of the Human Resource Competency Study, the survey questions were almost exactly the same as their first survey in 1989. Repeating the same survey enabled the HR field to track important trends as they occurred. This second round found the following:

- the importance of knowledge of finance and external market dynamics had increased;
- change management was becoming a more critical category of HR value contribution;
- interpersonal skills and communications emerged as important contributors to personal success;
- high-performing firms were spending increasingly more time and effort on strategic HR issues whereas the low-performing firms were focused relatively more heavily on operational-level HR issues.

The 1992 iteration verified that the three main types of HR competencies were management of change competencies, delivery of HR practices, and knowledge of the business (Ulrich et al. 1995).

In 1997, the third iteration of the Human Resource Competency Study (Brockbank et al. 2001) sought a larger cross-section of medium and smaller companies at the expense of fewer overall participants. In this round 3,000 respondents from 142 companies were involved. Utilizing findings from extensive pre-survey focus groups, this round examined the influence of two additional categories of HR competencies: personal credibility and culture management. The results identified the following trends:

- Many of those activities that HR professionals did best mattered least and some activities that HR professionals did not do so well had substantial influence on business performance. For example, HR professionals in the low-performing firms and the high-performing firms had similarly high levels of knowledge about HR practices. HR professionals in the high-performing firms distinguished themselves in their knowledge of external business realities. This contrasted with the relatively low knowledge of external market dynamics in the field as a whole, and especially among HR professionals in low-performing firms. This round established the importance of the personal credibility of HR professionals in working with their internal clients. They had to have good interpersonal skills, had to achieve their promised results, and had to contribute to business decisions.
- This round continued to confirm that HR matters most under conditions of change. In companies whose business environments were relatively stable, HR as a whole had little differentiating influence on business performance.

This current chapter relies on the 2002 data set and the fourth round of the Human Resource Competency Data. In this chapter we also introduce the preliminary findings of the 2007 data set.

Characteristics of the 2002 data set

Questions that have been included in our competency research have been identified through interviews with hundreds of HR professionals and line managers and through extensive reviews of the academic literature. We have asked questions about every mainstream HR competency.

In order to relate the competencies of HR professionals to business performance, we also asked about business performance: "Compared to *the major competitor* in 'your business' in the last three years, how has 'your business' performed financially[3]?" This question has clear limitations; however, it does embody three issues. It focuses on financial performance; it has a built-in time perspective; and it represents performance relative to the competition.

Our competency research applies a 360° methodology. Each HR participant evaluates herself or himself on a "participant survey". Each participant selects a set of three to seven associates who are familiar with the participant's functioning as an HR professional. Associates could be either from HR or not from HR. This chapter relies solely on the US non-HR associates[4] as data sources (N = 646). The following additional aspects of the data are noteworthy.

- Primary role of associate raters: The non-HR associates are dominated, in order, by general management, marketing and sales, finance, and manufacturing.
- Company size: The data set is relatively balanced in terms of size including small, medium and large sized companies.
- Industry of participation: The data set cuts across virtually all industry sectors.

Competencies for HR professionals

To identify the basic categories we applied exploratory factor analysis. This objective sorting of the data generated the competency model in Figure 5.1.

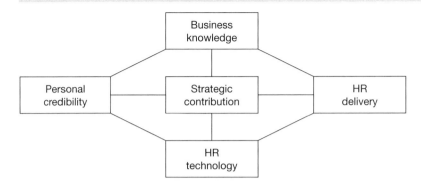

Figure 5.1 Competency model for the HR value proposition

This initial analysis identifies the competencies of HR professionals and establishes that these competencies may be divided into five categories or factors:

- strategic contributions (HR has influence on large-scale strategic contributions such as culture management, fast change, strategy decision making and market-driven connectivity);
- personal credibility (HR has personal credibility if they get results, have good inter-personal skills, and are effective communicators.);
- HR delivery (HR professionals deliver the foundational HR infrastructure of staffing, training and development, organization design, and performance management);
- business knowledge (HR professionals have knowledge of the integrated business value change, the business value proposition, and labor law);
- HR technology (HR professionals know how to apply technology to HR processes).

Having identified these factors, we then went on to address a second research objective: "What are the competencies of HR professionals in high-performing firms that are different from the competencies of HR professionals in low-performing firms?" In other words, we set out to identify those competencies that have the greatest influence on firm performance.

Table 5.1 provides information about two categories of performance.

Column 1 in Table 5.1 responds to the question, "How effective is HR at each competency category?" It shows that HR professionals are best at personal credibility (4.13). They achieve

Table 5.1 HR effectiveness in each competency category and the influence of each competency category on business performance

Competency category	HR effectiveness (1 = low; 5 = high) (Column 1)	Linear regressions of business performance on competency categories (Column 2)	Significance (Column 3)
Strategic contribution	3.65	.16	.000
Personal credibility	4.13	.11	.002
HR delivery	3.69	.06	.027
Business knowledge	3.44	.06	.029
HR technology	3.02	.04	.075

basic results; they have good interpersonal skills; they are effective communicators. There is a large drop-off in effectiveness for the next competency category – HR delivery. HR professionals do a moderately effective job at designing and delivering the foundational HR practices. Coming in at a very close third is HR's strategic contribution. This is followed by business knowledge and HR technology. These numbers reveal how well HR professionals undertake each competency category but they do not tell us which of these categories has the greatest influence on business performance.

Column 2 in Table 5.1 shows that the greatest influence of HR professionals on business performance is through the competencies of strategic contribution. HR professionals who are actively involved in culture management, fast change, strategic decision making, and market-driven connectivity have substantive influence on business performance.[5] The HR professionals in high-performing firms exhibit these competencies to a much greater degree than do the HR professionals in low-performing firms. The next category, personal credibility, accounts for significantly less business performance than strategic contribution. HR delivery and business knowledge account for approximately less than half of the business performance variance when compared to personal credibility. At a statistically insignificant R^2 of .04, the HR technology category has the least influence on business performance.

Thus what HR professionals do best (personal credibility) has moderate influence on business performance. And what HR professionals do only moderately well has greatest influence on business performance – when it is done well. These findings do not discount the importance of personal credibility, HR delivery and business knowledge. Rather, they suggest that to have the knowledge and legitimacy to be involved in strategic issues, HR professionals must first exhibit these more basic competencies. However, if HR professionals limit their professional aspirations and activities to personal credibility, HR delivery and business knowledge, they substantially limit their total influence that they might have on business performance.

With this awareness, we examine each of these five competency categories in more detail.

Strategic contribution

Our competency model emphasizes that the largest influence of HR on business performance is accounted for by strategic contribution. Through additional analyses, we identify four sub-factors that comprise the strategic contribution category.[6] In order of importance, these factors include culture management, fast change, strategic decision making, and market-driven connectivity.

Culture management

In high-performing firms HR professionals exhibit the competencies of culture management. Culture management consists of a number of steps that fit into an integrated framework. HR professionals in the high-performing firms make sure that they define the culture to be consistent with the balanced requirements of external customers, the business strategy, and employees. They ensure that the company's HR practices are designed and delivered to create and reinforce the desired culture by translating the desired culture into specific employee and executive behaviors.

Fast change

In high-performing firms, HR professionals make change happen successfully and thoroughly. They are centrally involved in planning and implementing change processes. But most critical is that they ensure that change happens quickly. They focus on getting decisions made quickly. They effectively involve key leaders in fast change. They ensure that the human, financial and informational resources required for effective change are aligned with the desired changes. They monitor progress of key change initiatives, capture important learnings and apply these learnings to improve future change efforts. They not only set the broad framework for effective change management but also have the facilitation skills to move change initiatives forward in a "hands-on" manner.

Strategic decision making

In high-performing firms, HR professionals play two roles in the making of key decisions. First, they know the business in enough detail that they are able to proactively set the direction of change. They walk into the strategy room with an opinion about the future of the business. They are willing to take strong stands. They not only facilitate change but they also set the direction of change. And, most interesting, they bring intellectual rigor to business decision making; that is, when HR walks into the room in the high-performing firms, the average of the "business IQ points" in the room goes up – not down. Second, they also play a reactive role relative to the business decision making. They ask insightful questions; they encourage others to be strategic; they forecast obstacles to achieving the strategy. In so doing they must have the interpersonal skills as well as the intellectual capacity to play an effective "devil's advocate".

Market-driven connectivity

The first three competency factors are reasonably well known in the HR literature. This last factor, market-driven connectivity, is new to the literature. To our knowledge, prior to the 2002 iteration of the HR Competency Study, the combination of specific competencies that make up this factor had not been empirically identified as an area for HR involvement. In this iteration of the Competency Study, it was not only identified as an issue but it was also identified as a distinguishing factor between the HR professionals in high-performing firms and those in low-performing firms. In high-performing firms, HR professionals play an important role in amplifying important signals (customer information) from the external environment and ensuring that these signals are fully disseminated throughout the company so that people may act in harmony with each other in responding to market place demands. Furthermore, they reduce the presence of less important information that frequently blocks attention to more critical information. By so doing HR professionals help to successfully "navigate" the organization through changing customer and shareholder requirements. We call the process of leveraging dynamic market information to create a unified and responsive organization "market-driven conductivity".

Personal credibility

Personal credibility has the second greatest influence on business performance. Our data indicate that there are a significant number of HR professionals who have personal credibility but who do not go to the next step of translating personal credibility into strategic contribution. However, to be allowed to make strategic contributions, HR professionals must first have credibility with the line managers with whom they work. Without credibility they will not be invited to strategy forums nor will they be able to generate commitment to the strategic agendas that they might bring to "the table". Personal credibility consists of three sub-factors: achieving results, effective relationships and communication skills.

Achieving results

The most important aspect of personal credibility is achieving a track record of results. HR professionals must have a reputation of meeting their commitments, of doing what they say and saying what they will do. The results they achieve should be error free. One important category in which results should occur is in the areas of asking important questions that help to frame complex ideas in useful ways. All of this must be done with personal integrity. It is noteworthy that in the Human Resource Competency Study, the integrity variables factored together with the "achieving results" variables. Therefore, in the minds of line executives, HR professionals must achieve results but they must do so in a way that meets the highest standards of integrity.

Effective relationships

Given that HR professionals focus on the human side of business, the expectation that HR professionals are able to foster and maintain effective interpersonal skills is reasonable. These skills enable them to work well with colleagues, with individual line executives and with the management team as a whole. They must be able to diagnose and improve, if necessary, intra-personal as well as interpersonal problems. They must be able to create an atmosphere of trust in their relationships. Trust comes about by being consistent relative to an agreed-upon set of behavioral and achievement standards. With trust comes the capacity to "have chemistry" with key constituents. In our work with effective HR executives we have noticed that "having good chemistry" occurs when core values are shared, when there are some elements of common interests that go beyond work boundaries, when HR executives are helpful and empathetic in addressing non-direct work-related concerns and when the HR executive can decompress tense interpersonal issues.

Communication skills

HR professionals must have effective written and verbal communication skills. Over the past twenty years, the average span of control has more than doubled. This requires that HR profess-ionals must be able to communicate effectively to large numbers of people in shorter time periods. In a world where the speed of information has increased approximately 16,000,000% in the past twenty-four years or so, the mandate to communicate clearly is obvious. Multiple messages compete for airtime in the limited mental space of virtually all organizations. To have personal credibility HR professionals must be able to accurately select and clearly communicate the most critical messages for organizational success. They must communicate not only through formal communication lines; they also recognize that virtually all activities in which HR is involved have an important communication component. When HR professionals hire, promote and fire certain people, when they design and implement measurement and reward systems, and when they offer specific training programs, they are sending powerful messages about what is important to the organization and to its success.

HR delivery

HR professionals deliver both traditional and operational HR activities to their businesses. The HR delivery category entails the HR activities that are traditionally associated with the HR function. They are the tools of the trade. These include staffing, training and development, organization design,[7] performance management, legal compliance and HR measurement.

This category of HR involvement is akin to one of the dominant HR frameworks of the 1970s and 1980s: "Right person, right people, right place, doing right things."

HR Delivery has a small though statistically significant influence on business performance. The conclusion is that increasingly the HR delivery tools do not highly differentiate the HR professionals in the high-performing firms from those in the low-performing firms. However, there is a fascinating and important conclusion that can be drawn when HR delivery is applied in the context of HR's strategic contribution. Recall that elements of the HR delivery tools are included in both culture management (i.e. alignment of HR with the desired culture) and fast change (i.e. alignment of people, information, measurement and incentives with fast change). Thus, when applied in the context of powerful cultural or change agendas, the foundational HR tools strongly contribute to business performance. When these foundational HR tools are applied without powerful business direction, their differentiating impact is weak. This does not suggest that these practices do not need to be done well. Rather, it suggests that the well-designed and delivered HR basics are the "price of entry" into the strategy game.

Staffing

HR professionals should have the ability to develop comprehensive staffing processes. They must competently design and deliver each phase of the staffing process; they must be able to hire, promote, transfer and fire people as individual and discrete steps. They must also be able to carry out these tasks as part of an overall staffing agenda. They must integrate the full breadth of staffing practices into a comprehensive system that supports the overall HR strategy as described above.

In a world of change, the required individual competencies and organizational capabilities need to be continually defined and created. Your company will need to keep some competencies and capabilities through aggressive programs that retain the key talent. Your company may need to develop other key competencies. Still other competencies and capabilities may no longer be needed because of the changing nature of the competitive environment. These need to be reduced through divestitures or through outplacement. Thus, staffing practices play a central role in continually updating the capabilities that are required by a company. Of the HR basics, staffing practices have greatest influence on financial performance.

Development

Effective development defines and integrates two key sets of activities: training and organization development. This is noticeable since it sometimes occurs that HR activities become dominated by psychologists with a decided bent toward individual development. On other occasions, developmental activities may be dominated by organizational development specialists who focus on organizational interventions. As a result of this distinction, some companies have experienced a fragmentation between the training specialists and the OD specialists. Occasionally the segmentation deteriorates into dysfunctional one-upmanship – each trying to outdo the other in importance, impact, and image. In the high-performing firms, these two sets of activities are integrated into a cooperative whole and are conceptually and practically linked into a single and comprehensive agenda. Training programs may consist of four major sets of activities:

- basic skills (reading, writing, arithmetic), technical skills (activity-based costing, inventory management), or leadership skills (strategy, organizing, coaching);
- training programs that promote overall cultural and strategic agendas;

- training that is linked to career development for individual participants;
- training that engages employees in high value-added and challenging work assignments.

Organization development is also a key component of an overall developmental agenda. In the HR field, there are probably as many different definitions of OD as there are companies that employ OD specialists. At a minimum, OD generally refers to change interventions at the organization and team levels. In the Human Resource Competency Study, we identified two key OD activities:

- developmental intervention programs that facilitate change;
- large-scale communication initiatives that help people to know where the organization is headed and how it will get there.

Structure

HR professionals assist in the design of effective organizations. The Human Resource Competency Study differentiates two aspects of organization design: organization structure and process design. To play a substantial role in restructuring activities, HR professionals must apply four key principles of organizational structure.

- First, the primary purpose of structure is to place those people together structurally who need to interact most to create the greatest wealth. This principle applies whether corporate wealth is created by developing a close relationship with customers (market-based structure), by creating and producing products (product-based structure), by being highly efficient (functionally based structure), by leveraging synergies (matrix structure) or by responding to regionally segmented markets (geographically based structure).
- Second, organizational structures bring people together to solve one problem but in so doing structures inevitably separate people who must still have working relationships. HR professionals can help design mechanisms that foster coordination among separated functions or products groups such as meetings, task forces and committees, common goals, measures and rewards, lateral and diagonal transfers, and work process integration.
- Third, we live in a world that mandates greater speed, flexibility, efficiency, empowerment, productivity and innovation. In this world, hierarchical delayering and staff reductions continue as an ongoing way of life in many organizations. When these occur, HR must establish control mechanisms which replace the traditional managerial hierarchy. Such control mechanisms include the following:
  - training programs that enhance technical, team and personal competencies, financial and process knowledge, and skills in conflict resolution;
  - team-based goal setting, measurement, feedback and incentives;
  - intensive communications about company direction and strategy, cultural and technical requirements, and financial and operational matters;
  - delegation of authority to make decisions and take action with minimal supervisory oversight (because there are fewer supervisors).
- Fourth, HR professionals should not only be experts in the structuring of organizations but should also be expert in the process of organizational restructuring. They should work with organization design teams to ensure that political considerations are minimized and that business logic receives predominant consideration. They should be the integrity shepherds and primary proponents of the pre-specified strategic objectives of

the restructuring. They should make sure that the right people are selected to be on the design team, that design team members have the correct instructions and that they have the opportunity to receive information and instructions from key stakeholders. Finally, HR professionals should ensure that measures are in place to evaluate the effectiveness of the new structure within pre-specified time frames.

The second aspect of organization design is process design. Redesigning organizations around processes is becoming a more prevalent trend. Two considerations are central in process redesign:

> First, process-based organization design generally presumes that the processes begin with a target customer or group of target customers in mind. With the target customer as the focal definer of the process, information and activities flow backward from the customer into the organization through sales and marketing, delivery, service, logistics, manufacturing (or the equivalent in a service-based company), product or service design, R&D, and market research. The key issue in this flow is the maintenance of consistency of customer focus.

> Second, processes must be concurrent and integrated. Concurrency requires that organizational processes be designed so that heretofore sequential steps are planned and executed simultaneously. Integration occurs, as processes are designed to move away from individual assembly line-based processes to more team-based workflow. As these are done, time, quality and costs are mutually improved.

HR measurement

As part of the basic HR delivery, HR professionals must be able to measure how much their activities add value. They must have a concept of the full HR value proposition. They must be able to provide measures for each component of the HR value proposition and verify the statistical relationship among the levels of the HR value proposition (Ulrich & Brockbank 2005).

As the mandate for greater productivity continues to impress itself on most corporations, HR departments are expected to provide quantitative indicators of value added. Two categories of HR measurement may be distinguished: efficiency measures and effectiveness measures.

> The HR measurement literature has traditionally been dominated by measures of efficiency. These measures tend to focus on how well HR does specific HR activities (e.g. costs per hire, time to fill a job, training hours per year per employee).

> In recent years substantial progress has been made in measuring the contributions of HR to business success. The premise of these recent trends is that measuring HR is easy; the difficult aspect of HR measurement is not the measurement but rather knowing what to measure. Before measurements can be taken, the dominant and focal contributions of HR to the firm must first be determined. Once these are decided then the measurement process may proceed rather easily by statistically connecting marketplace results, strategy implementation results, organizational capability results, and HR practice implementation results.

Legal compliance

To be effective in working with the human side of business, HR professionals must know the legal issues that influence and safeguard people at work:

- the rights of people to work free from discrimination based on gender, race, religion, sexual orientation, ethnicity, age or disability;
- legal protection of an environment that is free from physical threat or forms of psychological harassment;
- legal rights of people at work relative to testing, evaluation, discipline, compensation, and privacy;
- legal issues that have direct influence on labor relations;
- legal issues that have ethical overtones including honesty in financial and other kinds of reporting.

Performance management

HR professionals should have the ability to design and deliver performance management systems. Of the four sub-factors that constitute HR delivery, the performance management factor is the weakest predictor of business financial performance. There are probably several reasons for this result:

- other factors influence pay besides performance, such as seniority, guaranteed base pay, hierarchical level, and functional category;
- companies frequently pay large compensation packages as part of pre-employment agreements rather than solely on the basis of performance;
- many companies link compensation to performance when business is good and cash flow is strong; fewer companies substantially reduce total compensation when business is bad and cash flow is weak.

To be a driver of business performance, performance management systems must consist of two basic elements: measurements and rewards.[8] Effective measurement systems have four important features:

- high-performing teams and individuals from low-performing teams and individuals can be differentiated;
- measurements should be simple but complete; they should measure both results and behaviors including ethical integrity;
- measurements should come from several sources so as to be credible in the mind of the person being evaluated and to capture the full richness of multiple perspectives;
- measurements should be comparable to key benchmarks such as previous year-to-date performance, other individuals doing the same tasks, and preset targets or goals.

Effective reward systems also have seven important characteristics:

- effective reward systems acknowledge that certain components of the reward system are required to get people to go to work for you (e.g. benefits and some form of base compensation);
- rewards motivate when they are of value to the receiver and not to the giver;
- rewards are most motivating when they are visible to both the receiver and to those whose opinions are valued by the receiver;
- rewards that are given close to the achievement of the desired results or to the expression of the desired behaviors are more effective at reinforcing those desired results and behaviors;

- rewards are more effective if they are performance contingent and can therefore be taken away if performance is not sustained;
- non-financial rewards can be important sources of motivation; these include office size, titles, and public acknowledgement;
- of the non-financial rewards, one that is often overlooked and yet has great motivating influence is the option to do challenging and high value-added work that may be outside of the formal job description.

Business knowledge

Business knowledge likewise accounts for a small though statistically significant portion of HR's influence on business performance. It is not that business knowledge is unimportant but it is the case that HR professionals in low-performing firms tend to know as much about business as those in high-performing firms. Knowledge by itself is not a differentiator of performance. What does differentiate performance is not what you know but rather what you do with that knowledge. Specifically, what matters is how effectively you apply that knowledge to making strategic contributions to the business.

Knowledge of the value chain

HR professionals need to have knowledge of the full breadth of activities that comprise the value chain. The value chain consists of several elements which together link the market demand with internal supply. The value chain factor starts with knowledge of external customers, suppliers and competitors. The dynamics and requirements of the competitive environment are then translated into internal financial and production requirements. Finally, the supplied products and services are then distributed to the marketplace through alternative channels. By applying this knowledge a major contribution of HR is to make the value chain whole greater than the sum of the parts.

Knowledge of the firm's value proposition

The Human Resource Competency Study identifies three key categories of wealth creation that determine the context within which other value-creating activities occur and about which HR professionals should be knowledgeable.

- First, companies create wealth by developing a portfolio of businesses that maximize leverage and returns while concurrently mitigating risks. Company leaders (including HR leaders) determine which businesses they will buy, which they will keep, and which they will close or divest. This must be done with the focused consideration of the risk tolerance of the investment community. They must also determine which activities will be conducted through which internal channels (within business units, within corporate headquarters, and within shared services) or which should be outsourced.
- Second, in harmony with determining which businesses they will emphasize, companies must also determine which markets they will pursue and through which marketing activities they will approach their selected markets.
- Third, they must know the basic processes through which products and services will be provided and the quality standards to which these processes will be held accountable.

Labor knowledge

As might be anticipated, HR professionals need to have knowledge of labor issues. Labor issues may be divided into four categories:

- general infrastructure, personnel, and logic of unions;
- how to avoid disputes by knowing the issues that are of greatest importance to the work force, maintaining accurate mechanisms to track employee satisfaction relative to these key issues, ensuring that the company is proactive in meeting the key needs of employees, and maintaining ongoing two-way communications with the workforce;
- key legal and ethical issues of collective bargaining;
- how to effectively work within the provisions of the labor contract, acting within the spirit as well as within the letter of the law.

HR technology

In the last decade, there has been a substantial increase in the application of electronic technology to HR administrative services. HR departments are regularly inventing new applications to accomplish a multitude of HR goals. These goals focus on helping HR to be more efficient as well as more effective. Nonetheless, the Human Resource Competency Study has found that HR technology has a statistically insignificant influence on business performance. There are at least two reasons for this finding:

- First, approximately 10% of business IT projects is delivered on time and on budget. HR specific projects are probably consistent with this general statistic.
- Second, even if the projected cost savings are realized, it is likely that these cost savings are a relatively small percent of the firm's total cost structure.

The above logic does not, of course, lead to the conclusion that companies should not invest in HR technology. Rather, it does suggest that the likelihood of HR information systems directly and significantly impacting bottom-line financial performance is rather low. In fact, one might argue that the direct influence of HR technology on financial performance will never be very high. Rather, the influence of HR technology on financial performance will occur because it will free up the time, focus and energy of HR professionals so that they can make important strategic contributions (as discussed above).

Conclusions and what's next

This chapter indicates the competencies of HR professionals that relate to business performance. It, therefore, suggests the specific competencies that HR professionals should identify and master to fully contribute. These findings have important implications for the selection, development, and performance management processes for those in HR. If and when we know what is expected for an HR professional to contribute to business success, then HR leaders can use that information for investing in their HR professionals.

This study reported data from the 2002 data set. At this time, we are culling the data from the 2007 data set with about 10,000 total respondents. Our initial findings on the 2007 data set suggest that most of the key findings of this 2002 data set continue to be valid, with the 2007 data showing an ever-increasing importance of what we now call "credible activist" (in this chapter, personal credibility). It is not enought for HR professionals to be credible, they must also have a point of view on how to influence the business.

We anticipate further refinements as the HR profession continues to move forward.

Notes

1 We express our appreciation to Dave Yakonich and Jon Woodard for their contributions to this chapter.
2 During four iterations of the Human Resource Competency Study, we have had the opportunity to work with a number of outstanding colleagues. In 1987 and 1992, Arthur Yeung and Dale Lake contributed heavily to the project. In 1997, Connie James played a central role. In 2002, David Yakonich capably managed the increasing complexity of the project.
3 We consciously selected the concept of business for reasons that were consistent with the intent of the research project. The term "business" is used to describe the organizational units in which the HR participants generally provide services. Businesses are "identifiable units that are commonly understood within the firm". Thus, "business" could refer to corporate offices, group (Household Products group), division (Software Division), plant (Ann Arbor Manufacturing), function (Financial Services, or geography (Asia-Pacific Region). We avoided the term "business unit" due to the fact that "business unit" has different meaning in different firms. For example, in some companies Asia Pacific Region may be the "business" which an HR professional may serve but the Asia Pacific Region may not be a "business unit" in the vernacular of a specific firm.

We also consciously decided to focus on the participant's business rather than on the corporation as a whole. The rationale for this decision is based on the assumption that the HR practices and competencies that may be important for one business may be less relevant for another business even if they are part of the same corporation. However, companies were not willing to provide "business"-level performance measures such as ROI, margins, sales, profitability or revenue growth. Thus we were left with a perceived measure of financial performance.

To confirm the reliability of this indicator, the research team undertook a two-phase process:
   1. Data from multiple business units from the same corporation were aggregated to the corporate level.
   2. These aggregated data were then correlated with the publicly available ROA figures for the past three years (1999, 2000, 2001).

The resultant correlation is .5645. Given that virtually none of the companies for which ROA figures were available had 100% of their respective "businesses" involved in the study, this result supports the convergent validity assumption between the perceived and objective performance measures.
4 The entire 2002 data set consisted of 7082 respondents. In this chapter, we used only US and non-HR associates. The logic for the utilization of this sub-sample is as follows. In this analysis we are examining the influence of HR on business performance. Through the four rounds of the Human Resource Competency Study, we have found that non-HR associates view the work of HR professionals differently in important ways from how HR professionals view themselves. Non-HR professionals tend to be more critical and more business focused in their judgments of HR professionals. We chose to use the US portion of the sample because of the relatively more competitive business conditions that exist in the US when compared to many other parts of the world. For example, in controlled or developing economies, business performance may be primarily dependent on government influence rather than on the inherent competitiveness of the company.
5 The authors recognize that the data set is based on cross-sectional data from which it is difficult to attribute causality. What we know from the cross-sectional results is that the HR professionals in high-performing firms exhibit these competencies more than do those in the low-performing firms. Additional analysis will be conducted to further test the causal nature of our conclusions.
6 The additional analysis consists of second-level exploratory factors analysis of the items that comprise the strategic contribution category.

86

7   The "organization design" factor is the most complex of the entire study. Several variables factored together which make sense but only a very high level of conceptual abstraction. While they make conceptual sense as a single factor, from a practical standpoint it makes less sense to address them at the same time. Therefore, we divide this factor into three categories:
    organization design;
    HR measurement;
    legal compliance.
8   The criteria for effective measurements and rewards are based on the work of Steve Kerr whose substantial influence on the HR field we gratefully acknowledge.

References

Boyatzis, R., 1982a. *The Competent Manager*. New York: John Wiley & Sons.

Boyatzis, R., 1982b. Competence at work. In A. Stewart, ed. *Motivation and Society*. San Francisco: Jossey-Bass, pp. 221–243.

Brockbank, W., Sioli, A. & Ulrich, D., 2001. So . . . We are at the table! Now what? Available at http://webuser.bus.edu/Programs/hrcs/res_NowWhat.htm [accessed July 23, 2002].

Intagliata, J., Ulrich, D. & Smallwood, N., 2000. Leveraging leadership competencies to produce leadership brand. *Human Resource Planning*, Dec., 12–22.

Kenny, J., 1982. Competency analysis for trainers: a model for professionalization. *Training and Development Journal*, 36 (5), 142–148.

Kolb, D., 1984. *Experiential Learning*. New Jersey: Prentice-Hall, Inc.

Lippitt, G. & Nadler, L., 1967. Emerging roles of the training director. *Training and Development Journal*, 21 (8), 2–10.

Losey, M., 1999. Mastering the competencies of HR management. *Human Resource Management*, 38 (2), 99–102.

McClelland, D., 1973. Testing for competence rather than intelligence. *American Psychologist*, 28 (1), 1–14.

McClelland, D., 1976. *A Guide to Job Competency Assessment*. Boston: McBer.

McClelland, D. & Boyatzis, R., 1982. Leadership motive pattern and long-term success in management. *Journal of Applied Psychology*, 67 (6), 737–743.

McCullough, M. & McLagan, P., 1983. Keeping the competency study alive. *Training and Development Journal*, 37 (6), 24–28.

McLagan, P. & Bedrick, D., 1983. Models for excellence: The results of the ASTD training and development study. *Training and Development Journal*, 37 (6), 10–20.

McLagan, P. & Suhadolnik, D., 1989. *Models for HRD Practice: The Research Report*. Alexandria: American Society for Training and Development.

Morris, D., 1996. Using competency development tools as a strategy for change in the human resources function. *Human Resource Management*, 35 (1), 35–51.

Nadler, L. & Nadler, Z., 1989. *Developing Human Resources*. San Francisco: Jossey-Bass.

Schoonover, S., 1998. *Human Resource Competencies for the Year 2000: The wake up call!* Alexandria: Society for Human Resource Management.

Schuler, R., 1990. Repositioning the human resource function: Transformation or demise? *Academy of Management Executive*, 4 (3), 49–59.

Spencer, L. & Spencer, S., 1993. *Competence at Work*. New York: John Wiley.

Ulrich, D., 1987. Organizational capability as a competitive advantage: Human resource professionals as strategic partners. *Human Resource Planning*, 10 (4), 169–184.

Ulrich, D., 1997. *Human Resource Champions*. Boston: Harvard Business School Press.

Ulrich, D. & Brockbank, W., 2005. *The HR Value Proposition*. Boston: Harvard Business School Press.

Ulrich, D., Brockbank, W. & Yeung, A., 1989. Beyond belief: A benchmark for human resources. *Human Resource Management*, 28 (3), 311–355.

Ulrich, D., Brockbank, W., Yeung, A. & Lake, D., 1995. Human resource competencies: An empirical assessment. *Human Resource Management*, 34 (4), 473–495.

6

Compensation

Barry Gerhart

To be successful over time, organizations must be effective in formulating and executing their product market strategies. Although strategy is often framed as a macro topic, what happens at the organization level depends on the nature of decisions that are made by individuals at every level in the organization, as well as the success with which these decisions are executed. Although many factors influence the effectiveness of strategy formulation and execution, one key factor, and the focus of this chapter, is how people in the organization are compensated. Whether the goal is to have executives formulate and execute a strategy that benefits shareholders, or the goal is that of a first-level manager seeking to have his or her work group make a successful contribution to strategy execution and success, it is likely that the design of compensation for these groups (executives, managers, and employees) will play an important role in effectiveness. Thus, effective compensation design can play a major role in strategy formulation, execution and effectiveness.

Definition

Compensation, or remuneration, can be defined to include "all forms of financial returns and tangible services and benefits employees receive as part of an employment relationship" (Milkovich & Newman, 2008, p. 9). "Total rewards" include monetary compensation and nonmonetary rewards. This distinction and the related different general forms of compensation are shown in Figure 6.1 below.

Compensation can alternatively be defined and studied in terms of its key decision/design areas, which include (Gerhart & Milkovich, 1992; Milkovich & Newman, 2008): how pay varies across (and sometimes within) organizations according to its level (how much?); form (what share is paid in cash versus benefits?); structure (how is pay linked to job content, individual competencies, and progression and does pay vary across business units?); basis or mix (what is the share of base pay relative to variable pay/performance-based pay and what criteria determine payouts?); and administration (who makes, communicates, and administers pay decisions?).[1]

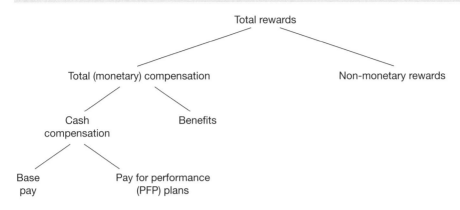

Figure 6.1 Dimensions of total rewards and total compensation

Alternatively, compensation can be organized around two broader dimensions: *how much* (total compensation level) to pay and *how* (e.g., cash or benefits, structure, degree of PFP) to pay (Gerhart & Milkovich, 1992; Gerhart & Rynes, 2003). Some evidence suggests that organizations may have more discretion regarding the how compared to the how much decision (Gerhart & Milkovich, 1990). Labor market competition pressures (the need to offer a competitive compensation package to attract and retain employees) and product market competition pressures (the need to control labor costs to keep product costs competitive) may set lower and upper bounds respectively on pay level for particular skills and occupations. In contrast, decisions regarding how payments are made (e.g., the mix of base versus variable pay) and the criteria used in awarding such payments (e.g., individual, group, organization effectiveness) can vary widely across (and within) organizations without necessarily generating significantly different labor costs. Or, if labor costs are higher, it is hoped that these higher costs are a natural consequence of higher productivity, quality, and/or other measures of effectiveness that are a result of a well-designed compensation strategy.

In addition to specifying the content of compensation decisions and thinking about where there is the most discretion in design choices, the compensation literature also seeks to understand their causes (e.g., organization strategy) and consequences (e.g., organization effectiveness). Additionally, the compensation literature has sought to understand whether the consequences (for effectiveness) of compensation decisions depend on alignment or fit with contextual factors (e.g., organization strategy, which is studied as both a causal and moderator variable).

Finally, it should be acknowledged that compensation could be defined to include non-monetary rewards as well. There is no doubt about the fact that both monetary and nonmonetary rewards are important in the workplace. However, monetary rewards are unique in at least a few ways (Gerhart & Rynes, 2003; Lawler, 1971; Rottenberg, 1956). First, compensation is one of the most visible aspects of a job to both current employees and job seekers. Second, unlike some other job characteristics (e.g., job responsibility, working in teams), most people prefer more money to less. Third, money can be instrumental for meeting a wide array of needs, including, where preferences differ, economic consumption, self-esteem, status, and feedback regarding achievement. Given the central importance of monetary compensation, as well as limits on what can be covered in a single chapter, the main focus here is on pay or monetary rewards.

Chapter plan

I organize this chapter around the "how much to pay" and "how to pay" decisions identified above.[2] I focus primarily on the "how to pay" decision, especially pay-for-performance (PFP) plans. Most of my attention is devoted to the potential consequences of PFP decisions (both good and bad) and how these consequences may depend on contextual factors (i.e., alignment) and on design choices. First, however, it is necessary to address the fundamental issue of money's role as a motivator.

Does pay motivate?

Campbell and Pritchard (1976) observe that motivation can be defined in terms of its intensity, direction, and persistence. (Together with ability and situational constraints/opportunities, motivation contributes to observed behavior.) Thus, to fully evaluate the impact of pay on motivation, one must look not only at (enduring) effort level, but also the degree to which effort is directed toward desired objectives.

The role of pay, specifically PFP, and its effect on the level and direction of motivation in the workplace has long been a source of debate.[3] In some psychology-based treatments, the view is that "money is the crucial incentive" (Locke et al., 1980, p. 379). In a similar vein, Lawler (1971) stated that "the one issue that should be considered by all organization theories is the relationship between pay and performance" (p. 273). Lawler presented a model showing that pay is important because it is instrumental for meeting so many needs, both tangible (e.g., Maslow's (1943) frequently mentioned "lower order" needs such as food and shelter) and less tangible (or "higher order" needs such as security, status, esteem, and feedback about achievement). The importance of compensation in economics-based theories is taken as a given, as a reading of agency, efficiency wage, and tournament theories reveals.

In contrast, especially in recent years, there has been a tendency to ignore compensation in treatments of motivation and performance management in the psychology-based literature. Rynes et al. (2005, p. 574) observe that "at least three historical theories of motivation have dampened psychological interest" in pay: Maslow's (1943) need hierarchy theory, Herzberg et al.'s (1957) motivator-hygiene theory, and Deci and Ryan's (1985) cognitive evaluation theory. The scholarly literature has, for the most part, come to the conclusion that many of the core propositions of the Maslow and Herzberg models have not been empirically supported, including the peripheral role given to pay in motivation. Likewise, while the empirical support for cognitive evaluation theory, specifically the idea that PFP undermines intrinsic motivation (in nonwork settings) is still being debated, Gerhart and Rynes (2003) argue that such an effect is unlikely in work settings and find no empirical evidence in such settings. Rynes et al. (2005) observe that these ideas nevertheless seem to have continued influence in both the academic and practitioner worlds.[4]

Finally, a third view does not question the motivational impact of pay as an incentive. To the contrary, the concern is that it sometimes motivates "too well" resulting in unintended consequences (e.g., lack of teamwork, lack of quality, gaming the system) caused by people (mis)directing their effort in a way that earns the incentive payout, but which is ultimately not beneficial to the organization. Thus, the concern is not with effort level, but with its direction. These potential problems have received a good deal of attention across disciplines and in both the academic and practice literatures (e.g., Gerhart, 2001; Kohn, 1993; Lawler, 1971; Pfeffer, 1998; Whyte, 1955).[5]

Each of the above perspectives on compensation has some validity and relevance in at least some situations. As I show below, the evidence clearly indicates that PFP can be a powerful motivator of effective behaviors. Just as important, I also discuss the evidence (often anecdotal, but compelling) of the risks associated with PFP and some of the things that can go wrong. In any event, the question of whether to use compensation as an incentive may be largely irrelevant, given that organizations around the world already, as a rule, use compensation to motivate *something*, whether it be high performance, promotion, seniority, or avoidance of discharge or other discipline.

Effects of pay: incentive, sorting, and other intervening mechanisms

There are many theoretical processes, both in psychology and in other social sciences that have been used to explain the impact of pay in organizations, including reinforcement, expectancy, equity, utility, agency, efficiency wage, and tournament theories. (For a summary and review, see Gerhart & Rynes, 2003.) To greatly simplify, these theories indicate that pay operates on motivation and performance in two general ways (Gerhart & Milkovich, 1992; Gerhart & Rynes, 2003; Lazear, 1986).

First, there is the potential for an *incentive effect*, which we define as the impact of PFP on current employees' motivational state. The incentive effect is how pay influences individual and aggregate motivation, holding the attributes of the workforce constant. The incentive effect has been the focus of the great majority of theory and research in compensation, especially in management and applied psychology (in earlier years when monetary incentives received more attention).

Second, there is the potential for a *sorting effect*, which we define as the impact of pay on performance via its impact on the attributes of the workforce. Different types of pay systems may cause different types of people to apply to and stay with an organization (self-select) and these different people may have different levels of ability or trait-like motivation, or different levels of attributes (e.g., team skills) that enhance effectiveness more in some organizations than in others. Organizations may also differentially select and retain employees, depending on the nature of their pay level and/or PFP strategies. The self-selection aspect of sorting and its application to the effects of pay is based primarily on work in economics (e.g., Lazear, 1986), but the idea is consistent with Schneider's (1987) attraction-selection-attrition (ASA) idea in the applied psychology literature.

The sorting and incentive idea provides one broad conceptual framework for thinking about intervening processes in studying the effects of compensation. Another is the ability-motivation-opportunity to contribute (AMO) framework (Appelbaum et al., 2000; Boxall & Purcell, 2003; Gerhart, 2007). Compensation seems most likely to influence workforce ability and motivation, less likely to come into play in the 'O' component, which has more to do with job design and participation in decisions. (As noted later, however, the 'O' component and the AMO dimensions in general are quite relevant in addressing horizontal alignment in HR and compensation.)

Gerhart and Milkovich (1992) called for compensation research to include intervening variables (and) at "multiple levels" of analysis in studying compensation and performance, because "if a link is found . . . possible mediating mechanisms can be examined to help establish why the link exists and whether (or which) causal interpretation is warranted" (p. 533). Beyond the general mediating mechanisms discussed above, more detailed intervening variables might include employee attitudes, individual performance and/or competencies, and employee turnover (broken out by performance levels). Other relevant mediators, depending on the particular goals of the unit or organization would be citizenship behavior, teamwork, climate for innovation, motivation, and engagement.

Effects of pay level

Higher pay levels result in higher labor costs per worker, which, by itself, makes a firm less price competitive in its product market. In addition, the costs of a high pay-level policy tend to be easier to measure and more certain than its benefits. Thus, as may be the case with human resource policies generally, it is possible that costs tend to be given more weight than benefits in deciding on a pay-level policy. While competitive pressures drive firms to minimize costs and maximize benefits, the cost side means that firms must control labor costs by controlling total compensation per employee and/or by controlling employee headcount. In a global world, cost control includes an ongoing search for the lowest cost location for production, all else being equal (e.g., proximity to customers and suppliers, worker skill levels) which is to varying degrees, depending on the product, technology, and work organization, a partial function of labor costs. As Table 6.1 makes clear, labor costs differ significantly across the world.

Efficiency wage and other economics-based theories argue that some firms, for a variety of reasons (e.g., their technology depends more heavily on having higher quality workers or monitoring performance is more difficult) do indeed have efficiency reasons to pay higher wages.[6] Higher pay levels, either for the organization as a whole or for critical jobs, may be well suited to particular strategies, such as higher value-added customer segments (e.g., Batt, 2001; Hunter, 2000). Similarly, evidence suggests that organizations making greater use of so-called high-performance work practices (teams, quality circles, total quality management, job rotation) and computer-based technology and having higher skilled workers also pay higher wages (Osterman, 2006).

The observable benefits of higher wages may include (Gerhart & Rynes, 2003): higher pay satisfaction (Currall et al., 2005; Williams et al., 2006; for a review, see Heneman & Judge, 2000), improved attraction and retention of employees (for a review, see Barber & Bretz, 2000), and higher quality, effort, and/or performance (e.g., Klaas & McClendon, 1996; Yellen, 1984).

Table 6.1 Average hourly labor costs for manufacturing production
workers, by country 2005 (in equivalent US dollars)

United States	$24
Canada	24
Germany	33
France	25
United Kingdom	26
Spain	18
Czech Republic	6
Japan	22
Mexico	3
Hong Kong[a]	6
Korea	14
Sri Lanka[b]	0.52
China[c]	0.57

Note: Wage rates rounded to nearest dollar except when rate is less than one dollar.

Sources: U.S. Bureau of Labor Statistics, www.bls.gov
[a] Special Administrative Region of China; [b] 2004; [c] 2002

I conclude the discussion of pay level at this point because it is only at an organization's peril that it follows a high pay-level policy without also linking high pay to high performance, whether it be the performance of the individual, team, unit, organization, or some combination. While it is possible to decouple pay level and performance in the short run, especially where there are forces that dampen market-based competition, by contrast, where market forces dominate, this decoupling is expected to work against organization survival and success in the longer run. In addition, as noted earlier, it may be that organizations have more discretion in terms of how they pay than in terms of how much they pay. Thus, the how to pay or PFP issue is perhaps the more strategic of the two decisions (Gerhart & Milkovich, 1990) and it is an issue that is (or should be) made in tandem with the how much to pay decision (Gerhart & Rynes, 2003).

Effects of pay for performance (PFP)

I begin by recognizing that PFP can take on many forms. When it is claimed that PFP did or did not work in a particular context, it is important to know the particular types of pay-for-performance programs being discussed, as different programs may be more or less suitable for different situations. Further, it is important to examine the impact of PFP plans on both incentive and sorting effects, as both are important and may operate differently.

Types of PFP programs include profit sharing, stock plans, gain sharing, individual incentives, sales commissions, and merit pay (Milkovich & Newman, 2008). As Figure 6.2 shows, these programs can be classified on two dimensions: level of measurement of performance (e.g., individual, plant, organization) and type of performance measure (results-oriented or behavior-oriented).

This distinction has also been drawn by Gerhart and Rynes (2003) and Milkovich and Wigdor (1991). It is important to note that, in practice, many employees are covered by what might be called hybrid pay programs. In other words, rather than working under either merit pay alone or under profit sharing alone, in many cases, employees will be covered by both types of plans and perhaps others as well.

Type of performance measure	Level of performance measure			
	Individual	Facility/plant	Organization	Multiple levels
Behavior-based	Merit pay		Merit pay for executives	Hybrid
Results-based	Individual incentives sales commission	Gain sharing	Profit-sharing stock plans	Hybrid
Results-based and behavior-based	Hybrid	Hybrid	Hybrid	Hybrid

Figure 6.2 Pay-for-performance (PFP) programs, by level and type of performance measure

Some of the many companies in the United States that are well known for their use of PFP include Lincoln Electric, Nucor Steel, Whole Foods, Hewlett-Packard, Southwest Airlines, and General Electric, to name just a few. Each uses a different form of PFP, with varying degrees of relative emphasis on individual, group/unit, and/or organization-level performance. Outside the United States, in countries with less of a tradition of PFP, there appears to be a movement in some cases (e.g. Japan, Korea) toward greater emphasis on PFP at all organization levels. In these and many other countries, there has been a clear movement toward greater use of PFP for selected employee groups (e.g., executives; Towers Perrin, 2006).

Incentive effects

In a meta-analysis of potential productivity-enhancing interventions in actual work settings, Locke, Feren, McCaleb, Shaw, and Denny (1980) found that the introduction of individual pay incentives increased productivity by an average of 30%. This meta-analysis is particularly compelling, since the authors only included studies that were conducted in real organizations (as opposed to laboratories), used either control groups or before-and-after designs, and measured performance via "hard" criteria (e.g. physical output) rather than supervisory ratings. Based on these multi-study findings, Locke et al. concluded that "money is the crucial incentive . . . no other incentive or motivational technique comes even close to money with respect to its instrumental value" (1980, p. 379).

Subsequent research also supports the powerful incentive effects of pay. Another meta-analysis by Guzzo, Jette, and Katzell (1985) also examined the average effects of both monetary incentives and work redesign on productivity (physical output). They found that financial incentives had a large mean effect on productivity (d = 2.12).[7] More recent meta-analyses (Jenkins et al., 1998; Judiesch, 1994; Stajkovic & Luthans, 1997) likewise provide strong support for a significant positive relationship between financial rewards and performance. Thus, there is compelling evidence that PFP, on average, is associated with substantially higher productivity in these settings.

In studies of executives, PFP plan design seems to influence a wide range of strategic decisions (Gerhart, 2000), including staffing patterns (Gerhart et al., 1996); diversification (Hitt et al., 1996; Phan & Hill, 1995); research and development investment (Galbraith & Merrill, 1991; Hill & Snell, 1989); capital investment (Larcker, 1983); and reaction to takeover attempts (Buchholtz & Ribbens, 1994; Kosnik, 1992; Mallette & Fowler, 1992). Likewise, over time, organizational strategy is more likely to change when (executive) pay strategy changes (Carpenter, 2000). Thus, there is consistent evidence that pay strategy does influence managerial goal choice.

Sorting effects

After reading the studies reviewed above, the reader would be well aware of the incentive mechanism, but quite possibly unaware of the sorting mechanism as a possible explanation for the observed effects. To the extent that the above studies track the same individuals before and after the intervention, they do indeed estimate incentive effects. However, to the degree that the individuals making up the workforce changed in response to a PFP intervention, then at least some of the improvement in performance might be due to a sorting effect. Lazear (2000), for example, reported a 44% increase in productivity when a glass installation company switched from salaries to individual incentives. Of this increase, roughly 50% was due to existing workers increasing their productivity, while the other 50% was attributable to less productive workers quitting and being replaced by more productive workers over time.

Cadsby, Song, and Tapon (2007) likewise found that both incentive and sorting effects explained the positive impact of PFP on productivity. Their study, set in the laboratory, was designed so that subjects went through multiple rounds. In some rounds, subjects were assigned to a PFP plan, while in other rounds they were assigned to work under a fixed salary plan. In yet other rounds, they were asked to choose either the fixed salary or the PFP plan to work under (i.e.,they were asked to self-select). Cadsby et al. found that by the last rounds in their experiment, the PFP condition generated 38% higher performance than the fixed salary condition and that the sorting effect (less risk-averse and more productive subjects being more likely to select the PFP condition) was actually about twice as large as the incentive effect in explaining this 38% difference. In explaining why they found a sorting effect that was larger than that found by Lazear (which was also substantial), Cadsby et al. observe that in the Lazear study, few employees chose to leave the organization, presumably because there was no down-side risk to the PFP plan implemented there. Thus, most of the sorting effect in the Lazear study was probably attributable to new hires being more productive than current employees on average, without much of the sorting effect being due to lower performing employees leaving the organization.

Evidence suggests that PFP is more attractive to higher performers than to lower performers. For example, Trank and her colleagues (2002) found that the highest achieving college students place considerably more importance on being paid for performance than do their lesser achieving counterparts. Likewise, persons with higher need for achievement (Bretz et al., 1989; Turban & Keon, 1993), and lower risk aversion (Cable & Judge, 1994; Cadsby et al., 2007) also prefer jobs where pay is linked more closely to performance. Since these are all characteristics that some or most employers desire, such individual differences are important for employers to keep in mind.

Other research shows that high performers are most likely to quit and seek other employ-ment if their performance is not sufficiently recognized with financial rewards (Salamin & Hom, 2005; Trevor et al., 1997). Conversely, low performers are more likely to stay with an employer when pay–performance relationships are weaker (Harrison et al., 1996).

Finally, to the degree that sorting effects are important, they may make it appear as though the relationship between pay and performance is weaker than it really is (Gerhart & Rynes, 2003). For example, to the degree that organizations are selective and valid in their decisions regarding who to hire and who to retain, the remaining group of employees will be unrepresen-tative in that their average performance level should be high as selectivity and validity increase (Boudreau & Berger, 1985). So, even if there is little observed variance in performance and/or pay within this group (i.e., there is range restriction), this selected group of employees may have above-market pay and above-market performance. Thus, in this example, there is no (observed) relationship between pay and performance within the firm, but there would be a significant relationship between pay and performance between firms. Similarly, on the employee side of the decision, it may be that high performers self-select such that they are more likely to join and remain with organizations that have PFP. In summary, even when there is little observed variance in performance ratings and/or pay within an organization, it may nevertheless be the case that PFP, via sorting effects, has resulted in major differences in performance between organizations (Gerhart & Trevor, 2008).

Concerns, cautions, and challenges

The discussion of the motivational impact of PFP might convey an impression that any organization can readily benefit from PFP and that there is little risk in such a strategy. That, however, is not the case, for reasons noted earlier. First, some critics say pay has no important impact because it is a secondary motivator. In other words, it does not energize and sustain motivation and behavior. While the value that employees attach to pay certainly does vary, we believe that in workplaces where PFP does not appear to motivate, it is often because there is not a sufficiently strong pay–performance link.

Consider the case of two employees, each earning US$50,000 per year. Suppose that the first receives an "excellent" performance rating and a 5% merit increase, while the second receives a "very good" rating and a 4% increase. On an annual basis, the differential is only 1%, or $500. On a weekly basis, the differential is $500/52 = $9.62. With a marginal tax rate of say 40%, the after-tax weekly differential is $5.77. Is this performance payoff sufficient to motivate Employee A to maintain the same level of high performance or to motivate Employee B to aspire to higher performance? Many people would say "no." Furthermore, given the imprecision of performance ratings, there is no assurance that better performance by Employee B would actually result in a higher rating and the modestly higher take-home pay.

Thus, even where (e.g., in the United States) most private sector organizations tend to claim that they have PFP policies (or researchers claim that they are studying PFP policies), there is, in fact, sometimes little meaningful empirical relationship between pay and performance (Gerhart & Milkovich, 1992; Gerhart & Rynes, 2003; Trevor et al., 1997). Not surprisingly then, when employees are asked about how much PFP there is in their own organizations, they tend to say "not very much." For example, in a survey of employees in 335 companies conducted by the HayGroup (2002), employees were asked whether they agreed with the statement, "If my performance improves, I will receive better compensation." Only 35% agreed, whereas 27% neither agreed nor disagreed, and 38% disagreed with this statement.

PFP, if weakly implemented, is not expected by anyone to have much impact. Thus, like any policy, its success depends on the success (including the strength) with which it is implemented. It is also worth noting that PFP is often narrowly defined as annual merit increases. If defined more broadly to include the cumulative effects over time of such increases and importantly, the effect of merit ratings on pay over time via their influence on promotion, the pay–performance relationship begins to look bigger. It is possible that doing a better job of communicating these facts would contribute to stronger performance–pay relationships among employees.

While the above concern focuses on the problem of PFP being too weak to motivate, a very different concern is that PFP motivates "too well" in other cases. Here, the danger is that a PFP program can act as a blunt instrument that may result in unintended and harmful consequences. Several supporting examples can be cited. One is the range of executive pay scandals in the United States, which have involved gaming of the system (e.g. manipulating profits, backdating stock options) as a means to maximize stock option and other incentive plan payouts for themselves. Other examples (see Gerhart (2001) for further details) have to do with "churning" practices in the insurance industry, miscoding health conditions at hospitals to get higher reimbursement from the government, and even auto repair shops finding (non-existent) mechanical problems with automobiles so they could sell more repairs, thus increasing sales and bonus payments, which depend on sales growth.

These and other examples make clear that people do respond to incentives, so great care must be taken in designing such incentives. This issue must, in our opinion, be accorded significant weight and be given serious consideration by any organization implementing or revising a PFP program. There are many potential pitfalls in the use of PFP. One general problem is that there are multiple objectives in organizations and a PFP system cannot maximize them all simultaneously. Thus, a balancing act is required. A system that too aggressively rewards one objective may compromise other objectives. People tend to do what is rewarded and objectives not rewarded tend to be ignored (Lawler, 1971; Milgrom & Roberts, 1992).

How long a PFP plan remains in place is sometimes used as a measure of its success. While a short-term gain in performance from a pay plan that does not last long should not be dismissed, a plan that generates longer term performance gains is preferred and changing plans too often can result in a counterproductive "flavor-of-the-month" perception among employees (Beer & Cannon, 2004). So, survival is a useful indicator.

In addition, evidence on survival is important in terms of drawing statistical conclusions for at least two reasons (Gerhart et al., 1996). First, plans that survive for shorter periods are more likely to be excluded from studies of pay plan effectiveness. To the degree that PFP plans have significant "failure" rates and this results in failed plans not being studied, it would result in a sample of plans that are more effective on average than the full population of plans. Second, while it is useful to know how effective different PFP plans are, on average, just like an investor looking at different types of investments, an organization should be interested in information not just on the average "return," but also information on the variance or risk of the PFP plan.

Beer and Cannon (2004) provide an analysis of 13 PFP "experiments" conducted at Hewlett-Packard in the mid-1990s. In 12 of the 13 cases, the program did not survive. They concluded that "Despite the undisputed instrumentality of PFP to motivate, little attention has been given to whether the benefits outweigh the costs or the 'fit' of these programs with high-commitment cultures like Hewlett-Packard was at the time" (p. 3). In the Hewlett-Packard case, the PFP initiatives had "unintended consequences" and managers eventually decided that performance could be more effectively improved "through alternative managerial tools such as good supervision, clear goals, coaching, training, and so forth" (p. 13). Beer and Cannon note that "This decision [did] not imply that managers believed that pay did not motivate or that it could not be used effectively in other settings" (p. 13). Rather, managers decided that at Hewlett-Packard, there were better alternatives.

Gerhart and colleagues have made similar observations on the risk in implementing PFP programs: "One must consider whether the potential for impressive gains in performance" from such plans is "likely to outweigh the potential problems, which can be serious" (Gerhart, 2001, p. 222) and that such plans are best thought of as representing "a high risk, high reward strategy" (Gerhart et al., 1996, p. 222).

While the risks of PFP programs must be acknowledged and understood, it is also necessary to use some caution here so that one does not get too carried away with the risk issue. Several points are in order. First, Ledford (2004) observed that we need to be clear regarding what specific types of PFP programs we are addressing. For example, the programs that Hewlett-Packard experimented with appear to be mostly team-based programs. Although these did not survive, as both Beer and Cannon and Ledford observe, Hewlett-Packard has for many years used other PFP programs such as broad-based stock options and profit sharing. These PFP programs have survived. So, it is not possible to make any broad statement about PFP programs overall. Second, the evaluation of PFP program success can depend on the timeframe. Beer and Cannon state that "Hewlett-Packard's performance since Carly Fiorina [its former chief executive] introduced pay-for-performance at the executive level has been less than stellar" (p. 16). That statement may have been accurate then, but looking back from the later vantage point of 2007, Hewlett-Packard's performance over the preceding several years was very strong relative to the market and its peers. Does that mean the introduction of more PFP for executives has actually been a success?

Third, it should be understood that in cases where PFP programs generate sorting effects (see earlier discussion), the risk element of PFP programs may be diminished in some respects.

For example, problems caused by a lack of fit with the current culture or employee preferences should be more avoidable in a start-up situation to the extent that an organization can exercise considerable control from day one over who it hires and how well they fit its PFP system.

Fourth, as Cannon and Beer (2004) and others (e.g., Gerhart & Rynes, 2003) have pointed out, risk, defined in terms of lack of fit, disruption, dissatisfaction, and so forth, is not necessarily a bad thing. Indeed, it may be a goal of the plan to reshape the workforce by replacing those that are less effective under a new PFP plan with those that would be more successful (Sturman et al., 2003).

Finally, whenever the risk of implementing a new PFP plan is discussed, it is also necessary to discuss the risk of not implementing such a plan as well (Gerhart et al., 1996). What are the costs and benefits of acting versus not acting? What is the cost of a program not surviving? Is it large enough that it should play an important role in the implementation decision? What happens if the status quo continues while competitors are making changes that, while not necessarily warmly received in the short run, do result in more long-run competitiveness, and thus returns to shareholders and continued employment and earnings for employees?

Factors in PFP success: alignment and performance measurement issues

Given the preceding discussion's emphasis on the need for caution in designing and implementing PFP plans, a couple of natural questions might be "What contextual factors affect whether a PFP plan is successful?" and "How should performance be measured for a PFP plan to succeed?" The former question has to do with alignment/fit and the latter question has to do with pros and cons of different performance measures.

Alignment

Terms such as alignment, synergy, fit, and complementarity describe the idea that the effects of two or more factors are nonadditive and dependent on contextual factors.[8] An example given by Gerhart and Rynes (2003) is where a gain-sharing program alone results in an average performance increase of 10%, while a suggestion system alone results in an average performance increase of 10%. However, when used in combination, their total effect is not additive (i.e., 20%), but is rather nonadditive (e.g., 30%). So, the effect of the gain-sharing program is contingent on a contextual factor, in this case, another aspect of HR (Gerhart & Rynes, 2003).

There are two general classes of contingency factors: person and situation. Our earlier discussion of sorting effects highlighted some of the relevant person factors (e.g., risk aversion, need for achievement, academic performance, performance) that predict preference for PFP. In addition, other person characteristics may predict preferences for particular types of PFP. For example, Cable and Judge (1994) found that individual-based PFP was preferred, on average, by those with high self-efficacy, but as might be expected, less preferred, on average, by those scoring high on collectivism.

There are three key aspects of pay strategy alignment or fit that focus on the situation or environmental context (Gerhart, 2000; Gerhart & Rynes, 2003): horizontal alignment (between pay strategy and other dimensions of HR management, as in the gain-sharing example above), vertical alignment with organizational strategy (i.e., pay strategy with corporate and business strategy), and internal alignment between different dimensions of pay strategy (e.g. pay level and pay basis). Only a brief review is provided here. (For more detail, see Gerhart, 2000; Gerhart & Rynes, 2003; Gomez-Mejia & Balkin, 1992; Milkovich, 1988.)

The primary focus of the pay strategy literature has been on vertical alignment. It has been shown that aspects of corporate strategy such as the process, degree and type of diversification (Gomez-Mejia, 1992; Kerr, 1985; Pitts, 1976) and the firm's life cycle (e.g., growth, maintenance; Ellig, 1981) are associated with different compensation strategies (Gomez-Mejia & Balkin, 1992; Kroumova & Sesis, 2006; Yanadori & Marler, 2006). Evidence also suggests performance differences based on fit such that growth firms perform better with an incentive-based strategy (Balkin & Gomez-Mejia, 1987) and that the effectiveness of an incentive-based strategy depends to a degree on the level of diversification (Gomez-Mejia, 1992). Alignment of pay strategy with business strategy (e.g., Miles & Snow, 1978; Porter, 1985) may also have performance consequences (e.g., Rajagopolan, 1996). Another stream of work on nonexecutives at the business unit level focuses on the alignment between pay strategy and manufacturing strategy (Shaw et al., 2002; Snell & Dean, 1994). Finally, other work shows, consistent with agency theory, that companies having more financial risk tend to have less risk sharing in their compensation for managers and executives (Aggarwal & Samwick, 1999; Bloom & Milkovich, 1998; Garen, 1994). Thus, both the risk aversion of the individual and risk properties of the situation are relevant (Wiseman et al., 2000).

In contrast to the work on vertical alignment, horizontal alignment of pay strategy with other employment practices has been studied mostly using nonexecutive employees and mostly in the context of work on so-called high-performance work systems and HR systems. The effect of an HR system on effectiveness is thought to operate via the intervening variables of ability, motivation, and opportunity, or AMO (Appelbaum et al., 2000; Batt, 2002; Boxall & Purcell, 2003; Gerhart, 2007). One problem with studying horizontal fit, however, is that the hypothesized role of pay and/or PFP, as well as the way these constructs are operationalized, tends to differ across studies, making it difficult to draw robust conclusions about what other HR strategy elements work best with particular pay and PFP approaches (Becker & Gerhart, 1996; Gerhart & Rynes, 2003).

Nevertheless, certain potential areas of fit and mis-fit can be identified (Gerhart & Rynes, 2003; Rynes et al., 2005). For instance, with respect to the 'O' component, it seems likely that group-based incentive plans (e.g., gain sharing, profit sharing) will be more effective in smaller groups (Kaufman, 1992; Kruse, 1993) than in larger groups or organizations. In addition, in situations where work is more interdependent, it may be that some shift in emphasis from individual performance to group performance will be more effective (e.g., Shaw et al., 2002). Nevertheless, it must be kept in mind that even where tasks are interdependent, if there are individual differences in ability and/or performance that are important, then placing too little weight on individual performance in compensation can lead to undesired sorting effects, such that high performers may not join or remain with the group or organization.

To use a sports example, by not paying high competitive rates for high individual performance in basketball, football/soccer, American football, or hockey, a team may find itself left with a set of individuals with less talent, on average, than on other teams. The lack of dispersion in pay may generate some form of harmony and cooperation, but can a team low on talent and high on harmony be competitive? And, if not, how long will the harmony last? If it does last, is it harmony in the form of resignation to the lack of competitiveness?

The third area of fit, internal alignment, has been the least studied. The work of Gomez-Mejia and Balkin (1992) has sought to identify overarching compensation strategies, but more work is needed to document which aspects of pay tend to cluster together in organizations and whether certain clusters are more effective and/or what contingency factors are most important. In any event, the modest evidence that exists concerning the degree of actual alignment between pay and other HR strategy dimensions suggests that there is less alignment than one might wish (Wright et al., 2001).

Although it could be included as a part of vertical alignment, another type of alignment that is important is that between pay strategy and country. Countries differ on a multitude of dimensions that can affect management practice (Dowling et al., 2008), including the regulatory environment (e.g., requirements for worker participation in firm governance), institutional environment (e.g., strength of labor unions, accepted HR practices in areas like compensation), and cultural values (e.g., Hofstede's (1980) dimensions of individualism/collectivism, long-term orientation, masculinity–femininity, power distance, and uncertainty avoidance). As such, a good deal of attention has been devoted to the constraints that organizations face when it comes to choosing which HR and pay strategies (a) can be implemented, and (b) if able to be implemented, which will be effective. Thus, organizations must decide how best to balance standardization and localization in designing HR and pay practices.

While practices that are effective in one country are not necessarily going to be effective or even feasible in another country due, for example, to legal or strong institutionalized traditions, I would like to caution against giving too much weight to contingency factors generally, including country. For example, in the case of the five cultural values dimensions made famous by Hofstede (1980, 2001), evidence shows that country actually explains only a small percentage of variance in individual employee cultural values (Gerhart & Fang, 2005). There is good reason to believe that organizations have considerable room to be different from the country norm in many countries in at least some key areas of HR and pay strategy (Gerhart, 2007). Also, country norms as they relate to HR and pay strategy can and do change. As mentioned earlier, one example is executive compensation. Countries like Germany, South Korea, and Japan changed from essentially no use of long-term incentives (e.g., stock options, stock grants) for top executives in 1998 to substantial use by 2005 (Towers Perrin, 2006). Another example mentioned earlier is the significant change in South Korea (Choi, 2004) and in Japan (Jung & Cheon, 2006; Morris et al., 2006; Robinson & Shimizu, 2006) away from seniority-based pay toward PFP. A third example is the dramatic decline in private sector unionism in the United States, which stands at 7.4% of the workforce in 2006. A fourth example is the decentralization (e.g., from industry to firm or plant level) of collective bargaining in many parts of the world (Katz et al., 2004).

Some of these examples are changes that occurred over the long run. So, a fair question is, how relevant are these examples of changing national conditions in the somewhat shorter run that organizations and managers must survive to make it to the longer run? My point is only that it is important to recognize not only institutional pressures toward conformity in a country, but also that at least in some respects, depending on the country, the timeframe, and the particular policy, there can be room to be unique and the strategy literature tells us that being the same as everyone else is unlikely to generate anything more than competitive parity, whereas being different, while perhaps being more risky, has the potential to generate sustained competitive advantage (e.g., the resource-based view of the firm; Barney, 1991). Some evidence indicates that there is indeed substantial variability in employment practices within countries (Katz & Darbishire, 2002).

Turning to methodology, a challenge in studying contextual or contingent effects is that if only firms and units that achieve some minimal level of alignment survive (Hannan & Freeman, 1977), alignment may be so important that it is almost impossible for the researcher to observe substantial departures from alignment (Gerhart et al., 1996; Gerhart & Rynes, 2003). In this case, restricted range in alignment would reduce the statistical power available to observe a relationship between alignment and performance. This may help explain why the idea of fit, while often thought to be critical, has not received as much support as might be expected in HR research broadly and in the area of compensation specifically (Gerhart et al., 1996; Gerhart, 2007; Wright & Sherman, 1999).

A final observation, on the conceptual side, as alluded to earlier, is that pay strategy work needs to think about how the resource-based view (RBV) of the firm may be relevant to pay strategy. The RBV emphasizes how firms "look inside" for resources that are rare and difficult to imitate and that can be leveraged to build sustained competitive advantage. Industry characteristics and business strategy are still important under the RBV because they place some limits on managerial discretion. However, within these limits, firms are viewed as having considerable discretion in how they compete. Some work has been done addressing how the RBV is relevant to HR strategy broadly (Barney & Wright, 1998; Becker & Gerhart, 1996; Colbert, 2004), but beyond Gerhart et al. (1996), there has not been much application to pay strategy.

Performance measurement issues

A limitation of the meta-analytic evidence reviewed earlier on the effects of PFP is that in most of the studies included, physical output measures of performance (e.g., number of index cards sorted, number of trees planted) were available, (related to this) tasks were simple, and individual contributions were usually separable (Gerhart & Rynes, 2003). In contrast, in many jobs, some or all of these three characteristics do not apply. The widespread use of merit pay and its subjective performance measures is, to an extent, a result of this fact (Milkovich & Wigdor, 1991).

In deciding on which performance measures to use in PFP programs, there are at least two key choices. First, how much emphasis can or should be placed on results-oriented performance measures (e.g., number of units produced) relative to behavior-based ones (e.g., supervisory evaluations of effort or quality)? Second, how much emphasis should be placed on individual contributions relative to collective contributions (an issue discussed briefly above)? Although we discuss each choice separately, in practice, many organizations use multiple performance measures to balance multiple (and sometimes conflicting) objectives.

Behavior-based (subjective) and results-based (objective) measures

Behavior-oriented measures (such as traditional PE ratings) offer a number of potential advantages relative to results-based measures (Gerhart, 2000). First, they can be used for any type of job. Second, they permit the rater to factor in variables that are not under the employee's control, but that nevertheless influence performance. Third, they permit a focus on whether results are achieved using acceptable means and behaviors. Fourth, they generally carry less risk of measurement deficiency, or the possibility that employees will focus only on explicitly measured tasks or results at the expense of broader pro-social behaviors, organizational citizenship behaviors, or contextual performance (see e.g., Arvey & Murphy, 1998; Wright et al., 1993).

On the other hand, the subjectivity of behavior-oriented measures can limit their ability to differentiate employees (Milkovich & Wigdor, 1991). In addition, meta-analytic evidence finds a mean inter-rater reliability of only .52 for performance ratings (Viswesvaran, Ones & Schmidt, 1996), making it difficult for organizations to justify differentiating employees based on such error-laden performance measures, especially if a single rater, often the immediate supervisor, is the source. (A 360-degree appraisal, with its multiple sources/raters, may be helpful in this regard.)

Even if subjectivity in PE could be sufficiently controlled and performance reliably and credibly differentiated, managers may be reluctant to do so because of concerns about adverse consequences for workgroup cohesion, pro-social behaviors, and management–employee relations (Heneman & Judge, 2000; Longenecker et al., 1987). Perhaps for these reasons, as we saw earlier, evidence indicates that most employees do not believe that better performance results in higher compensation (HayGroup, 2002).

At first blush, objective measures of performance, such as productivity, sales volume, shareholder return, and profitability, would seem to provide the solution to the above problems. However, relevant objective measures are not available for most jobs, especially at the individual level. Moreover, agency theory emphasizes that results-based plans (e.g., individual incentives, gain sharing, profit sharing) increase risk bearing among employees (Gibbons, 1998). Because most employees derive the bulk of their income from employment, they cannot diversify their employment-related earnings risk, making them more risk averse than, say, investors. This then is the classic trade-off between designing plans that maximize incentives while keeping the negative effects of risk under control.

Risk aversion is less of a problem where objective measures are seen as credible and performance on such measures is high, providing significant payouts to employees. However, poor performance on such measures (and thus decreasing or disappearing payouts), especially if attributed to factors employees see as beyond their own control (e.g., poor decisions by top executives), often results in negative employee reactions (Gerhart & Milkovich, 1992). Often, there will be pressure to revise (e.g., the experience at GM's Saturn division, Gerhart, 2001) or abandon the plan (e.g., Petty et al., 1992).

Finally, even though objective measures are possibly more reliable, they may also be more deficient. Lawler (1971) warned that "it is quite difficult to establish criteria that are both measurable quantitatively and inclusive of all the important job behaviors," and "if an employee is not evaluated in terms of an activity, he will not be motivated to perform it" (p. 171).

Individual versus group (or collective) performance

Criticisms have been leveled at organizations for focusing too much on individual performance and rewards. For example, Pfeffer (1998b) critiqued individual merit and incentive plans as being ineffective, inciting grievances, and reducing product quality. Similarly, Deming (1986) argued that management's "excessive" focus on individual performance often obscures apparent differences in individual performance that "arise almost entirely from the system that (people) work in, rather than the people themselves" (p. 110). Deming and Pfeffer also argue that focusing on individual performance discourages teamwork: "Everyone propels himself forward, or tries to, for his own good . . . The organization is the loser" (Deming, 1986, p. 110).

While the potential pitfalls of individually based PFP are important, the literature is quite clear that group-based plans also have their own drawbacks. One is that most employees (at least in the U.S.) prefer that their pay be based on individual rather than group performance (Cable & Judge, 1994; LeBlanc & Mulvey, 1998). Another is that this preference is strongest among the most productive and achievement-oriented employees (e.g., Bretz et al., 1989; Lazear, 1986; Trank et al., 2002; Trevor et al., 1997). These facts suggest, as noted earlier, that group-based pay can have unfavorable sorting effects, causing the highest performers to choose alternative opportunities where individual results will be rewarded more heavily.

Yet another drawback has to do with the potential for weakened incentive effects under group plans among those that do join and stay with the organization: "Unless the number of individuals in a group is quite small, or unless there is coercion or some other special device to make individuals act in their common interest, rational self-interested individuals will not act to achieve their common or group interests" (Olson, 1965, pp. 1–2).

This last phenomenon has been widely studied (Kidwell & Bennett, 1993) and goes by many names (e.g., the common-resource problem, public-goods problem, free-rider problem, or social loafing problem). The general idea is that when people share the obligation to provide a resource (e.g., effort), it will be undersupplied because the residual returns (e.g., profit-sharing payouts) to the effort are often shared relatively equally, rather than distributed in proportion to contributions. Evidence suggests that the free-rider problem is sufficiently important (see Gerhart & Rynes (2003) for a summary of evidence) that researchers have devoted considerable attention to how free-rider effects might be mitigated.

One potential solution is to give differentiated rewards to group members based on their individual contributions (an approach used for many years by Lincoln Electric). As mentioned earlier, differentiating rewards based on performance can yield benefits via both incentive and sorting effects (Bishop, 1984). In the same vein, differentiating pay on the basis of individual performance, even within group systems, may reduce the tendency of high-performing employees to leave organizations that switch to group-based pay systems (e.g., Weiss, 1987).

In summary, there are important trade-offs involved in choosing how to measure performance. Performance measures must have a meaningful link to what the organization is trying to accomplish, be sufficiently inclusive of key aspects of performance, balance sometimes competing objectives, and be seen as fair and credible by employees. As noted earlier, organizations often attempt to achieve these goals by using multiple measures of performance, aggregate and individual, results and behavior-oriented (e.g., as in a Balanced Scorecard), and adjusting incentive intensity, to an important extent, on the degree to which valid and credible performance measurement is believed to be achievable.

Conclusion

Compensation involves decisions in multiple areas. My focus in this chapter has been on PFP and, to a lesser extent, pay level. I have highlighted the potential for well-designed PFP plans to make a substantial contribution to organization performance through effects on intervening mechanisms such as incentive and sorting. I have also noted the potential for PFP plans to cause serious problems, often as a result of unintended consequences. I suggested that the probability of success of PFP plans might be improved by effective alignment with contextual factors such as organization and human resource strategy, as well as through careful selection and balancing of performance measures. Still, it may be that the stronger the incentive intensity of such plans, the greater their potential positive impact as well as their potential negative impact. Finally, regardless of how well designed the PFP plan is, its probability of success also rests on how well it is executed and communicated.

Notes

1 Benefits represent a substantial share of compensation cost to employers in the United States, for example, given that many (especially larger) companies fund retirement and health care for employees.

2 Another approach is to organize around the level of analysis and/or type of employee being studied. Studies of executives often use the organization as the level of analysis, whereas studies of non-executives use organization, unit, or individual levels. I focus primarily on non-executive compensation. There is a very large literature on executive compensation. (Publicly traded companies are required in the United States by the Securities and Exchange Commission to publicly disclose how and how much they pay their five highest paid officers.) For reviews, see Devers et al., 2007.

3 This section draws freely on Gerhart and Rynes (2003) and Rynes et al. (2005).

4 It is certainly the case that not all people have pay as their primary motivator and also that the motivational impact of pay is contingent to a degree on these individual differences as well as on situational contingencies (e.g., declining marginal utility at higher pay levels, the strength of the link between pay and performance) (Rynes et al., 2004).

5 One of the more formal treatments of incentive problems and challenges is provided by agency theory and its central focus on agency costs, which are seen as arising from goal incongruence and information asymmetry. Milgrom and Roberts (1992) provide a helpful review.

6 A strict traditional neoclassical economics view would find the notion that employers (at least within a particular market) have a choice when it comes to pay level to be misguided, because the forces of supply and demand yield, in the long run, a single going/market wage that all employers must pay to avoid too high costs in the product market on the one hand and the inability to attract and retain a sufficient quantity and quality of workers in the labor market on the other. The only way that an employer could pay higher wages than other employers would be if better quality workers were hired. In that case, the ratio of worker quality to cost would be unchanged, meaning both that the apparent difference in pay levels was not real, disappearing upon appropriate adjustment for worker quality and that employers would not necessarily realize any advantage from using a high-wage, high-worker quality strategy. However, evidence of persistent and arguably non-illusory differences in compensation levels (see Gerhart & Rynes (2003) for a review) between companies operating in the same market has resulted in greater attention to why such differences exist and more general acknowledgment, including in economics (Boyer & Smith, 2001), recognition that employers have some discretion in their choice of pay level. In response, efficiency wage theory provides an economics-based rationale for why some firms may benefit from higher (lower) wages.

7 The d statistic is defined as the difference between the dependent variable mean for Group A versus Group B, divided by the pooled standard deviation of Groups A and B. Thus, it gives the difference between Group A and B in terms of standard deviation units.

8 This section draws freely on Gerhart and Rynes (2003).

References

Aggarwal, R.K. & Samwick, A.A. (1999). The other side of the trade-off: The impact of risk on executive compensation. *Journal of Political Economy, 107*, 65–105.

Appelbaum, E., Bailey, T., Berg, P. & Kalleberg, A. (2000). *Manufacturing Advantage: Why high performance work systems pay off*. Ithaca, NY: Cornell University Press.

Arvey, R.D. & Murphy, K.R. (1998). Performance evaluation in work settings. *Annual Review of Psychology, 49*, 141–68.

Balkin, D.B. & Gomez-Mejia, L.R. (1987). Toward a contingent theory of compensation strategy. *Strategic Management Journal, 8*, 169–82.

Barber, A.E. & Bretz, R.D. Jr. (2000). Compensation, attraction and retention. In S.L. Rynes & B. Gerhart (Eds), *Compensation in Organizations* (pp. 32–60). San Francisco, CA: Jossey-Bass.

Barney, J.B. (1991). Firm resources and sustained competitive advantage. *Journal of Management, 17*, 99–120.

Barney, J.B. & Wright, P.M. (1998). On becoming a strategic partner: The role of human resources in gaining competitive advantage. *Human Resource Management, 37*, 31–46.

Batt, R. (2001). Explaining intra-occupational wage inequality in telecommunications services: Customer segmentation, human resource practices, and union decline. *Industrial and Labor Relations Review, 54*(2A), 425–49.

Batt, R. (2002). Managing customer services: Human resource practices, quit rates, and sales growth. *Academy of Management Journal, 45*, 587–97.

Becker, B. & Gerhart, B. (1996). The impact of human resource management on organizational performance: Progress and prospects. *Academy of Management Journal, 39*, 779–801.

Beer, M. & Cannon, M.D. (2004). Promise and peril in implementing pay-for-performance. *Human Resource Management, 43*, 3–20.

Bishop, J. (1984). The recognition and reward of employee performance. *Journal of Labor Economics*, *5*, S36–S56.

Bloom, M. & Milkovich, G.T. (1998). Relationships among risk, incentive pay, and organizational performance. *Academy of Management Journal*, *41*, 283–97.

Boudreau, J.W. & Berger, C.J. (1985). Decision-theoretic utility analysis applied to employee separations and acquisitions. *Journal of Applied Psychology*, *73*, 467–81.

Boxall, P. & Purcell, J. (2003). *Strategy and Human Resource Management*. Basingstoke, UK: Palgrave Macmillan.

Boyer, G.R. & Smith, R.S. (2001). The development of the neoclassical tradition in labor economics. *Industrial and Labor Relations Review*, *54*, 199–223.

Bretz, R.D., Ash, R.A., & Dreher, G.F. (1989). Do people make the place? An examination of the attraction-selection-attrition hypothesis. *Personnel Psychology*, *42*, 561–81.

Buchholtz, A.K. & Ribbens, B.A. (1994). Role of chief executive officers in takeover resistance: Effects of CEO incentives and individual characteristics. *Academy of Management Journal*, *37*, 554–79.

Cable, D.M. & Judge, T.A. (1994). Pay preferences and job search decisions: A person-organization fit perspective. *Personnel Psychology*, *47*, 317–48.

Cadsby, C.B., Song, F., & Tapon, F. (2007). Sorting and incentive effects of pay-for-performance: An experimental investigation. *Academy of Management Journal*, *50*, 387–405.

Campbell, J.P. & Pritchard, R.D. (1976). Motivation theory in industrial and organizational psychology. In M.D. Dunnette (Ed.), *Handbook of Industrial and Organizational Psychology*. Chicago, IL: Rand McNally.

Carpenter, M.A. (2000). The price of change: The role of CEO compensation in strategic variation and deviation from industry strategy norms. *Journal of Management*, *26*, 1179–98.

Choi, J.T. (2004). Transformation of Korean HRM based on Confucian Values. *Seoul Journal of Business*, *10*, 1–26.

Colbert, B.A. (2004). The complex resource-based view. *Strategic Management Journal*, *29*, 341–58.

Currall, S.C., Towler, A.J., Judge, T.A., & Kohn, L. (2005). Pay satisfaction and organizational outcomes. *Personnel Psychology*, *58*, 613–40.

Deci, E.L. & Ryan, R.M. (1985). *Intrinsic Motivation and Self-determination in Human Behavior*. New York: Plenum.

Deming, W.E. (1986). *Out of the Crisis*. Cambridge, MA: MIT, Center for Advanced Engineering Study.

Devers, C.E., Cannella, A.A., Reilly, G.P., & Yoder, M.E. (2007). Executive compensation: A multidisciplinary review of recent developments. *Journal of Management*, *33*, 1016–72.

Dowling, P.J., Festing, M., & Engle, A.D. Sr. (2008). *International Human Resource Management* (5th Edition). London: Thomson Learning.

Ellig, B.R. (1981). Compensation elements: Market phase determines the mix. *Compensation Review* (Third Quarter), 30–8.

Galbraith, C.S. & Merril, G.B. (1991). The effect of compensation program and structure of SBU competitive strategy: A study of technology-intensive firms. *Strategic Management Journal*, *12*, 353–70.

Garen, J.E. (1994). Executive compensation and principal-agent theory. *Journal of Political Economy*, *102*, 1175–1200.

Gerhart, B. (2000). Compensation strategy and organizational performance. In S.L. Rynes & B. Gerhart (Eds), *Compensation in Organizations*. San Francisco: Jossey-Bass.

Gerhart, B. (2001). Balancing results and behaviors in pay for performance plans. In C. Fay (Ed.), *The Executive Handbook of Compensation*. New York: Free Press.

Gerhart, B. (2007). Horizontal and vertical fit in human resource systems. In C. Ostroff & T. Judge (Eds), *Perspectives on Organizational Fit*. SIOP Organizational Frontiers Series. New York: Lawrence Erlbaum Associates, Taylor & Francis Group.

Gerhart, B. & Fang, M. (2005). National culture and human resource management: Assumptions and evidence. *International Journal of Human Resource Management*, *16*, 975–90.

Gerhart, B. & Milkovich, G.T. (1990). Organizational differences in managerial compensation and financial performance. *Academy of Management Journal*, *33*, 663–91.

BARRY GERHART

Gerhart, B. & Milkovich, G.T. (1992). Employee compensation: Research and practice. In M.D. Dunnette & L.M. Hough (Eds), *Handbook of Industrial & Organizational Psychology*, 2nd edn (pp. 481–570). Palo Alto, CA: Consulting Psychologists Press, Inc.

Gerhart, B. & Rynes, S.L. (2003). *Compensation: Theory, evidence, and strategic implications*. Thousand Oaks, CA: Sage.

Gerhart, B. & Trevor, C.O. (2008). Merit pay. In A. Varma, P.S. Budhwar, & A. DeNisi (Eds), *Performance Management Systems: A global perspective*. London, UK: Routledge.

Gerhart, B., Trevor, C., & Graham, M. (1996). New directions in employee compensation research. In G.R. Ferris (Ed.), *Research in Personnel and Human Resources Management*, pp. 143–203.

Gibbons, R. (1998). Incentives in organizations. *Journal of Economic Perspectives, 12*, 115–32.

Gomez-Mejia, L.R. (1992). Structure and process of diversification, compensation strategy, and firm performance. *Strategic Management Journal, 13*, 381–97.

Gomez-Mejia, L.R. & Balkin, D.B. (1992). *Compensation, Organizational Strategy, and Firm Performance*. Cincinnati, OH: Southwestern Publishing.

Guzzo, R.A., Jette, R.D., & Katzell R.A. (1985). The effects of psychologically based intervention programs on worker productivity: A meta-analysis. *Personnel Psychology, 38*, 275–91.

Hannan, M.T. & Freeman, J. (1977). The population ecology of organizations. *American Journal of Sociology, 82*, 929–64.

Harrison, D.A., Virick, M., & William, S. (1996). Working without a net: Time, performance, and turnover under maximally contingent rewards. *Journal of Applied Psychology, 81*, 331–45.

HayGroup. (2002). Managing performance: Achieving outstanding performance through a 'culture of dialogue.' Working Paper.

Heneman, H.G. III & Judge, T.A. (2000). Compensation attitudes. In S.L. Rynes & B. Gerhart (Eds), *Compensation in Organizations*. San Francisco: Jossey-Bass.

Herzberg, F., Mausner, B., Peterson, R.O. & Capwell, D.F. (1957). *Job Attitudes: Review of research and opinion*. Pittsburgh: Psychological Service of Pittsburgh.

Hill, C.W.L. & Snell, S.A. (1989). Effects of ownership structure and control on corporate productivity. *Academy of Management Journal, 32*, 25–46.

Hitt, M.A., Hoskisson, R.E., Johnson, R.A., & Moesel, D.D. (1996). The market for corporate control and firm innovation. *Academy of Management Journal, 39*, 1084–119.

Hofstede, G. (1980). *Culture's Consequences: International differences in work-related values*. Beverly Hills, CA: Sage.

Hofstede, G. (2001). *Culture's Consequences: Comparing values, behaviors, institutions, and organizations across nations*, 2nd edn. Thousand Oaks, CA: Sage.

Hunter, L.W. (2000). What determines job quality in nursing homes? *Industrial & Labor Relations Review, 53*, 463–81.

Jenkins, D.G. Jr., Mitra, A., Gupta, N., & Shaw, J.D. (1998). Are financial incentives related to performance? A meta-analytic review of empirical research. *Journal of Applied Psychology, 83*, 777–87.

Judiesch, M.K. (1994). *The Effects of Incentive Compensation Systems on Productivity, Individual Differences in Output Variability, and Selection Utility*. Unpublished doctoral dissertation. Iowa City, IA: University of Iowa.

Jung, E. & Cheon, B. (2006). Economic crisis and changes in employment relations in Japan and Korea. *Asian Survey, 46*(3), 457–76.

Katz, H.C. and Darbishire, O. (2002). Convergences and divergences in employment systems. In S. Estreicher (Ed.), *Global Competition and the American Employment Landscape as We Enter the 21st Century*. New York: Kluwer.

Katz, H.C., Lee, W., & Lee, J. (2004). *The New Structure of Labor Relations: Tripartism and decentralization*. Ithaca, NY: ILR Press/Cornell University.

Kaufman, R.T. (1992). The effects of Improshare on productivity. *Industrial and Labor Relations Review, 45*, 311–22.

Kerr, J.L. (1985). Diversification strategies and managerial rewards. *Academy of Management Journal, 28*, 155–79.

106

Kidwell, R.E. & Bennett, N. (1993). Employee propensity to withhold effort: A conceptual model to intersect three avenues of research. *Academy of Management Review, 18*, 429–56.

Klaas, B.S. & McClendon, J.A. (1996). To lead, lag, or match: Estimating the financial impact of pay level policies. *Personnel Psychology, 49*, 121–41.

Kohn, A. (1993). Why incentive plans cannot work. *Harvard Business Review, 71*(5): 54–63.

Kosnik, R.D. (1992). Effects of board demography and directors' incentives on corporate greenmail decisions. *Academy of Management Journal, 33*, 129–50.

Kroumova, M.K. & Sesis, J.C. (2006). Intellectual capital, monitoring, and risk: What predicts the adoption of employee stock options? *Industrial Relations, 45*, 734–52.

Kruse, D.L. (1993). *Profit Sharing: Does it make a difference?* Kalamazoo, MI: Upjohn Institute.

Larcker, D. (1983). The association between performance plan adoption and corporate capital investment. *Journal of Accounting and Economics, 5*, 3–30.

Lawler, E.E. III (1971). *Pay and Organizational Effectiveness.* New York: McGraw-Hill.

Lazear, E.P. (1986). Salaries and piece rates. *Journal of Business, 59*, 405–32.

Lazear, E.P. (2000). Performance pay and productivity. *American Economic Review, 90*, 1346–61.

Le Blanc, P.V. & Mulvey, P.W. (1998). How American workers see the rewards of work. *Compensation & Benefits Review, 30*, 24–8.

Ledford, G.E. (2004). Commentary on "Promise and peril in implementing pay-for-performance". *Human Resource Management, 43*, 39–41.

Locke, E.A., Feren, D.B., McCaleb, V.M., Shaw, K.N., & Denny, A.T. (1980). The relative effectiveness of four methods of motivating employee performance. In K.D. Duncan, M.M. Gruenberg, & D. Wallis (Eds), *Changes in Working Life* (pp. 363–88). New York: Wiley.

Longnecker, C.O., Sims, H.P., & Gioia, D.A. (1987). Behind the mask: The politics of employee appraisal. *Academy of Management Executive, 1*(3), 183–93.

Mallette, P. & Fowler, K.J. (1992). Effects of board composition and stock ownership on the adoption of "poison pills". *Academy of Management Journal, 35*, 1010–35.

Maslow, A.H. (1943). A theory of human motivation. *Psychological Review, 50*, 370–96.

Miles, R.E. & Snow, C.C. (1978). *Organizational Strategy, Structure, and Process.* New York: McGraw-Hill.

Milgrom, P. & Roberts, J. (1992). *Economics, Organization, & Management.* Englewood Cliffs, NJ: Prentice-Hall.

Milkovich, G.T. (1988). A strategic perspective on compensation management. *Research in Personnel and Human Resources Management, 6*, 263–88.

Milkovich, G.T. & Newman, J.M. (2008). *Compensation,* 9th edn. Boston: McGraw-Hill/Irwin.

Milkovich, G. & Wigdor, A. (1991). *Pay for Performance: Evaluating performance appraisal and merit pay.* Washington, DC: National Academy Press.

Morris, J., Hassard, J., & McCann, L. (2006). New organizational forms, human resource management and structural convergence? A study of Japanese organizations. *Organization Studies, 27*, 1485–1511.

Murphy, K.J. (1999). Executive compensation. In O. Ashenfelter & D. Card (Eds), *Handbook of Labor Economics,* Volume 3. Amsterdam: Elsevier.

Olson, M. (1965). *The Logic of Collective Action: Public goods and the theory of groups.* Cambridge, MA: Harvard University Press.

Osterman, P. (2006). The wage effects of high performance work organization in manufacturing. *Industrial & Labor Relations Review, 59*, 187–204.

Petty, M.M., Singleton, B., & Connell, D.W. (1992). An experimental evaluation of an organizational incentive plan in the electric utility industry. *Journal of Applied Psychology, 77*, 427–36.

Pfeffer, J. (1998). Six dangerous myths about pay. *Harvard Business Review, 76*, 108–20.

Phan, P.H. & Hill, C.W. (1995). Organizational restructuring and economic performance in leveraged buyouts: An ex post study. *Academy of Management Journal, 38*, 704–39.

Pitts, R.A. (1976). Diversification strategies and organizational policies of large diversified firms. *Journal of Economics and Business, 8*, 181–8.

Porter, M. (1985). *Competitive Advantage.* New York: Free Press.

Rajagopalan, N. (1996). Strategic orientations, incentive plan adoptions, and firm performance: Evidence from electric utility firms. *Strategic Management Journal*, *18*, 761–85.

Robinson, P. & Shimizu, N. (2006). Japanese corporate restructuring: CEO priorities as a window on environmental and organizational change. *Academy of Management Perspectives*, *20*(3), 44–75.

Rottenberg, S. (1956). On choice in labor markets. *Industrial & Labor Relations Review*, *9*, 183–99.

Rynes, S.L., Gerhart, B., & Minette, K.A. (2004). The importance of pay in employee motivation: Discrepancies between what people do and what they say. *Human Resource Management*, *43*, 381–94.

Rynes, S.L., Gerhart, B., & Parks, L. (2005). *Annual Review of Psychology*, *56*, 571–600.

Salamin, A. & Hom, P.W. (2005). In search of the elusive U-shaped performance-turnover relationship: Are high performing Swiss bankers more liable to quit? *Journal of Applied Psychology*, *90*, 1204–16.

Schneider, B. (1987). The people make the place. *Personnel Psychology*, *40*, 437–53.

Shaw, J.D., Gupta, N., & Delery, J.E. (2002). Pay dispersion and workforce performance: Moderating effects of incentives and interdependence. *Strategic Management Journal*, *23*, 491–512.

Snell, S.A. & Dean, J.W. Jr. (1994). Strategic compensation for integrated manufacturing: The moderating effects of jobs and organizational inertia. *Academy of Management Journal*, *37*, 1109–40.

Stajkovic, A.D. & Luthans, F. (1997). A meta-analysis of the effects of organizational behavior modification on task performance, 1975–1995. *Academy of Management Journal*, *40*, 1122–49.

Sturman, M.C., Trevor, C.O., Boudreau, J.W., & Gerhart, B. (2003). Is it worth it to win the talent war? Evaluating the utility of performance-based pay. *Personnel Psychology*, *56*, 997–1035.

Towers Perrin. (2006). Worldwide Total Remuneration, 2005–2006.

Trank, C.Q., Rynes, S.L., & Bretz, R.D. Jr. (2002). Attracting applicants in the war for talent: Differences in work preferences among high achievers. *Journal of Business and Psychology*, *17*, 331–45.

Trevor, C.O., Gerhart, B., & Boudreau, J.W. (1997). Voluntary turnover and job performance: Curvilinearity and the moderating influences of salary growth and promotions. *Journal of Applied Psychology*, *82*, 44–61.

Turban, D.B. & Keon, T.L. (1993). Organizational attractiveness: An interactionist perspective. *Journal of Applied Psychology*, *78*, 184–93.

Viswesvaran, C., Ones, D.S., & Schmidt, F.L. (1996). Comparative analysis of the reliability of job performance ratings. *Journal of Applied Psychology*, *81*, 557–574.

Weiss, A. (1987). Incentives and worker behavior: Some evidence. In H.R. Nalbantian (Ed.), *Incentives, cooperation, and risk taking*. Lanham, MD: Rowman & Littlefield.

Whyte, W.F. (1955). *Money and Motivation*. New York: Harper & Row.

Williams, M.L., McDaniel, M.A., & Nguyen, N.T. (2006). A meta-analysis of the antecedents and consequences of pay level satisfaction. *Journal of Applied Psychology*, *91*, 392–413.

Wiseman, R.M., Gomez-Mejia, L.R., & Fugate, M. (2000). Rethinking compensation risk. In S.L. Rynes & B. Gerhart (Eds), *Compensation in Organizations* (pp. 32–60). San Francisco, CA: Jossey-Bass.

Wright, P.M. & Sherman, W.S. (1999). Failing to find fit in strategic human resource management: Theoretical and empirical problems. In P. Wright, L. Dyer, J. Boudreau, & G. Milkovich (Eds), *Strategic Human Resources Management in the Twenty-first Century*. Supplement to G.R. Ferris (Ed.), *Research in Personnel and Human Resources Management*. Stanford, CT: JAI Press.

Wright, P.M., George, J.M., Farnsworth, S.R., & McMahan, G.C. (1993). Productivity and extra-role behavior: The effects of goals and incentives on spontaneous helping. *Journal of Applied Psychology*, *78*, 374–81.

Wright, P.M., McMahan, G., Snell, S., & Gerhart, B. (2001). Comparing line and HR executives' perceptions of HR effectiveness: Services, roles, and contributions. *Human Resource Management*, *40*, 111–24.

Yanadori, Y. & Marler, J.H. (2006). Compensation strategy: Does business strategy influence compensation in high-technology firms? *Strategic Management Journal*, *27*, 559–70.

Yellen, J.L. (1984). Efficiency wage models of unemployment. *American Economic Review*, *74*, 200–5.

7

Strategic performance management

Issues and trends

Manuel London and Edward M. Mone

Performance management refers to the process of goal setting, performance monitoring for feedback and development, and performance appraisal for evaluation as input to compensation and other administrative decisions. As a process, performance management is not a single event or a series of discrete events, but rather an integrated series of interactions. As a system, the components relate to each other in a continuous cycle that is affected by external factors (e.g., demands and opportunities) and internal factors (e.g., self-expectations and monitoring). At the individual level, we speak of an employee's or manager's goals and performance in relation to the strategies of the organization and department. At the group level, we speak of the department's or work team's goals and performance as affected by organizational expectations and the demands from other work groups. Departmental goals affect individual employees' goals and performance, which in turn affect those of the department, other departments, and the entire organization. In this chapter, we present critical issues for practitioners and researchers for today and the future. We also present a case that illustrates the design and implementation of an organization-wide performance management process.

The performance management cycle, depicted in Figure 7.1, evolves as people perceive and evaluate environmental conditions, determine others' and their own expectations, set goals, seek and digest feedback, participate in developmental experiences, change behavior, alter their performance, and benefit from the consequences of goal achievement and/or suffer the consequences of failing to achieve goals. It involves others, such as one's supervisor, peers, and customers, who convey expectations, participate in goal setting and performance monitoring, provide feedback and coaching, and deliver rewards. It is continuous or ongoing in that it occurs over time, and it is repetitive or cyclical, with multiple and overlapping components. Goals are revised as expectations change, competition shifts, feedback is received and interpreted, and training is experienced. Performance management tools and tactics are designed by the human resource department to support each step of the process from guidelines for joint goal setting to rating forms for performance appraisal. The design process includes ensuring that the methods are reliable (meaning, for example, that behaviors are perceived similarly by multiple raters who have similar roles) and valid (meaning, for example, that performance ratings accurately reflect important performance outcomes).

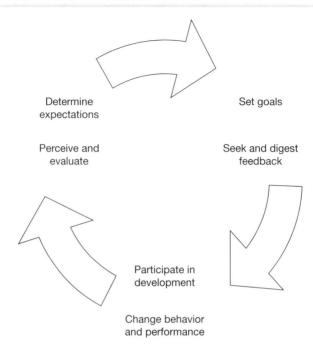

Figure 7.1 The performance management cycle

Table 7.1 lists theories that guide the elements of performance management, describes implications for practice, and provides key references. These theories address key processes in the performance management cycle, such as goal setting, feedback, motivation and self-regulation, social cognition, feelings of fairness about how rewards are distributed, and self-verification and impression management. Theories also deal with processes that support performance management, such as rater accuracy, multi-source ratings, coaching, supervisors' and coaches' implicit views about whether people can be developed, and methods for creating a feedback-oriented, performance-centered work environment. The citations in the table indicate that there is a rich body of knowledge from which to draw in understanding how to formulate and implement effective performance management programs.

Performance management processes apply to groups and organizations as well as to individuals. We usually think of performance management from the standpoint of an individual's performance (e.g., individual employees setting goals jointly with supervisors, supervisors appraising their performance, etc.). However, groups and organizations also engage in goal setting, performance measurement, and feedback giving, seeking, and receiving. Performance management can and should be strategic in that at each level of analysis (individual, group, or organization), it is tied to accomplishing higher level objectives (for example, those of specific functions or the overall organization) and overall organization results. So, for instance, an individual manager's goals need to be aligned with the goals of the department, and the department's goals need to be aligned with the goals of the function and the overall organization. More generally, the nature of an individual's goals and dimensions of performance will depend on the function of the department and the role of the individual. Examples of organization strategies guiding performance expectations, goals, and measurement include: moving from a domestic to global business; becoming number one in the marketplace; increasing return on investment (ROI) by 10%; and building a culture that values integrity, open communication, fair treatment, and differences. We illustrate these relationships in Table 7.2 with an example of an HR department and manager, in this case, a manager of recruiting, whose efforts are in alignment with the organization's goals of reducing costs by 10%. The table indicates how each main component of the performance management process requires action at the organizational, departmental, and individual managerial level. So, for instance, the human resource department can find ways to reduce its costs, including reengineering the company-wide recruitment process. The recruiting manager can set a time line for accomplishing this and track cost data per candidate recruited. The performance appraisal will measure the extent to which the manager completed the reengineering project and is rewarded accordingly.

This chapter focuses primarily on methods for assessing and improving individual performance. Comprehensive performance management programs include support mechanisms and guidelines for use. Comprehensive, strategic performance management programs that incorporate appraisal, feedback, and compensation at multiple levels are Management by Objectives (MBO) (Drucker, 1993; Odiorne, 1968), Balanced Scorecards (Kaplan & Norton, 1996), and Dashboards (Alexander, 2006). These strategic performance management (SPM) programs facilitate setting goals in relation to larger objectives, measuring results, and seeking improvement. These programs usually start from the top of the organization and cascade down, conveying organization-wide goals that should be reflected in department and team goals, which in turn should be reflected in each individual's goals and performance.

SPM programs evolve over time as strategies change and as instruments for measurement and methods for linking the components together are fine-tuned. As a result, SPM affects the culture of the organization, making employees and managers more comfortable with discussing performance issues, providing and receiving feedback, and supporting and engaging in development for performance improvement. SPM programs in one organization or setting may not work in another because of the organization's history of using performance management methods, the management philosophy of the organization's leaders, and the resources and emphasis placed on the investment in performance management tools and processes. Overall, SPM is a developmental process that promotes individual and organizational learning.

Periodically, the strategic performance management system may need to be refreshed to reflect (a) changes in organizational objectives and strategies (e.g., moving from a domestic to a global business), (b) changes in key elements of performance (which may evolve as technology changes), (c) the need to create a performance management culture and awareness of key organizational goals and performance dimensions, (d) take advantage of employees' increasing commitment to performance improvement and comfort with, and sophistication in dealing with, feedback and coaching, and (e) increase the value of the organization's investment in performance measurement, feedback, development, and continued performance improvement.

Issues for practitioners

Based on the authors' experience and the literature (cf. Table 7.1), we have identified five concerns of practitioners who design and support SPM: (1) eliciting the active involvement and buy-in of executives and managers to the design, roll-out, and ongoing use of the program elements, (2) linking the components of the program to the strategy of the organization overall while maintaining relevancy to departments and individuals throughout the organization, (3) keeping the program current so that managers and employees will find it valuable and will be motivated to use it, (4) capturing the learning so that managers and employees become more able to focus on performance issues and creating an environment in which it is acceptable to

Table 7.1 Examples of seminal theories and research guiding performance management policies and programs

Theories	Implications for practice	Key references
Goal setting theory	Help employees set specific, difficult, yet achievable goals which focus attention; easy, "do your best," and assigned goals result in lower performance.	Locke & Latham (1990, 2002)
Feedback intervention theory	Provide feedback that focuses on specific behaviors and goal progress. Avoid giving feedback that focuses on personal characteristics, threatens self-esteem, and lowers performance.	Kluger & DeNisi (1998)
Temporal motivation theory (integration and extension of expectancy, prospect, and need theories)	Recognize time as a motivational factor along with expectancy of goal achievement, loss aversion, values of success, and needs. Enhance motivation by parceling tasks into subgoals that focus behavior, avoid temptation to be distracted, and clarify expectancy and value of achievement. However, avoid subtasks that are so small, immediate, and easy to achieve that they lose their tie to the whole and decrease motivation.	Steel & Cornelius (2006)
Social cognitive theory; control theory	Enhance motivation, increase self-esteem, and attain goals by helping people adopt goal challenges (proactive discrepancy production) and then reduce the discrepancy (i.e., meet their goals). (Note that this contradicts control theory's position that people maintain self-esteem by setting low challenges for themselves.) Support employees' self-efficacy by reinforcement, training, and encouraging setting realistic, achievable, yet challenging goals. Self-efficacy influences managers' goal achievement both directly and through its effects on their goal setting and analytic thinking.	Bandura & Locke (2003); Wood & Bandura (1989)
Fairness of process and outcome (equity theory)	Provide clear explanations for performance ratings. Ratings that enhance the employee's self-concept are perceived to be the most fair, indicating the importance of explanations in enhancing perceptions of fairness. Both the perceived fairness of the ratings process and the fairness of the rating are important to understanding an employee's reaction to the appraisal. The process includes (a) the structure, policies, and support of the formal appraisal system, and (b) the appraisal-related interactions that occur throughout the year between supervisors and subordinates.	Giles, Findley, & Field (1997); Greenberg (1991)
Self-verification and impression management	Give employees an opportunity to describe their strengths and weaknesses to others and seek feedback to test how well the people with whom they interact know them. Generally, people want to verify their self-concept by (a) providing others with an accurate view of their capabilities, and (b) seeking feedback from others	Polzer, Milton, & Swann (2002)
Rater accuracy—self-ratings	Recognize that employees will not immediately agree with an appraisal of their performance. People, in general, and especially lower performers, tend to rate themselves higher than others rate them. Also, they, in general, overestimate the similarity between how they see themselves and the way they think others see them.	Atwater, Rousch, & Fischthal, (1995); Harris & Schaubroeck (1988); Mabe & West (1982)

Topic	Description	References
Rater accuracy – ratings from supervisors, peers, and others	Use easily measured and observable, behaviorally based performance dimensions to increase the accuracy of employees' self-ratings and ratings from supervisors and peers. Train raters in ways to observe key behaviors, request clarifying information, and search for disconfirming evidence. Provide raters with a frame of reference (e.g., standards, norms, expectations, examples) for evaluating the accuracy of ratings. Hold people accountable for their ratings (chance they will have to justify them) so they perceive a cost as being inaccurate.	Klimoski & Donahue, (2001); London (2003); London, Smither, & Adsit (1996); Mone & London (2003)
Multisource (360-degree) feedback surveys, self-other agreement, and setting developmental goals	Use 360-degree feedback surveys (ratings from subordinates, peers, supervisors, customers, and self) to support and direct manager development; avoid its use for making administrative decisions about managers since raters are less likely to be honest if they know that the ratings will be used for this purpose. Recognize that people tend to overrate themselves compared to how others see them.	London (2003); London & Smither (1995); Smither, London, & Reilly (2005)
Supplement feedback with coaching	Use coaching to increase the value of multisource feedback by encouraging managers to set specific goals, ask for ideas for improvement, and improve their performance over time.	Smither, London, Flautt, Vargas, & Kucine (2003)
Supervisors' implicit personality theories and their role as coach and developer	Demonstrate to supervisors that employees' personal attributes can be changed and developed (recognizing that supervisors who believe that employees' key characteristics can't be changed will not be effective coaches). Train managers in coaching techniques to provide guidance, facilitation, and inspiration.	Dweck (1999); Heslin, Vandewalle, & Latham (2006)
Acceptance of feedback and the likelihood of behavior change	Consider the effects of individual characteristics on reactions to performance appraisal. People who are mastery learners (those who are motivated to learn and improve continuously for the sake of their development) are more likely to seek feedback and react positively to it compared to those who are performance oriented (those who demonstrate competence and avoid failure). Self-monitors are more sensitive to feedback and more willing to respond constructively to it; low self-monitors do not modify their behavior to meet the needs of the situation. People are more likely to change their behavior when they accept others' evaluations of their weaknesses.	Stamoulis & Hauenstein (1993); Vandewalle, Brown, Cron, & Slocum (1999)
Creating a feedback-oriented, performance-centered environment	Foster an environment that provides resources for and rewards continuous learning and performance feedback.	London & Mone (1999); London & Smither (2002); Sessa & London (2006)

Table 7.2 Example of strategic performance management relationships – an HR department and recruiting manager

Performance management component	The organization	The HR department	The recruiting manager
Goal setting	Reduce overall costs by 10%.	Reengineer HR processes and systems to reduce costs by 10%.	Reengineer the company-wide recruitment process to reduce costs by 10% and increase process efficiency and effectiveness.
Feedback and development	Review financial reports for each department and the overall organization at monthly intervals. Take appropriate action if interim targets are not being met.	Review department finance and measures of internal customers' satisfaction with HR processes and systems monthly to monitor overall performance. Take appropriate action if performance and satisfaction levels are not being achieved.	Meet time lines for reengineering initiative and monitor overall effort monthly for increased efficiency and satisfaction of internal customers' with the recruiting process. Take appropriate action if time lines are not being met and/or if satisfaction levels are not being achieved.
Appraisal	Measure the extent to which the overall organization met the cost reduction goal of 10%.	Measure extent to which financial and customer satisfaction measures where achieved.	Measure extent to which reengineering was completed on a timely basis, costs were reduced and customer satisfaction with the recruiting process increased.
Connection to compensation and rewards	Improved financial position for the company; allows for an organization-wide, all employee cash bonus if key targets are met.	HR department enjoys eligibility for participation in company-wide and departmental-level bonus awards if targets are met at the company-wide and/or department level.	Recruiting manager eligible to receive various bonus awards based on individual, HR department and organization-wide performance in meeting or exceeding targets.

discuss difficult performance issues, and (5) evaluating the program, assessing its impact on individual, departmental, and organizational performance and regularly fine-tuning the program to improve its effectiveness.

Human resource and/or organizational development professionals are likely to be responsible for the design and implementation of the SPM program. However, these professionals need the active engagement of the employees and managers who will use the program. The elements of the program need to be helpful in doing their jobs. Their active involvement in designing the process is likely to ensure the right aspects of performance are measured and rewarded. If they believe the program is imposed from above and is the work of outside consultants who have little understanding of their organization's goals and their individual roles and functions, then they are not likely to take the process seriously. Their involvement in the program design may be critical because they know the organization and the performance expectations that need to be measured by the program. Off-the-shelf performance rating forms and 360-degree performance surveys that measure generic dimensions of performance are likely to have little specific relevance to the organization and will excite little interest. Customizing performance dimensions and incentive plans to the organization, and having the people who will use the program involved in the customization, is likely to result in a program that will be accepted and valued.

The performance management process should be viewed as developmental and evolutionary. Working on its design, educating managers and employees during its initial roll-out, and supporting the use of the program over time helps educate managers about the meaning of performance management. They can then grow more comfortable dealing with performance issues and incorporate performance discussions into their daily activities. Over time, performance management becomes part of the way the organization does business. A performance-based culture is created. However, this is not a natural process. People usually shy away from giving and seeking feedback because it is potentially threatening to their self-esteem and leads to defensiveness and uncomfortable interpersonal situations (London, 2003). Consider a program that emphasizes an annual performance appraisal followed by a formal performance interview with the supervisor and an accompanying change in salary. This puts the supervisor and subordinate on edge. Both are likely to be defensive, unclear, and unhappy. Next, consider a program that emphasizes feedback for development throughout the year. The supervisor and subordinate can become a team focused on enhancing performance. They can be creative in suggesting performance improvement strategies, trying them out, and jointly evaluating their effects. They are "in this together." The formal annual evaluation is a culmination of these formative processes, and the results are not a surprise and an occasion to feel threatened or be defensive. Indeed, individuals will feel more responsible for monitoring their own performance in conjunction with their supervisors. Their self-evaluations will likely be critical and accompanied by ideas for behavior change. Human resource professionals can help managers and employees be ready to participate in the excitement of ongoing improvement by providing resources that help managers to be better coaches and help both managers and employees to participate in constructive feedback discussions.

Overall, when creating strategic performance management programs, HR professionals can generate higher degrees of commitment to both the program and the process of performance management by inviting managers and employees to contribute to the design, implementation, and evaluation of the program. HR professionals should strongly consider forming a design task force for development and implementation with representatives from different functions and levels of the organization. This will not only help build commitment, it will also help to ensure that key components (e.g., performance dimensions) that are important to the overall

115

organization, as well as those that are unique to specific departments or functions, will be included in the program. After the program has been implemented, HR professionals should consider forming a performance management council to oversee the program's assessment and use. As a result, monitoring the use of the program becomes more than the bureaucratic exercise of being sure forms are completed; rather, it becomes an examination of how people are using the process, what they think about it, and ways they would like it changed to be even more valuable.

Sustaining interest in the process and ensuring compliance are two different things. Compliance can be enforced by requiring that annual appraisal forms be completed before salary increases or other administrative changes, such as promotions, can be implemented. However, completing appraisals because they are required can result in a pro forma exercise with little meaning or effect. Sometimes organizations try to refresh their programs by changing formats, rating methods, and performance dimensions. Training can be used to explain these changes and create more awareness of performance issues and how the process might be used to evaluate and improve performance. However, both employees and managers may become jaded quickly when new performance programs are introduced every year or two.

Performance management programs that are redesigned to reflect changes in organizational strategy can go hand-in-glove with the implementation of the new strategy. For instance, an organization that is implementing a new global strategy may expect employees to acquire and use multicultural competencies and will want to incorporate this expectation in the performance management process, perhaps in setting and evaluating development goals.

Another potential reason for redesigning a performance management program is to build on the skills and competencies both employees and managers have developed in performance management. For example, as managers become adept at giving feedback and supporting development, they may need to rely less on formal processes, such as 360-degree surveys. Instead of a semi-annual 360-degree survey for all managers, for instance, the organization may implement a just-in-time, online process that allows managers to formulate their own surveys when they believe they need feedback to understand how their peers, subordinates, or customers are responding to their decisions and actions. In other words, they learn when to ask "how am I doing," and how to gather information that will help them guide their efforts.

Knowing when to adapt or devise an entirely new performance management program requires constant assessment. Assessment is usually the job of the human resource or organization development professionals in the organization. They need to devise and implement methods for assessment, and they need to convince top executives of the importance of investing in assessment. Perhaps the best way to do this is to conduct a trial program and study to demonstrate its effectiveness. The program might be implemented in one department in one region of the company. A similar department in the same region and the same department in another region might be used for comparison purposes. In general, assessment should be built into the design of the program itself so that it is expected and recognized as an integral part of the program.

There are four types of assessment data: (1) attitude surveys that ask about the perceived value of the performance management program; (2) behavioral data, which may be self-report (part of a survey that asks not only about value but use; for instance, "Did you complete the annual performance appraisal form for all your subordinates?," "How often do you and your manager discuss your job performance?"), or it may be frequency counts of use (e.g., number of managers who completed appraisal forms for their employees); (3) behavior change reflected in changes in performance ratings over time or external measures (e.g., number of times a behavior was carried out, such as a successful sales call); and (4) improvement in bottom–line performance and outcomes associated with the organization's strategic goals (e.g., change in profits, sales, new clients, employees hired, employees retained, etc.) and objectives (methods for accomplishing the goals).

Each of these measurements has potential problems. Ratings may be subject to response biases, such as central tendency (ratings in the middle of the scale) or halo (ratings at the top end of the scale). In either case, the result is that managers are not truly differentiating between dimensions of performance but instead rating one employee or all employees the same on all performance dimensions. So when the data are averaged across employees to consider performance change in a department or the organization as a whole, the results would be confounded by rater error. Behavioral and performance ratings may be a function of many factors other than an honest assessment of performance as defined by the performance management program in place. This is why multiple measures are needed to understand the performance management program from different perspectives and to recognize the diverse factors that influence performance, including faulty measurement. Insights result as data from different sources and indicators converge to tell a consistent story. So, for instance, attitude survey results may indicate that performance dimensions are difficult to understand or too time consuming to complete. This may explain why managers leave items blank, fill out the appraisal forms in a cursory way, or don't meet with employees to discuss performance results.

Program evaluation, alternatively called action or applied research, faces greater challenges than basic research because program evaluation is not designed to eliminate alternative explanations. So the data are likely to be subject to a variety of unavoidable confounds. However, consistent measurement procedures repeated over time that take into account subgroup differences are likely to produce meaningful results. These results can be used to understand how people are using and reacting to the elements of a performance management program, and can also be used to fine-tune the program. When the program undergoes a major transition in response to changes in the organization's strategic goals, or to increase awareness of performance issues, or to reinvigorate motivation to apply performance management techniques, the assessment methods can be changed accordingly. Some measures may stay the same in order to assess change over time. Others may be added to reflect performance relative to the new goals and program objectives. In the case we present at the end of the chapter, the organization development group used the results of the company-wide employee opinion survey to track use and satisfaction with its performance management process, and to design specific training to meet skill gaps in setting strategic goals, giving and receiving feedback, and conducting the performance appraisal conversation.

Issues for researchers

Here we raise five concerns of basic and applied researchers who are interested in understanding how people and groups monitor and change their performance, including: (1) generating theory that informs practice – that is, expressing theories that underlie, and so predict, human and organizational behavior that suggest fruitful directions for methods to improve performance; (2) formulating and carrying out research designs that clearly identify the unique and joint effects of the elements of performance management as a longitudinal, systemic process; (3) developing and applying reliable and valid measures of behaviors and outcomes at the individual, group, and organizational level; (4) finding opportunities to partner with organizations to conduct research; and (5) generating results that inform theory and practice.

Basic research explains the reasons for phenomena and improves our ability to predict and control performance behaviors and interactions that contribute to the performance improvement of individuals and groups. There is no shortage of theories that inform performance management. Each component has its own set of theoretical frameworks, including those listed in Table 15.1. So, for example, theories suggest that goals should be specific, challenging but possible to achieve, and involve the employee in setting them (e.g., Locke & Latham, 2002). Feedback should be specific, occur soon after the event that occasioned the feedback, and behaviorally focused (Ilgen et al., 1979; London, 2003).

Performance management theories are continuously being tested, revised, and extended. In fact specific research shows how the program components work together to develop comprehensive approaches to performance management. Research designs in the laboratory and the field have examined the joint effects of goal setting and feedback (e.g., see Locke & Latham, 2002), feedback and coaching (Smither et al., 2003, 2005), and leadership schemas and ratings (Lord & Maher, 1993). As an example, one study in a major global bank collected 360-degree performance survey data from more than 700 senior managers (Smither et al., 2003). Managers rated themselves and were rated by their peers, subordinates, and immediate supervisor. A portion of the sample received the results from an executive coach and then worked with the coach to establish a development plan for performance improvement. The results showed that those who worked with a coach had statistically significant higher ratings a year later when the 360-degree performance survey was repeated compared to the group that did not receive coaching, but the difference accounted for only 4% of the change in performance. Although small, even practically, 4% of the bottom line controlled by each of these managers was substantial (in millions of dollars) and well worth the investment in the performance management process. The research had practical suggestions for the value of external coaching and suggested to the bank that it could train managers to be coaches to lower level managers and employees, thereby cascading coaching throughout the organization.

Performance measures need to be reliable and valid for use in basic and applied research. One difficulty is that changes in performance ratings over time may be due to changes in perceptions of the instrument, performance standards, or changes in the level of difficulty of goal achievement. Measures that are external to the performance management system (e.g., objective indicators of individual performance, such as sales data) may be needed to validate improvements in performance ratings.

Although basic research strives to control conditions to isolate effects, this is often difficult to do, especially in field studies. Laboratory studies (for example, undergraduate students rating descriptions of managers' performance) are often artificial, and the results do not necessarily transfer directly to work settings, although these results usually have implications for work that needs to be tested in the field. On the other hand, isolating individual effects is difficult in research on comprehensive performance management programs that may be influenced by multiple factors. Also, comparison groups may be hard to find, the program may not be randomly assigned to groups but may be used in groups that need it the most, and measures may be influenced by a variety of factors that are external to the program, such as market or economic conditions.

Basic and applied research are not necessarily distinct. Program evaluations to examine reactions of raters and employees to feedback tell us something about how sensitive individuals are to various elements of a performance management program and suggest the extent to which goal setting, ratings, and/or feedback are likely to affect behavior.

Basic research is likely to be artificial and not directly transferable to all work settings. Applied research is likely to use measures of questionable reliability or validity and compare results to groups that are not equivalent and so produce ambiguous results. Still, as long as we recognize the limitations of research results and continue to conduct research to build a repository of knowledge, we are likely to increase our understanding of performance management from a variety of perspectives and under different conditions. So, for instance, we will learn when and how organizational goals inform individual goals, the extent to which performance dimensions need to be customized to specific functions and positions or can be general and apply across departments and functions, and when and why different types of feedback and coaching are useful.

Challenges for future research and practice

Before presenting a case example, we conclude with five challenges for the future.

(1) Business is global, and managers and executives need to interact effectively with people from multiple cultures. This suggests that designing and implementing performance management programs that reflect cultural issues will be a challenge, especially in multinational organizations. Performance expectations and dimensions will need to be communicated clearly especially when multiple languages are involved. Cultural issues may affect raters' willingness to participate and provide meaningful feedback. For example, subordinates rating supervisors may not be viewed in the same way in hierarchical, collectivistic cultures, for instance, in Asia, compared to individualistic cultures in which there is power equalization, for instance, in Scandinavian countries (Hofstede, 2003).

(2) We now have online methods of conveying and gathering information about performance management. As a result, challenges include developing and using online ratings, feedback through emails and other forms of electronic communication, survey generation systems that allow managers to seek feedback themselves when they want it, and comparative data on a host of performance topics that become public information.

(3) Organizations will face the challenge of understanding performance management from the standpoint of new-generation (e.g., X and Y) employees. This may encompass dealing with discontinuities between organizational expectations for performance, standards, and behavior and the thinking of new generation employees regarding career goals, concerns for work–life balance, and modes of communication. Younger generations may not have the same performance standards, career goals, and desires for development compared to older generations. Of course, this is a continuously evolving picture (Huntley, 2006).

(4) Another challenge is linking performance management programs to the many interfaces that employees and managers have, including input from customers, suppliers of outsourced functions, and joint venture partners, to name a few stakeholders in performance management. These are constantly shifting, yet these various constituencies all have a stake in the performance management process. They contribute to an individual's performance and are able to provide a perspective about the individual's performance (Amabile & Kramer, 2007). So performance management systems need to recognize the contributions of others to an individual's performance and also collect information about the individual's performance from people who make these contributions.

(5) Overall, a principal challenge is preparing for, and creating, the workplace of the future. Strategic performance management systems can help create a learning, feedback-oriented culture that incorporates the above shifts in globalization, technology, and workforce attitudes, and attract, develop, and retain talent to maintain high standards and strive for continuous performance improvement.

Case study: GHT Corporation

The following describes the evolution of strategic performance management (SPM) at a global, high-tech company (GHT), a firm with more than 10,000 employees and revenues in billions of dollars.

Background

GHT was a successful company, but it was undergoing a transition. To remain an industry leader, it created a new business model, restructured operating units, and began to shift away from a heroic, founder-driven view of leadership toward becoming a professionally managed organization. GHT had a culture of compliance. Employees, in general, did what they were asked to do, often rallying resources to meet unique business challenges and events. If you were to ask most GHT employees about their next job or career aspirations, the answer, most likely, was "whatever GHT wants me to do." At the same time, GHT did not have a process focus, viewing, for example, performance appraisal as an event rather than being part of an overall performance management process. In fact, the company's human resource (HR) function, as well as its HR processes and systems, were immature. To say the least, HR was not considered a strategic business partner.

Although the company was successful it lacked a clearly articulated vision, mission and overarching goals. As a result, its performance management process was less than effective from a goal-setting perspective. In addition, the form used for the year-end appraisal had a number of faults, including poor scale design, unclear scale definitions, no established set of competencies for evaluating behavior, and a system-generated overall rating that had no consistency to its meaning across different parts of the organization.

The beginning

After the hiring of a successful, senior HR professional several years ago to lead HR, and the subsequent staffing of other senior HR and organization development (OD) professionals in key functions, the OD team was charged with creating a new performance management process while the compensation team was charged with building a total rewards strategy and program. Both teams were expected to and did work together and align efforts.

The current automated performance management process, in its design, was more an outcome of IT system designers than performance management experts. The system design drove what could and could not be done from a performance management perspective. The changes to performance management at GHT, described next, occurred over a four-year period.

Early work

There were a number of factors inhibiting effective performance management at GHT. These are outlined in Table 7.3. Also identified in Table 7.3 are those factors, over years two and three in this journey, that helped to make performance management a more successful and effective process at GHT.

In spite of the lack of an explicit corporate mission, vision and overarching goals, work was done to transform the performance management process. The new appraisal process would now include a focus on both behavior and performance, with all employees being assessed against the behaviors supporting the company's values, and behaviors explicitly defined for both

Table 7.3 Strategic performance management at GHT

Initial inhibiting factors	Later factors promoting a strategic performance management process
A non-professional management team	A professional management team
Insular, limited-experienced HR team	International, experienced HR team
Leader-founder driven	Leadership team driven
Sales focus	Business focus
Lack of robust strategic plan, budget-driven focus	Strategic planning process in place, strategic focus
Implicit, not widely shared, strategic direction	Explicit mission, vision and key priorities
No cross-functional planning	Cross-functional planning part of strategic planning process
Poor performance appraisal and process	Appraisal focusing on goal achievement, development and behavior
Lack of HR process integration	Key HR process integration, e.g., compensation and appraisal
No explicit statement about culture and performance	Key priority established as "building a performance-based culture"
Minimal training on performance management process	Regular, updated training available on aspects of performance management process
Appraisal and performance management process not clearly linked to rewards	Clear link between year-end appraisals and rewards
Appraisal ratings influenced by distribution expectations	Overall appraisal ratings based on objective measures of performance

managers and individual contributors. Along with a strong emphasis on performance goals, these two aspects became the focus of the new appraisal, which also included a development action plan.

The new appraisal process was approved by senior management, and within one year, a system was built to automate the new process. The overall performance management process now formally included goal setting, feedback, and mid-year and year-end appraisals.

Compliance culture

Although we stated previously that GHT had a culture of compliance, its managers did not feel a strong need to comply with the requirements of the new performance management process and its related time lines. In fact, managers' prevailing belief backed by experience was that extensions would be granted for all deadlines, as managers and employees always considered themselves "too busy" to meet the official time lines. As a result, setting goals and completing appraisals was typically a "right down to the wire" exercise.

As outlined in Table 7.4, GHT achieved nearly 100% completion of year-end appraisals (though not always within the official timeframe) because overall ratings were required for compensation administration. And to move to the compensation phase, both managers and their employees had to sign the official year-end appraisal. At first, the HR department was reluctant to push for firmer deadlines for completion because of the extraordinary changes going on in the business. However, it was not until the policy was changed to "no extensions will be

121

Table 7.4 Improvement in "compliance to deadlines" over time

- GHT had both a mid-year appraisal process that managers could adopt for their departments ("strongly recommended") and a required year-end appraisal.
- Generally, several transmittal letters, reminder emails, etc., needed to be sent to managers and employees to achieve compliance with the policy and timelines.
- Initially extensions were typically granted and expected (part of the culture).
- Near 100% compliance was attained for year-end appraisal completion as overall ratings were required for compensation administration.
- In year one, due to issues in business, only 75% voluntary compliance with mid-year appraisal completion was attained, even after extending the period from the normal two months to four and a half months.
- In year two, 90% compliance was reached for mid-year appraisals, with only a one-month extension granted (three months' total). The extension was granted because there was a change in the timing of the appraisal process, moving from a calendar-year-based to a fiscal-year-based process.
- In year three, the policy was changed and extensions were no longer granted; this was communicated at the beginning of the process. An 83% completion rate for mid-year appraisals was achieved in two months. However, a 93% rate was achieved if those appraisals completed up to one week past the deadline were included.
- Before the year-end appraisal phase in year four, employee opinion survey ratings showed a significant increase in satisfaction (as measured by percent favorable response) with the set of performance management-related questions, although still in the 60%–70% favorable range.
- In year four, 92% of year-end appraisals were completed on time.

granted" that practically all managers complied by meeting the official deadlines for both mid-year and year-end appraisals. In fact, for the most recent year-end appraisal period, year four of the journey, more than 92% completed appraisals *on time*, the highest percentage ever at GHT.

Performance management process support

During this period of transition, the OD team provided extensive communication and training on performance management including how to set strategic goals, complete appraisal forms, and conduct a performance appraisal discussion. In addition, the development of an explicit mission and vision, as well key priorities, including "establishing a performance-based culture," went a long way toward creating the framework for team and individual goal setting. Again, Table 7.3 describes those promoting factors, which in the case of GHT, helped to make performance management a more effective and respected process.

Lessons learned

As in most case studies, there are specific lessons learned at GHT that can be applied elsewhere. These lessons are described in Table 7.5 and focus mostly on the need for training managers and employees in the performance management process and regular communication about the process throughout the year. Not included in the table, however, is a very critical lesson learned as a result of GHT's most recent employee opinion survey.

The survey included six questions on performance management. The prior year's results averaged a 60% favorable response – fair but not outstanding. The current results showed a statistically significant increase, but still averaged only 63% favorable, lower than HR had anticipated given all the recent training efforts for, and process improvements to, performance management and positive changes in the business. In fact, a new question was added to the current year's survey, "Is performance management valued at GHT?", to which there was only a 53% favorable response.

Table 7.5 Lessons learned from GHT

- Need to clearly articulate the process for each phase of performance management (goal-setting feedback, development planning, appraisal).
- Need to train managers and employees for how to effectively conduct each phase – tell them what to do and how to do it.
- HR/OD must regularly support the process with:
  - emails;
  - websites with tools, techniques, strategies for performance management;
  - HR partners counseling leaders throughout the performance management process.
- Using systems-based vs. paper-based processes creates an additional set of concerns:
  - the system must be designed to be both user-friendly and the process it supports must be based on sound HR practices;
  - system changes and maintenance impact usage and may be difficult to support, as dedicated IT resources are required;
  - managers and employees, and particularly senior leaders, need to take time to learn the system, regardless of its perceived ease of use.
- As the business changes, performance management process changes have to be made.
- It takes time to change behavior (almost four years).

What happened? Open-ended comments revealed that employees did not see a strong connection between their overall performance ratings and their subsequent merit increases. Many felt the positive feedback they had received throughout the performance year and their overall ratings justified a higher increase. Increases were moderated, however, by a relatively small merit increase budget driven by business conditions, so distinguishing and rewarding strong performance was difficult. As a result, a strong performer might not have received the level of rewards he or she expected. Managers did not adequately explain this situation, adding to the general dissatisfaction with and confusion about the performance–pay relationship. Some employees also expressed the feeling that their ratings were suppressed because of an implied "20–70–10" ratings distribution, where only 20% of employees could achieve a rating of "exceeded expectations." From a corporate perspective, "20–70–10" was a general guideline, not an absolute; it helped to express a "pay-for-performance" philosophy. Although there was an explicit connection at GHT between pay and performance, managers in general did not adequately communicate how they were related, and they did not communicate the purpose of the distribution guidelines and how they were to be used.

Given increasing manager and leadership support for the performance management process, the ongoing training and communication provided by OD, the focus on building a performance-based culture, and recent efforts to further clarify for all employees the linkage between pay and performance, GHT anticipates increased satisfaction with performance management over the next year. Current senior leadership are counting on this fact. They see performance management as critical to achieving business results, maintaining GHT's industry leadership position, and driving the overall success of GHT in the marketplace.

Finally, based on lessons learned, the OD team will also be taking additional steps to:

- better align and integrate performance management with business planning and strategic goal setting to make the connections more transparent;
- drive a paradigm shift regarding performance management from one of "a bureaucratic, compliance-oriented process" to "a process of business value";
- make performance management the way of doing business;
- help managers to understand and be able to customize general ratable behaviors to reflect individual job performance;

help managers (train them) to establish and formulate goals where performance measures may be more qualitative, for example, in staff roles such as finance, marketing, software and administration.

Conclusion

Our case illustrates challenges for practice, theory, and the future that we described earlier in the chapter. Performance management requires executive buy-in, clearly articulated program elements with strong linkages with each other and with organizational goals, and a system to track success and improve the process over time. Performance management components draw on a strong theoretical foundation, and this case demonstrates the value of goal setting, evaluation, feedback, and development as integrated functions. The case recognizes the changing corporate world, utilizing technological advances for program delivery and communications. It also recognizes the dynamic nature of performance management in a business-focused, internationally experienced, growing organization. Senior leaders learn the system along with the new generation of managers entering the business, building a fluid yet focused culture of performance assessment and improvement. Organization culture change through performance management takes time, commitment, and involvement of staff at all levels, with human resource professionals closely aligned with business functions to implement a system that all employees respect and value. This is not an easy process, but it is one that can result in dividends through improved performance and the ability to adapt to future needs.

References

Alexander, J. (2006). *Performance dashboards and analysis for value creation*. New York: Wiley.

Amabile, T. M., & Kramer, S. J. (2007). Inner work life: Understanding the subtext of business performance. *Harvard Business Review, 85*(5), 72–83.

Atwater, L., Roush, P., & Fischthal, A. (1995). The influence of upward feedback on self and follower ratings of leadership. *Personnel Psychology, 48*, 34–60.

Bandura, A., & Locke, E. A. (2003). Negative self-efficacy and goal effects revisited. *Journal of Applied Psychology, 88*, 87–99.

Drucker, P. F. (1993). *Management: Tasks, responsibilities, practices*. New York: Collins.

Dweck, C. S. (1999). *Self-theories: Their role in motivation, personality, and development*. Philadelphia, PA: Psychology Press.

Giles, W. F., Findley, H. M., & Field, H. S. (1997). Procedural fairness in performance appraisal: Beyond the review session. *Journal of Business, 11*, 493–506.

Greenberg, J. (1991). Using explanations to manage impressions of performance appraisal fairness. *Employee Responsibilities and Rights Journal, 4*, 51–60.

Harris, M. M., & Schaubroeck, J. (1988). A meta-analysis of self-manager, self-peer, and peer-manager ratings. *Personnel Psychology, 41*, 43–62.

Heslin, P. A., Vandewalle, D., & Latham, G. P. (2006). Keen to help? Managers' implicit person theories and their subsequent employee coaching. *Personnel Psychology, 59*, 871–902.

Hofstede, G. (2003). *Culture's consequences: Comparing values, behaviors, institutions, and organizations across nations* (2nd edn). Newbury Park, CA: Sage Publications.

Huntley, R. (2006). *The world according to Y: Inside the new adult generation*. Crows Nest, New South Wales, Australia: Allen & Unwin.

Ilgen, D. R., Fisher, C. D., & Taylor, M. S. (1979). Consequences of individual feedback on behavior in organizations. *Journal of Applied Psychology, 64*, 349–371.

Kaplan, R. S., & Norton, D. P. (1996) *The balanced scorecard: Translating strategy into action*. Boston: Harvard Business School Press.

Klimoski, R. J., & Donahue, L. M. (2001). Person perception in organizations: An overview of the field. In M. London (Ed.), *How people evaluate others in organizations* (pp. 5–43). Mahwah, NJ: Erlbaum.

Kluger, A. N., & DeNisi, A. (1998). Feedback interventions: Toward the understanding of a double-edged sword. *Current Directions in Psychological Science, 7*, 67–72.

Locke, E. A., & Latham, G. P. (1990). *A theory of goal-setting and task performance*. Englewood Cliffs, NJ: Prentice-Hall.

Locke, E. A., & Latham, G. P. (2002). Building a practically useful theory of goal setting and task motivation: A 35 year odyssey. *American Psychologist, 57*, 705–717.

London, M. (2003). *Job feedback*. Mahwah, NJ: Erlbaum.

London, M., & Mone, E. M. (1999). Continuous learning. In D. R. Ilgen & E. D. Pulakos (Eds), *The changing nature of work performance: Implications for staffing, personnel actions, and development* (pp. 119–153). San Francisco, CA: Jossey-Bass.

London, M., & Smither, J. W. (1995). Can multi-source feedback change self-awareness and behavior? Theory-based applications and directions for research. *Personnel Psychology, 48*, 803–840.

London, M., & Smither, J. W. (2002). Feedback orientation, feedback culture, and the longitudinal performance management process. *Human Resource Management Review, 12*(1), 81–101.

London, M., Smither, J. W., & Adsit, D. J. (1996). Accountability: The Achilles Heel of multisource feedback. *Group and Organization Management, 22*, 162–184.

Lord, R. G., & Maher, K. J. (1993). *Leadership & information processing: Linking perceptions and performance*. New York: Routledge.

Mabe, P. A., & West, S. G. (1982). Validity of self-evaluation of ability: A review and meta-analysis. *Journal of Applied Psychology, 67*, 280–296.

Mone, E. M., & London, M. (2003). *Fundamentals of performance management*. London: Spiro Press.

Odiorne, G. S. (1968). *Management by objectives: A system of managerial leadership*. New York: Pitman Publishing Corporation.

Polzer, J. T., Milton, L. P., & Swann, W. B., Jr. (2002). Capitalizing on diversity: Interpersonal congruence in small work groups. *Administrative Science Quarterly, 47*, 296–324.

Sessa, V. I., & London, M. (2006). *Continuous learning in organizations*. Mahwah, NJ: Erlbaum.

Smither, J. W., London, M., & Reilly, R. R. (2005). Does performance improve following multisource feedback? A theoretical model, meta-analysis, and review of empirical findings. *Personnel Psychology, 58*(1), 33–66.

Smither, J. W., London, M., & Richmond, K. R. (2005). The relationship between leaders' personality and their reactions to and use of multisource feedback: A longitudinal study. *Group & Organization Management, 30*, 181–210.

Smither, J. W., London, M., Flautt, R., Vargas, Y., & Kucine, I. (2003). Can working with an executive coach improve multisource feedback ratings over time? A quasi-experimental field study. *Personnel Psychology, 56*, 23–44.

Stamoulis, D. T., & Hauenstein, N. M. A. (1993). Rater training and rating accuracy: Training for dimensional accuracy versus training for rate differentiation. *Journal of Applied Psychology, 78*, 994–1003.

Steel, P., & Cornelius, J. K. (2006). Integrating theories of motivation. *Academy of Management Review, 31*, 889–913.

Vandewalle, B., Brown, S. P., Cron, W. L., & Slocum, J. W. Jr (1999). The influence of goal orientation and self-regulation tactics on sales performance: A longitudinal field test. *Journal of Applied Psychology, 84*, 249–59.

Wood, R., & Bandura, A. (1989). Social cognitive theory of organizational management. *The Academy of Management Review, 14*, 361–384.

Employee engagement

John Storey, Dave Ulrich,
Theresa M. Welbourne and Patrick M. Wright

The aspiration to involve, engage and win commitment from employees has long been high on the agenda of a select portion of enlightened management. However, there has been a notable resurgence of interest in employee engagement in recent times and it seems that the phenomenon has evolved and been redrawn. Distinctive posts are now advertised which call, for example, for 'Directors of Employee Engagement' rather than, or sometimes in addition to, Director of HR. Recent conferences linking employer branding to employee engagement also indicate the nature of the trend, and the professional associations for HR professionals in the USA and the UK have both paid close attention to the issue (Chartered Institute of Personnel and Development 2006, 2007; SHRM 2008). The Australian Human Resource Institute has engagement as a key component of its 'Model of Excellence' which incorporates the latest research results from the HR Competency Model developed by Dave Ulrich and Wayne Brockbank of the University of Michigan. The practices and the remit are being reimagined and reinvented. The intensity of interest has been such that the Editor of T&D has moved to ask: 'What's the Big Deal About Employee Engagement?' (Ketter 2008). The purpose of this chapter is to explore the meanings and manifestations of employee engagement in its revitalized mode. We will answer four questions about employee engagement:

1. What does employee engagement mean?
2. What are the outcomes?
3. What are the methods?
4. What are the future theoretical and practical challenges?

Answering these four questions will help academics and consultants synthesize and advance engagement work and assist managers and HR professionals to make wiser choices about employee engagement activities and investments.

The meaning of employee engagement

We want to begin by seeking to clarify the meaning of employee engagement. Because it has grown so quickly in popularity, many consultants, companies, and researchers have developed their own definitions of engagement, resulting in confusion of meanings and of approaches. We begin with some commercial definitions and then move on to consider some academic definitions.

The Caterpillar Company defines it as: 'The extent of employees' commitment, work effort, and desire to stay in an organization.' Dell Inc declares that, 'To compete today, companies need to win over the minds (rational commitment) and the hearts (emotional commitment) of employees in ways that lead to extraordinary effort.' The Corporate Leadership Council defines it as 'The extent to which employees commit to something or someone in their organization, how hard they work and how long they stay as a result of that commitment.' The Gallup Organization simply states that it 'is the involvement with, and enthusiasm for, work' (Vance 2006a, b). The Gallup Organization (2006) has elaborated their understanding by referring to 'engaged employees' as those who 'work with a passion and feel a profound connection to their company and drive innovation and move the organization forward'. In the UK, the CIPD (2007) refers to it as 'passion for work' and the willingness to go the extra mile.

Academic researchers have defined employee engagement as 'the harnessing of organization members' selves to their work roles; in engagement, people employ and express themselves physically, cognitively, and emotionally during role performances' (Kahn 1990). Others have noted the centrality of 'vigor' in the idea of engagement – that is, feelings of strength and emotional energy in the workplace (Shirom 2003). Shaw (2005) defined engagement as 'translating employee potential into employee performance and business success'. This means changing the way employees perform 'by utilizing the tools in the armoury of internal communication professionals'.

International Survey Research (ISR) defines employee engagement as 'a process by which an organization increases commitment and continuation of its employees to the achievement of superior results'. The ISR separates commitment into three parts: cognitive commitment, affective commitment and behavioral commitment. In other words, the three dimensions are: think, feel and act.

The challenge with most of these definitions is that they define the construct in terms of its outcomes more than the construct itself. The definitions also suggest an overlap between engagement and commitment and yet the argument has been posited that engagement exists 'as a distinct and unique construct that consists of cognitive, emotional, and behavioral components that are associated with role performance' (Saks 2006: 602). When applied to organizational settings, however, the concept tends to exhibit considerable overlap with constructs such as affective organizational commitment and organizational citizenship behavior (OCB). There are overlaps too with ideas about (i) role expansion, (ii) the taking of initiative and (iii) the voluntary giving of discretionary – and even extraordinary – effort. Thus, employee engagement is hard to distinguish conceptually from this range of constructs relating to cognitive and emotional commitment. It is also important to ask 'engagement in or to what?' – the answer could be the immediate task, the social life of the group, the department or the organization as a whole. Each of these behaviours is of course rather different from the others.

For the purposes of this chapter 'employee engagement' is understood to mean the affective commitment which employees make in practice. Affective commitment implies discretionary energy and working hard on the job versus 'satisfaction' which focuses on 'liking' a job. There are cognitive, emotional and physical dimensions to engagement. We can demonstrate the distinction of satisfaction versus commitment with a simple illustration. When conducting a company workshop, we often ask participants the satisfaction question: 'Do you like your job (boss, pay, or other job features)'? To get at commitment means asking a different set of questions such as: 'To what extent do you go beyond your job description to do your best for the organization?' Someone can like or be satisfied with their job, but not work very hard at doing it well. Conversely, someone may work hard but not like the work they do. Thus, we define engagement as: *a set of positive attitudes and behaviours enabling high job performance of a kind which is in tune with the organization's mission.* To bring this about usually requires a mix of human resource practices built around involvement, perceived appropriate rewards, a set of learning and development opportunities and good leadership at multiple levels.

Contemporary approaches to employee engagement in practice almost invariably involve some systematic attempt to measure the phenomenon and to act upon the results over a series of iterations. We have undertaken a wide-ranging assessment of such surveys. The questions used in engagement surveys indicate the nature of the construct. Some typical core questions are shown below (these are normally accompanied by a Likert scale of responses):

- I am proud to work for this company
- I put my heart into the job
- I would recommend this company to a friend
- Our company is energizing and exciting
- I enjoy the challenges in my work
- I like to stay until the work is done.

This affective commitment should, and as we will show under the appropriate conditions does, impact employee behaviour in ways that can result in positive organizational outcomes. There are of course conditional factors such as team leader behaviour, job design and energy. We will focus later in the chapter on the 'energy' variable as we have conducted extensive research in this area both with managers' energy and that of employees.

The outcomes from employee engagement

When employees experience engagement or commitment, a number of positive outcomes occur. Some of the outcomes of engagement link to other employee affective responses to work. For example, the UK Workplace Relations Survey found that more engaged employees had higher employee participation in company programs, retention, receptiveness to change, and loyalty. In addition, employee engagement has also been found to be related to less:

- role conflict and stress;
- cynicism about the organization and its goals;

and more:

- sense of control over one's work environment;
- confidence in the future of the organization;
- sense of self-confidence in the ability to make change happen in the organization;
- willingness to learn and experiment;
- willing to stay with the company (lower turnover or higher retention);

- motivation;
- creative ideas and solutions; continuous improvement;
- team working;
- organization identity.

Most people can reflect on a personal experience when they felt more engaged with the organization and when conversely they felt less engaged or even disengaged. These feelings of engagement are associated with a greater willingness to work hard, feeling connected to both the work and cohorts doing the work, there is a sharper focus on achieving the goals of the organization, and a feeling of being part of the 'flow' of the organization. Researchers have confirmed and generalized these personal experiences. For example, work by Saks (2006: 613) revealed that engagement levels are predicted by perceived support granted to employees by the organization and that measures of engagement themselves predict levels of job satisfaction, commitment measures, intentions to quit, and positive behaviours within the organization.

In addition to these personal outcomes, when an organization has more engaged employees, the organization performs better. The relationship between employee engagement and performance seems to have been found in much of the empirical research that has tried to relate it to business unit or firm outcomes. For instance, the following quotes illustrate these empirical findings:

> Companies in which 60 percent (or more) of the workforce is engaged have average five-year total returns to shareholders (TSR) of more than 20 percent. That compares to companies where only 40 to 60 percent of the employees are engaged, which have an average TSR of about six percent.
>
> (Baumruk et al. 2006: 24)

> Highly engaged employees achieve 12 percent more of their goals than employees with low engagement. Twelve percent of an employee salary of $35,000 equates to $4,200. When considering the impact on an organization with 10,000 employees, the value of engagement can yield a major impact of $42 million.

A meta-analysis by Harter et al. (2002) of data collected by the Gallup Organization produced similar findings. This revealed the strong effects employee engagement can have on levels of customer satisfaction and loyalty. A weaker, but practically significant, effect was also found between measures of engagement and satisfaction and business-level outcomes. In another meta-analytic study, Riketta (2002) found a correlation between measures of attitudinal organizational commitment – defined as 'the relative strength of an individual's identification with and involvement in a particular organization' (Mowday et al. 1979: 226) – and job performance. Interestingly, the strength of this correlation was found to be moderated by the type of data collected and was stronger when self-ratings were used as compared to objective and/or supervisor-rated measures. Additionally, Luthans et al. (2002) examined the role of managers with regard to employees' levels of engagement and determined that levels of manager self-efficacy partially mediated the relationship.

Thus, research conducted by both academic and consulting firms seems to suggest that engagement (or commitment) is related to outcomes that are considered important by managers of organizations at both individual and organization levels.

Ways of achieving employee engagement

Many consulting firms, such as Accenture, Concours, Gallup, Hewitt, Mercer, Towers Perrin, Watson Wyatt and others, have created engagement surveys. We have assessed each of these products and we have identified seven common factors, briefly defined and then developed below.

- *Vision*: The work unit has a clear sense of the future that engages hearts and minds and creates pride among employees.
- *Opportunity*: The work on offer provides a chance to grow both personally and professionally, through participation in the work unit's activities.
- *Incentive*: The compensation package is fair and equitable, including base salary, bonus, and other financial incentives.
- *Impact*: The work itself makes a difference or creates meaning, particularly as it connects the employee with a customer who uses the employee's work.
- *Community*: The social environment includes being part of a team when appropriate, and working with co-workers who care.
- *Communication*: The flow of information is two-way, so employees are in the know about what is going on.
- *Experimentation*: The work hour, dress, and other policies are flexible and designed to adapt to the needs of both the firm and the employee.

We call these inducements VOICE. This framework stems from the work of Anthony Rucci and it has been elaborated in Ulrich and Brockbank (2005). Each of the elements represents a set of choices which leaders can make to increase employee engagement. An individual may differ on his/her interest in each of these seven factors (e.g., some may be more interested in community than in communication). Over a career span, employees may also vary on the relative weighting of each of these elements (e.g., early in a career, incentives or financial rewards may be more important than later in a career). These seven elements can be woven into an employee value proposition, representing what employees get in return for their dedication to the firm. They are shown diagrammatically in Figure 8.1.

In the following commentary on the figure we discuss the meaning of each term and we also in each case focus especially on the implications for leaders of teams, departments and organizations.

Vision

Defining a future direction for an organization unit goes by many names: strategy, goals, objectives, aspirations, themes, values, milestones, mission, intent, and purpose. While there are nuances of differences among these concepts, they all focus on a future direction and investments to make tomorrow's direction real today.

When employees understand, accept, and align their actions to the direction of the organization, they are more likely to be engaged. There are a number of specific dimensions of the vision that lead to employees being more engaged:

- *Clarity*. Visions should combine analytics which lay out statistical projections of the future and stories which capture the impact of the future investments on employees and customers. In consulting, we often ask members of a management team to write in

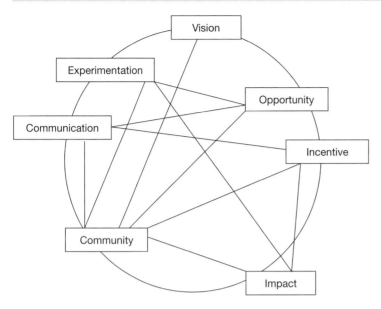

Figure 8.1 The VOICE framework

20 words or less 'What are we trying to accomplish?' We can quickly discern the extent to which there is a shared vision among the managers of the management team. Visions engage employees when they offer them a sense of purpose that has meaning to each of them.

- *Line of sight*. Visions in the abstract remain at the hoped-for-but-not-likely level. When visions translate to employee actions, they become real. Employees who can see how their day-to-day behaviour links to longer term organization visions become more engaged. This is consistent with expectancy theory which advocates the alignment between an employee's effort and performance and performance and outcomes. When this line of sight exists, employees feel engaged because they believe that their work will have impact.
- *Future focused*. Visions focus on what can be, not what has been. By creating the future, visions engage employees in working together to deliver a desired result.
- *Emotive and cognitive*. Visions create energy by generating passion among employees about what can be. Energy often comes from emotions that may exist within a company or from the leaders of the company. Cognitive visions ensure that the passions are grounded in reality.

When leaders build purpose-driven organizations, employees are more engaged. Employees in these organizations act like volunteers because they believe in the cause or purpose of the organization. At times, a crisis may create a temporary purpose-driven organization. In utility firms, when a storm creates power outages, utility employees find a clear and unifying purpose to their work. Employees think much less about distracting politics or policies and focus on restoring power. These employees are engaged. The greater challenge for leaders is to ensure a continuity of engagement with the benefit of an external crisis.

Implications for leaders

Leaders who create visions that lead to employee engagement should identify and connect with leading customers, anticipate technology and industry trends, determine how to leverage their core competencies to move into new markets, and find ways to involve employees in defining and shaping their strategy. Nokia leaders knew that the cellular phone devices strategy which had been so successful had to morph to being an internet company where content on the devices defined their future. They held broad-based employee 'café' meetings where employees throughout the company could learn about the future and engage in discussing the strategy. As the Nokia internet strategy emerges, employees who participated in it will be more engaged with it.

Opportunity

Opportunity means that employees are given the chance to learn and grow through their participation in the work's activities. Opportunities to participate may come from direct participation involving individual employees, indirect or representative participation through the intermediary of employee representative bodies, such as works councils or trade unions, and financial participation. Each of these forms is discussed in more detail below. Through all of these forums, employees participate in decision making and work impact.

- Direct participation can be seen as taking two main forms: *consultative participation* where management encourages employees to make their views known on work-related matters, but retains the right to take action or not; and *delegative participation* where management gives employees increased discretion and responsibility to organize and do their jobs without reference back.

  Both *consultative* and *delegative participation* can involve individual employees or groups of employees. The two forms of consultative participation can be further subdivided. Individual consultation can be 'face-to-face' or 'arm's-length'; group consultation can involve temporary or permanent groups.

- Indirect or representative participation includes co-determination or rights of works councils in some EU member countries, notably Germany. The decision forums make social policy decisions jointly with management. Joint consultation may also exist, where management seeks the views of the union and takes them into account in making its decision. The most obvious example of a 'dual system' is to be found in Germany where it is enshrined in the legal framework. Joint regulation is largely the responsibility of the employers' organizations and trade unions and takes place outside the workplace at the level of the industry or the Land. Inside the workplace, the task of representing the interests of employees is taken over by the statutory works councils, which have limited rights of joint regulation but extensive powers of joint consultation as well as information, which means a much wider range of issues is discussed between management and employee representatives.

As these forums for participation increase, employees are given more opportunities to join in how the organization defines and delivers work. When employees participate, they feel more engaged. Research on commitment among self-employed workers shows that their engagement scores are higher because they participate in and have control over decisions.

Opportunity also means that employees have prospects of learning and growing at work. This growth may come from formal training and development experiences, but it may also come from work assignments. Learning also comes when a culture exists that encourages risk taking and reflection. Employees are more engaged when they have opportunities to learn.

Implications for leaders

Leaders lead by doing, but also by getting others to do. Leaders recognize that their ultimate responsibility is to help others nurture and grow their talents. The participation and learning opportunities for employees should be a constant leadership action item. As decisions are made, leaders can ask questions such as: Who should be involved in this decision? Who are the next generation of talented employees and how do we give them learning opportunities? What is our workforce plan and how do we make sure we have employees prepared for what is coming? As leaders open their decision processes to more employees, these employees will be more engaged.

Impact

Hackman and Oldham's (1974) work on motivation showed that when employees could see the outcome of their work, they were more likely to be committed to it. Impact means that employees feel that their hard work will lead to desired results. In this present volume, the chapter by Bowen and Pugh (Chapter 30) shows the impact of employees seeing that their work will affect customer response to the firm. When employees realize that their attitude and behaviors will show up in customer attitude and behaviours, these employees are more engaged as they know that what they do makes a difference.

Leaders can help employees see the impact of their work by helping them understand how their work fits into the overall process of customer service. Every employee has a customer, either inside or outside the organization. When an employee can see the ways in which his or her work delivers value to customers, the employee is more likely to be emotionally engaged in delivering the work.

Some of the nature of this impact can be found in the empowerment literature especially in relation to those circumstances where employees are empowered to make decisions that affect customers. But good empowerment is not just about decentralizing decision making and sharing authority; it also means making sure that employees have the information required to make good decisions and the competencies to use that information to serve customers.

Implications for leaders

Leaders often have information about the connection of activities inside a company to users of the activities. Leaders can see the beginning of the processes to the end. As they open these processes to employees, employees become equally engaged with the impact that they have. This means getting more employees touching and thinking like customers. A large retail chain asked all of its 200,000 sales associates to interview ten people in a thirty-day period and ask questions like: Why do (or don't) you shop at our company? How would you rate your last experience in our store? What could we do to improve? What do you tell your friends about our company? At first, the leaders were excited about building a data base with all this data, but then they realized that the real impact was having employees throughout the company connecting with customers so that they could better experience the impact of their work.

Rewards and incentive

Few like to admit publicly that they are motivated by something so crass as money but, as the chapter in this volume by Barry Gerhart suggests (Chapter 14), financial incentives can shape employee behaviour. There are two main forms of financial participation: profit sharing and share ownership. Both have a long history in the UK. The John Lewis Partnership, for example, which embraces Waitrose, the multiple food retailer, as well as the general household stores, has long been a strong advocate of profit sharing and the organization in recent years has outperformed the industry sector.

Although a regular feature in the remuneration of many managers, however, profit sharing and share ownership among employees in general has not been extensively practised. In the UK, for example, the number of workplaces with an employee share ownership scheme for non-managerial employees amounts to no more than 15 per cent, while profit-sharing schemes cover about 30 per cent of workplaces. Typically, too, the amounts of money involved in profit sharing or the number of holdings in share ownership are relatively small.

Employee engagement increases when employees receive financial benefits from their engagement. Remuneration sends communication signals about what matters, serves as a scorecard for performance, and also meets the needs of some employees. Profit sharing and share ownership can be very useful in sensitizing employees to the state of the business. It is a moot point, however, whether they do a great deal for involvement and participation on a day-to-day basis. Arguably, they need to be raised to the levels available to senior managers to have a serious impact in this respect.

Implications for leaders

Creating an incentive system that drives the right behaviour starts by being very clear about the behaviour that reflects the strategy. Behaviours or standards that put strategic directions into actions that employees understand may come when leaders share directions with employees and then ask employees what they should do more or less of to make the direction actionable. The responses to these questions become the basis for employee standards. Then, as employees reach these standards, they receive positive financial or non-financial consequences. If employees miss these standards, this has negative consequences. Leaders need to continually audit their incentive systems to make sure that they are measuring the right things, having clear standards, connecting rewards to standards, and providing employees with feedback on how they are doing.

Community

Community affects employee engagement in two ways. First, a community represents cohorts of teams with whom the employee works. Peer pressure and social networks encourage employees to commit to their job. Gallup's finding of having a friend at work as a source of engagement implies a reciprocal relationship between the employee and his/her peers. Because of personal relationships, employees have goodwill towards their peers and will try to not let them down, and to make sure that they are not the weak link on the team. Richard Hackman's (2002) research on high-performing teams shows that when employees feel like they are part of a social network, or community, they allocate more effort to supporting the goals of the team.

Community is often rooted in leadership. Clearly, leadership matters. When an employee works for a respected and admired leader, the leader is able to engage the employee to work hard by personal relationship or influence. Leaders who engage employees, listen, reinforce positive behaviour, help employees meet their personal goals, care for employees, and deliver results, are generally surrounded by employees who reciprocate by being more engaged. Obviously visible and immediate leaders have more impact than distant leaders who are higher in the hierarchy. However, we are finding that with internet blogs and other corporate transparency, employees in the bowels of the organization relate to the leaders at the top of the organization. When senior executives communicate an environment of openness and caring, employees throughout the organization feel more engaged.

Implications for leaders

Leaders who build community, model what they want others to do. Employees hear what leaders say, but they watch closely what leaders do. Leaders who build the right community start with customer expectations by answering the question: What do we want to be known for by our best customers in the future? The answers to this question then should be translated into leadership behaviours that leaders should model. If customers want a firm to be innovative, leaders need to take risks, ask questions, spend time on new products, and be open to change. In addition, leaders set the tone for the community they serve. This team work shows up in how the team makes decisions, processes information, manages relationships, and learns from good and bad experiences. Leaders who build community have employees who are more engaged.

Communication

Employees are more engaged when they know what is going on and why. Communication systems that inform employees help employees feel more a part of the organization. Communications can, of course, be two-way. Thus there can be channels of communicating *with* employees and channels for 'listening' *to* employees Sometimes the terms 'top-down' and 'bottom-up' are used. For the purposes of analysis and exposition, however, it makes sense to use the term communications or information disclosure to describe the former and consultation the latter. The importance of communications hardly needs emphasizing. Lack of understanding is a major source of inefficiency and lack of motivation. More worrying from a management perspective is that, in the absence of clear information, the infamous 'grapevine' takes over.

Leaders who build top-down, bottom-up, side-to-side, and inside-out communication plans ensure that employees understand what is expected and why it is expected. Employees are more engaged when they are more informed. Some employees like to be at the centre of the information network and become transmitters of information to others. Engaging these employees happens when they become spokespeople for the organization.

Implications for leaders

Leaders who communicate well have clear messages that they share redundantly. They share at both the cognitive and emotive levels. They are open to feedback and are constantly trying to improve. They use multiple tools to share information, from one-on-one meetings, to town hall meetings, to blogs, to videos, to e-mails depending on the purpose of their communication. They think carefully about the audience for their messages and tailor common messages to different audiences.

Entrepreneurship or flexibility

Finally, we know that employees, particularly the next-generation employees, enjoy flexibility. The playlist generation of employees has been raised on choices through computer technology.

In the work setting, flexibility about terms and conditions of work may help engage employees. Flexibility might include work hours, benefits, work location, work attire, office space, and other policies that give employees more choice over their work setting.

Flexibility gives employees choice. When an employee makes a choice about his or her work setting, they are more engaged because they have a feeling of ownership.

Implications for leaders

Leaders who encourage flexibility focus on the outcomes of an activity more than the activity. They are open to innovative and creative ways to accomplish the outcomes. They invite employees to find new ways to deliver on important goals. They are willing to experiment and learn by trying new things, and then learning from those experiments. They treat each employee as an individual, with clear performance expectations, but with flexibility on how to reach business goals.

Three future challenges

Our research and consultancy work in the domain of employee engagement suggests a need for more concentrated effort along three dimensions. These are challenges mainly for leaders and managers, though by implication there are also research challenges involved here.

Challenge 1: Leadership energy

We find that despite the exhortations, in practice many managers are often resistant to employee engagement programs. This can be for two underlying reasons – first, some inherent uncertainty about the implications for the leader role and second, due to the perceived additional work required by the leader. It can be argued from afar that engagement would in fact lighten the leader's role, but the perception is real and is a barrier to be overcome. We have found that those leaders who feel overburdened tend to judge that an 'engagement' programme will be an added cost to them personally. Our research also suggests that unless these interpretations are faced at the outset, it is difficult to embed and sustain a major engagement initiative in any organization.

The awareness-raising elements of an employee engagement initiative such as training, surveys, posters, action planning and the like are in fact the easy bits. Then comes the problem of implementation proper. This may be simple in an environment where leaders have the time for the additional work required for engagement initiatives; however, our work shows that many leaders are overworked and may even be burned out. They have little energy to embed the initiative in any meaningful sense. One of us in particular (Welbourne) has focused on this problem. Data have been collected from 4,000 leaders every two months since 2003 to track their energy at work[1] and gather comments about what is affecting energy. Using this data we can show that over the past few years, the measure of overall leadership energy has in fact been declining among this sample. These leaders are reporting their energy levels are at a rate that is lower than where they are most productive. These leaders say they have no time to get the most critical elements of their core work jobs done, and this is the key factor they report as negatively affecting their personal energy levels at work. Given that engagement implies activity 'above and beyond' (a common expression used for engagement), the problem is that these leaders are working at suboptimal energy levels and cannot even engage themselves properly because they are too busy just trying to cope with their personal workloads; still less do they feel that they have time or inclination to engage others.

The leadership study described above was inspired by two separate research initiatives. The first was a longitudinal study covering over a thousand firms which examined the predictors of earnings growth, stock price growth and firm survival. The second was the case study work within organizations that grew from the firm-level research. The key finding in the firm-level work was that organizations with higher, long-term performance had high energy cultures. The work involved surveying individual employee energy levels over time – in some cases at weekly intervals. The case study data found that, using the individual employee measure of energy established for the project, energy measures predicted levels of labour turnover, absenteeism, productivity, safety outcomes, patient satisfaction in hospitals, and customer satisfaction.

The case study also discovered that leader energy predicted employee energy. And so it is especially disconcerting to find in the ongoing leader study (that began in 2003) that leader energy is not optimal. If leader energy is falling and/or suboptimal, the overall outcome is negative for bottom-line productivity and firm performance because leader energy predicts employee energy, and high energy cultures predict organizational outcomes (stock price growth, survival). Therefore, exploring and dealing with the root causes of suboptimal leader energy is important for understanding long-term firm performance and the potential for employee engagement initiatives to work in any organization.

In order to provide some context for the above leader energy findings and the link of falling leader energy to employee engagement, we now briefly describe how it was measured for the studies mentioned. 'Energy' is a construct that is different from the constructs explored through traditional questions used in most employee surveys and it has been shown to be predictive in some unique ways. First, the ideal energy level varies from individual to individual and from occupation to occupation. The measurement process uses a 0 to 10 scale, where 0 = no energy, 8 = high energy, and 10 = too much energy.[2] Thus, energy is an optimization versus a maximization scale. A point can be reached where people are exerting so much energy they cannot find time to replenish themselves fast enough. An employee can have too much stimulus at work, and this can result in burnout. However, the definition of 'too much' differs from person to person, and it is important when measuring energy to ask more than one question. The measurement process used in the above-mentioned studies produces a variety of scores: energy overall, most productive energy level, and the gap between where one is most productive and where one is today.

When energy is measured, a few unique things are done: employees are asked to rate their energy frequently (bimonthly or even weekly); they rate where they are most productive using the same energy question; the 'most productive' rate is used to establish control zones, which are zones where the employee is most productive (similar to target heart zones when exercising); and variance over time in energy is measured and tracked.

Challenge 2: Role-based performance to define engagement

Leaders cannot get their core jobs done when they are overworked and near burnout. What does that mean for engagement? In order to delve into this question in more detail and add a theoretical perspective to the topic of engagement, we introduce the role-based performance model.

Five different categories of work behaviour can be defined via the roles that employers set up at work and reward within organizations. Short descriptions of each and an overall model follow:

1. Core job holder role (what is in the job description);
2. Entrepreneur or innovator role (improving process, coming up with new ideas, participating in others' innovations);
3. Team member role (participating in teams, working with others in different jobs);
4. Career role (learning, engaging in activities to improve your skills and knowledge);
5. Organizational member role (citizenship role or doing things that are good for the company).[3]

(Welbourne et al. 1998)

When the role-based approach to work is combined with a resource-based view of the firm, a link between role-based behaviour and firm performance can be derived. The resource-based view of the firm states that firms 'win' when they create long-term competitive advantage from resources that are valuable, rare, inimitable, and for which substitutes do not exist (Barney 1991, 1995). Researchers in human resource management strategy applied this work, suggesting that employees are a key strategic asset that meets the requirements of providing competitive advantage.

However, it is what people are doing at work specifically (or what roles they are engaged in) that drives results. If the role-based model of performance is applied, long-term competitive advantage does not come with people simply doing their core jobs. If employees are only doing core jobs (for which job descriptions are easily available), the competition can hire people, train them to do those same jobs, and do this in a location where wages and other costs are much lower.

But, if employees engage in behaviours above and beyond the core job, then true competitive advantage from people materializes. When employees have firm-specific knowledge and use that information to develop new ideas, to improve the organization, to assist new team members, and to continue to escalate their careers, then the synergy that comes from all of these above and beyond behaviours starts to drive long-term competitive advantage, which then affects firm performance.

If one starts with firm performance in mind and works backwards, then it becomes clear why employee engagement is so popular today. It makes sense that 'emotional commitment', 'above and beyond' behaviours, or 'discretionary' efforts (all terms found in the work on employee engagement) are desirable. A clear understanding of what these words mean is essential for anyone who expects to improve engagement and improve performance through their employees' efforts. Also, the link between extra role (entrepreneur, team, career, and organizational member) and core-job role performance needs to be clearly understood because if employees cannot find enough time to do the core job role, then the odds on engaging in any non-core roles are very low.

Going back to the leadership findings, leaders are saying they are de energized because they do not have enough time to get their core jobs done. In such an environment, how can these leaders be expected to work on an employee engagement initiative? By adding yet one more piece of work to overburdened leaders, organizations run the risk of further de-energizing them.

Thus, the lesson learned from all of this discussion of energy and research is that engagement programmes need to start at the top. Start with leader energy and leader role-based performance. Leaders themselves need to have time to go 'above and beyond' so that they exemplify what employee engagement can be by being engaged leaders. Only when leaders have the time they need will they be able to help the managers and employees who report to them reach their own optimal energy levels, balance their work in core and non-core job roles and engage in the behaviours that will drive the organization's strategy.

Challenge 3: Engaging low energy employees

As noted above, seeking to engage low energy leaders can be a problem; in a supplementary stream of research we also found that engaging non-manager employees can decrease employee performance. At the Society for Industrial and Organizational Psychology conference in 2007, several consulting firms presented tales of employee engagement noting that there is 'something more' going on with the data. In other words, there was a non-specific but consistent reference to engagement not being enough, at least when discussed in terms of raising engagement survey scores. Additional research linking engagement to energy in non-leader populations helps translate what is now becoming a concern or 'feeling' about employee engagement work (Welbourne 2007). The findings of a series of in-depth case studies with organizations in multiple organizations indicates that raising employee engagement survey scores for low energy employees has a negative effect on their performance. Figure 8.2 shows an example of what the resulting interaction effect looks like.

Although these same results were found in multiple within-organization case studies done with surveys developed by our team, with traditional, engagement-like survey questions, perhaps the more interesting study is with an organization that has been doing its own engagement survey, using its own questions, for the last five years. In addition to running their traditional employee engagement survey, the organization collected monthly energy data for a subpopulation of about 1,200 employees. At the end of the project, an analysis was done using data collected for the change in the firm's own employee engagement scores, average employee energy (over 12 months), change in the employees' performance appraisal scores and a series of control variables (location, job level, salary, gender, ethnicity). The analysis predicts change in employee performance appraisal scores as a function of both the change in their employee engagement scores and average energy. As can be seen from Figure 8.2, increasing employee engagement scores of high energy employees had a positive impact on their performance over the year. However, increasing employee engagement scores for employees with low energy scores backfired – it lowered their performance.

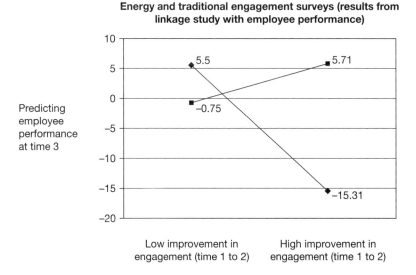

Figure 8.2 Interactive effect of energy and engagement on individual employee performance

It should be noted that this organization may or may not be increasing 'real' employee engagement in this situation; we are improving employee engagement survey scores. According to Macey and Schneider (2008: 11–12) who did a very extensive literature review of the academic work surrounding employee engagement:

> The measures of "engagement" we have seen in the world of practice are highly similar to measures used for assessments of job satisfaction (or climate or culture), albeit with a new label. While there may be room for satisfaction within the engagement construct, engagement connotes activation while satisfaction connotes satiation . . . [these surveys] do not directly tap engagement.

There are two potential reasons for the negative outcome. The first may be the same cause uncovered in the leader studies. The employees with low energy scores may have been reporting low levels of energy due to burnout and not getting their core work done. Trying to engage these low energy employees could have led to more distractions from the core job and resulted in lower performance appraisal scores because, in reality, most performance appraisals focus on core job (vs. non-core job roles). There is, however, a second possibility that has been borne out in some of our interview data with non-manager employees.

This second possibility only makes sense if we consider that much of what is studied in the engagement survey are really factors related to satisfaction or 'satiation'. Low energy employees are given better communications, more attention, made to feel more valued, cared about and nurtured, while all the time, employers may be simply enhancing the comfort level of the already 'low energy' employees.

If this were the case, then clearly there could be problems associated with including employee engagement survey scores as part of a balanced score card. There could be conditions under which the employer is doing more harm than good.

Taken together, we think that two key processes need to be added to employee engagement initiatives. First, start with the leaders. Second, improve energy before trying to increase employee engagement.

What these cautionary tales are telling us

Too often in HR there is a search for the 'holy grail', the thing that will improve performance overnight. There is a worry that employee engagement has the potential to become yet one more HR fad because after millions of dollars being spent on this intervention, there is still a lack of a clear, actionable, definition. In addition to being a field with many fads, HR also often generalizes more than is warranted or needed. Not everyone needs to be retained, trained, motivated, or indeed engaged at the same time. The faster we move to clear understanding of interventions and when they work and do not work, the better.

We believe that employee engagement should be treated as any other HR intervention. It should be a strategic programme, derived from an organizational need to change behaviour in order to achieve a strategic outcome. This means the starting point is not engagement. We should not be implementing 'engagement' because it is now in vogue.

The most important question anyone contemplating spending time and money on employee engagement should be asking is: 'Engaged in what?' Only when this question is asked first will employee engagement be a useful part of an organization's strategy.

Conclusions

Employee engagement is attracting a great deal of interest from employers across numerous sectors. In some respects it is a very old aspiration – the desire by employers to find ways to increase employee motivation and to win more commitment to the job and the organization. In some ways it is 'new' in that the context within which engagement is being sought is different. One aspect of this difference is the greater penalty to be paid if workers are less engaged than the employees of competitors, given the state of international competition and the raising of the bar on efficiency standards. A second aspect is that the whole nature of the meaning of work and the ground rules for employment relations have shifted and there is an open space concerning the character of the relationship to work and to organization which employers sense can be filled with more sophisticated approaches.

But there is reason to worry about the lack of rigor that has, to date, often characterized much work in employee engagement. If we continue to refer to 'engagement' without understanding the potential negative consequences, the core requirements of success, and the processes through which it must be implemented, and if we cannot agree even to a clear definition of what people are supposed to be engaged in doing differently at work (the engaged 'in what' question), then engagement may just be one more 'HR thing' that is only here for a short time. On a positive note, there is now a wider array of measurement techniques with which to assess trends in engagement and an associated array of approaches to effect some change. Thus, aspiration can more feasibly be translated into action.

Notes

1   Energy is defined as the degree to which they are energized or motivated at work. The construct has been validated (predicts turnover, productivity, customer service scores, and more) by numerous studies done since 1993. References to this work are available at www.eepulse.com.
2   The energy metric used in these studies is trademarked and copyright protected; use of the measure requires the written permission of Dr. T.M. Welbourne.
3   Validation research for this approach is available in: Welbourne, T.M., Johnson, D., & Erez, A. (1998). 'The role-based performance scale: Validity analysis of a theory-based measure of performance', *Academy of Management Journal*, 41(5): 540–55.

References

Barney, J. (1991). 'Firm resources and sustained competitive advantage', *Journal of Management*, 17: 99–120.
Barney, J. (1995). 'Looking inside for competitive advantage', *Academy of Management Executive*, 9(4): 49–61.
Baumruk, R., Gorman, Jr., B., & Gorman, R.E. (2006). 'Why managers are crucial to increasing engagement: Identifying steps managers can take to engage their workforce', *Strategic HR Review*, 5(2): 24–7.
Chartered Institute of Personnel and Development (2006). *Working Life: Employee Attitudes and Engagement*, London: CIPD.
Chartered Institute of Personnel and Development (2007). *How Engaged are British Employees?* London: CIPD.
Gallup (2006). 'Engaged employees inspire company innovation', *Gallup Management Journal*, http://gmj.gallup.com/content/default.aspx?ci=24880&pg=1.

Hackman, J.R. (2002). *Leading Teams: Setting the Stage for Great Performances*, Boston, MA: Harvard Business School Books.

Hackman, J.R. & Oldham, G.R. (1974). 'Motivation through the design of work', *Organizational Behaviour and Human Performance*, 16(2): 250–79.

Harter, J.K., Schmidt, F.L., & Hayes, T.L. (2002). 'Business-unit-level relationship between employee satisfaction, employee engagement, and business outcomes: a meta-analysis', *Journal of Applied Psychology*, 87(2): 268–79.

Kahn, W.A. (1990). 'Psychological conditions of personal engagement and disengagement at work', *Academy of Management Journal*, 33(4): 692–724.

Ketter, P. (2008). 'What's the big deal about employee engagement?', *American Society for Training & Development*, January: 45–49.

Luthans, F., Peterson, S.J., & Farmer, R.T. (2002). 'Employee engagement and manager self-efficacy', *Journal of Management Development*, 21(5): 376–87.

Macey, W.H. & Schneider, B. (2008). 'The meaning of employee engagement', *Industrial and Organizational Psychology: Perspectives in Science and Practice*, 1(1): 3–30.

Mowday, R.T., Steers, R.M., & Porter, L.W. (1979). 'The measurement of organizational commitment', *Journal of Vocational Behavior*, 14: 224–47. In M. Riketta (2002). 'Attitudinal organizational commitment and job performance: a meta-analysis', *Journal of Organizational Behavior*, 23: 257–66.

Riketta, M. (2002). 'Attitudinal organizational commitment and job performance: A meta-analysis', *Journal of Organizational Behavior*, 23: 257–66.

Saks, A.M. (2006). 'Antecedents and consequences of employee engagement', *Journal of Managerial Psychology*, 21(7): 600–19.

Shaw, K. (2005). *Employee Engagement: How to Build a High-performance Workforce*, Chicago, IL: Melcrum Publishing Limited.

SHRM (2008) White Paper: Employee Engagement and Organizational Performance: How do you know your employees are engaged? www.shrm.org/hrresources/whitepapers_published/CMS_012127.asp.

Shirom, A. (2003). 'Job-related burnout: A review', in J.C. Quick & L.E. Tetrick (Eds.), *Handbook of Occupational Health Psychology* (pp. 245–65). Washington, DC: American Psychological Association.

Ulrich, D. & Brockbank, W. (2005) *HR Value Proposition*. Cambridge, MA: Harvard Business Press.

Vance, R. (2006a). *Employee Engagement and Commitment*. Alexandria, VA: SHRM.

Vance, R.J. (2006b). 'Employee engagement and commitment: A guide to understanding, measuring and increasing engagement in your organization', *Society for Human Resource Management*, 1–45.

Welbourne, T.M. (2007). 'Employee engagement: Beyond the fad and into the executive suite', *Leader to Leader*, spring: 45–51.

Welbourne, T.M., Johnson, D. & Erez, A. (1998). 'The role-based performance scale: Validity analysis of a theory-based measure of performance', *Academy of Management Journal*, 41(5): 540–55.

142

9

Human resources, organizational resources, and capabilities

Patrick M. Wright and Scott A. Snell

This chapter examines the role of human resources and HR practices in building organizational resources and capabilities. It then discusses how these resources can be integrated at different levels of the firm in building capabilities. The implications for research are then discussed.

In a world characterized by global markets and rapid change, the importance of firms acquiring, developing, and leveraging resources to build capabilities for competitive advantage has become increasingly evident. Because these strategic resources may likely include human capital, and because a firm's people are integral to any capability, researchers have increasingly focused on HR practices as critical levers – or investments – through which firms might build resources and capabilities.

The extant literature on HR and firm performance has fairly well documented the empirical connection between HR practices and various financial measures such as sales growth, profitability, and market value (cf., Delerey and Doty, 1996; Huselid, 1995; Snell and Youndt, 1995; Wright et al., 2003). Even so, there is a recognized gap in the literature that examines the mechanisms through which this relationship occurs. Authors have generally referred to this as the "black box" phenomenon, and have called for more research and theory that improves our understanding of the mechanisms through which HR practices influence organizational performance (Becker and Gerhart, 1996).

A recent stream of thinking in this area has focused on the ways in which HR practices can build the resources (human capital and social capital) that underlie the capabilities of the firm. The purpose of this chapter is to provide some background on the ways in which this connection occurs, the logic that drives the decisions, and the HR practices that may be most useful for an overview of the kinds of resources and capabilities that might be those impacted by HR practices, and through which those practices might impact firm performance. In sum, this chapter will propose that HR practices have their most direct impact on the human capital resources of the firm. These human capital resources are critical to certain kinds of capabilities that firms seek to build, and, if focused strategically, HR practices can influence these capabilities.

The problem with HR and performance research

As previously discussed, an established body of research exists examining the relationship between HR practices and performance. Such research has been conducted at the corporate (e.g., Huselid, 1995), business (e.g., Wright et al., 2003) and plant level (e.g., Youndt et al., 1996). Studies have examined multiple industries (e.g., Guthrie, 2001), a single industry (e.g., MacDuffie, 1995) or even a single corporation (Wright et al., 2003). While the observed effect sizes may differ across studies, qualitative reviews of this literature conclude that in almost all cases HR practices are found to be at least weakly related to performance (Boselie et al., 2005; Wright et al., 2005). This conclusion is supported by a recent meta-analysis concluding that the mean effect size for the HR–performance relationship is approximately .14 (Combs et al., 2006) implying that a one standard deviation increase in the use of high-performance work systems is associated with a 4.6% increase in return on assets.

One major problem with this research is that, while performance is certainly a strategic outcome, the basic tenet of strategic HRM is that HRM systems need to be aligned with the strategy of the business. For instance, Cappelli and Singh (1992) early on suggested that strategic HRM assumed that (a) different strategies require different employee requirements (e.g., skills and behaviors), and (b) different employee requirements are elicited by different HRM systems.

Much subsequent theorizing has attempted to describe the types of alignment one might observe between different firm strategies and HR systems. For instance, Miles and Snow (1994) suggested that firms engaged in prospector (innovation) strategies would focus on rewarding outcomes rather than behaviors, whereas defender firms would be more likely to reward behaviors than outcomes. Many others have suggested frameworks that might indicate how HR systems might differ across different organizational strategies (Delery and Doty, 1996; Schuler and Jackson, 1987; Snell, 1992; Wright and Snell, 1991; Youndt et al., 1996).

In spite of the mass of theorizing, sadly, the empirical research fails to demonstrate consistent support for the "fit" between HR and strategy (Becker and Huselid, 2006). Wright and Sherman (1999) suggested that the failure to find "fit" in the HR–performance relationship most likely stemmed from the focus on measuring generic HRM practices (e.g., pay for performance) rather than the products or targeted outcomes that the practices aimed at eliciting what might differ across strategies. For instance, pay for performance might constitute a basic principle of good HRM, but a firm engaging in innovation might tie pay to new products whereas cost-focused firms might tie pay to cost reduction or cost control. Respondents across those two firms would both report the existence of a pay for performance system, revealing no differences across strategies, when, in fact, differences certainly exist, just at a more molecular level than the measure captures.

While we still believe that the specificity of the measures helps to explain why past research has failed to reveal the "fit" effect, more recently, authors have begun to also question the specificity of strategy measures. A focus on strategic processes and capabilities may be a more specific and therefore productive target for understanding the alignment of HR practices and performance (Becker and Huselid, 2006; Delery and Shaw, 2001; Wright et al., 2001). In order to more deeply explore the role of HR in enhancing organizational capabilities, we will first discuss the Resource-Based View of the firm and its treatment of capabilities.

The Resource-Based View of the firm

The Resource-Based View (RBV) of the firm (Barney, 1991; Wernerfelt, 1984) has become the predominant paradigm driving Strategic Human Resource Management (SHRM) research and thinking (Wright et al., 2001). The RBV has its roots in the work of Penrose who referred to the firm as a "collection of productive resources" (1959: 24). Rubin (1973) was also one of the early researchers who focused on firms as bundles of resources before the formal conceptualization of the RBV by Wernerfelt (1984). Barney (1991) later extrapolated from Wernerfelt, integrating what had become a fragmented literature on the RBV. He presented a formal RBV framework which proposes that firms that possess resources which are valuable, rare, inimitable, and non-substitutable will be able to sustain their competitive advantage over the long term. While the basic framework has not necessarily changed, the applications and examinations of resources have progressed significantly over the past 15 years. In general, the evolution of thinking in this area has been around resources, capabilities, and dynamic capabilities.

A focus on resources

Early RBV work focused, not surprisingly, on resources. Amit and Schoemaker defined resources as

> stocks of available factors that are owned or controlled by the firm. Resources are converted into final products or services by using a wide range of other firm assets and bonding mechanisms such as technology, management information systems, incentive systems, trust between management and labor, and the like. These Resources consist, inter alia, of know how that can be traded (e.g., patents and licences), financial or physical assets (e.g., property, plant, and equipment), human capital, etc.
>
> (1993: 35)

Barney (1991) categorized these resources as being either human, physical, or organizational.

SHRM researchers have taken two broad tracks in utilizing the RBV for research. The primary track that SHRM researchers have taken is to focus on the HR practices themselves; that is, the organizational resources. Lado and Wilson (1994), for example, suggested that because HR practices are complex and path dependent, they could be valuable, rare and costly to imitate; therefore a source of competitive advantage. Most of the empirical research linking HR and firm performance is based on this premise, though few have tested the theory directly (cf., Becker and Gerhart, 1996; Becker and Huselid, 1998; Guthrie, 2001).

The other track taken by SHRM researchers is to focus directly on the people rather than the practices; that is, the human capital. Wright et al. (1994) argued that the larger a firm's human capital pool, the more likely that it would have superior skills and behavior that would be valuable, rare, and costly to imitate. Wright et al. (1995) examined the skills and strategies of NCAA basketball teams, and found some support for the match between skill types and strategies for determining their team's performance.

Similarly, Lepak and Snell (1999, 2002; Lepak et al., 2003) used the RBV to examine the link between valuable and unique human capital and firm performance. In a similar way, researchers such as Hitt et al. (2001), Sherer (1995), and Hatch and Dyer (2004) have demonstrated how firms leverage different forms of human capital to drive firm performance.

Whether the focus is on the HR practices or the human capital itself, much of the SHRM literature has used the RBV to focus on resources as a source of competitive advantage (Wright et al., 2003). However, research by Newbert (2007) suggested that this approach may be missing the mark. In an exhaustive review of research using the RBV, he found that of the 232 empirical examinations of the relationship between resources (not just human) and either competitive advantage or performance, only 85 (37%) were found to be significant. Newbert concluded that "the empirical results seem to suggest that while capabilities and core competencies do indeed contribute significantly to a firm's competitive advantage and/or performance, resources do not" (p. 136).

A focus on capabilities

Over time, strategy researchers have focused more broadly on the *organizational* resources, particularly examining routines and capabilities. And increasingly, the strategy literature has come to equate resources and capabilities so that they "are used interchangeably and refer to the tangible and intangible assets firms use to develop and implement their strategies" (Ray et al., 2004: 24). However, in order to more clearly focus SHRM researchers, we more fully explore the concept of capabilities.

While Penrose (1959) and Rubin (1973) viewed firms as collections of resources, they did not specifically argue that the resources alone would impact a firm's ability to compete. For instance, Penrose argued that resources could only contribute to a firm's ability to compete if they were exploited by the firm. In addition, Rubin stated that "firms must process raw resources to make them useful" (p. 937). Prahalad and Hamel (1990) argued that it was not just static resources, but rather the inimitable skills, technologies, knowledge, etc. with which these resources were deployed that determined the value of those resources. Finally, while Barney's (1991) conceptualization focused on resources, he later noted that such a static view was too narrow. In response to criticism (Priem and Butler, 2001) that the RBV had become static in concept, he stated that "once a firm understands how to use its resources . . . implementation follows almost automatically" as if the actions necessary to exploit the resources were obvious (Barney, 2001: 53). In essence, the focus within much of the strategy literature has evolved from that of resources, to that of capabilities.

According to Amit and Schoemaker, "Capabilities refer to a firm's capacity to deploy resources, usually in combination, using organizational processes, to effect a desired end" (1993: 35). Eisenhardt and Martin described them as a "set of specific and identifiable processes such as product development, strategic decision making, and alliancing" (2000: 1106). In this sense, capabilities can be thought of as information-based tangible or intangible processes that are developed over time through complex interactions among the firm's resources. They can abstractly be conceived of as "intermediate goods" generated by the firm to provide enhanced productivity of its resources, as well as strategic flexibility and protection for its final product or service. Capabilities might be developed in functional areas (e.g., brand management or marketing) or by combining physical, human, and technological resources at the business or corporate level. For instance, firms may build such "corporate capabilities as highly reliable service, repeated process or product innovations, manufacturing flexibility, responsiveness to market trends, and short product development cycles" (Amit and Schoemaker, 1993: 35).

In this sense, the concept of capabilities parallels Porter's (1996) emphasis on value chain analysis. Porter had suggested that each phase in the value chain consisted of a set of activities that the firm engaged in, and that a firm's strategic orientation suggested differential abilities to perform certain activities better than their competitors. For instance, when Dell entered the PC industry, most of the firms in the industry used intermediary distributors as partners to sell and/or deliver computers to corporate clients. Dell's "direct" model circumvented this distribution step in the value chain, as Dell created its "premiere pages" enabling corporate clients to order and receive shipments directly without a distributor taking a commission. In addition, Dell leveraged a superior supply chain management system to control inventories more efficiently than the existing competitors. It was these "activities" (or capabilities) that provided Dell with a lower cost business model that distinguished it from competitors (Dell and Fredman, 1999).

The "capabilities" concept may provide both a more specific and comprehensive frame for the connection between HR and performance. Because capabilities combine processes and resources they can serve as non-tradeable assets which develop and accumulate within the firm (Dierickx and Cool, 1989). It is not just the processes themselves, but the tacit and complex learning that takes place among individuals who execute and improve those processes over time that can distinguish a firm. Such a conceptualization led Prahalad and Hamel (1990) to argue that core competencies, particularly those based in collective learning and knowledge, improve as they are applied.

The focus on capabilities has only recently been addressed in the SHRM literature. Such a focus requires examining human capital resources, not in isolation, but in conjunction with organizational routines, processes, and systems/technologies.

Researchers such as Lepak and Snell (1999, 2003), Delery and Shaw (2003), and Becker and Huselid (2006) have suggested that identifying critical processes, talent pools, and job families helps to more clearly link HR and firm performance.

Becker and Huselid (2006) argue that taking a "capability"-based approach to SHRM leads to a focus on concrete business processes as the intermediate outcome to reflect strategy implementation. In fact, they note that Ray et al. (2004) suggested that business processes "are the way that the competitive potential of a firm's resources and capabilities are realized and deserve study in their own right" (2004: 26). They present a conceptual model in which the market positioning strategy leads to a set of strategic business processes. In their model, each business process requires a different HR system to build the necessary human capital and elicit the required employee behaviors which translate into strategic implementation effectiveness. We agree with the basic tenets, but think that the value chain provides a more comprehensive approach to understanding the differentiated HR systems.

As shown in Figure 9.1, analysis of the value chain identifies the key business processes and activities that underlie a firm's core capabilities.

Certainly, numerous sub-processes take place at each stage in the value chain, but our focus is on those that are most critical in order to deliver an end product or service. Two implications derive from this.

First, examining processes within the value chain suggests that different strategies require superior capabilities at different stages in the value chain. For instance, Dell's operational excellence strategy requires a superior capability in supply chain management relative to PC industry competitors. On the other hand, Ritz Carlton's customer intimacy requires significantly greater capability in customer service relative to its hotel competitors. Thus, the value chain points to the first step in linking HR to strategy by providing a tool for identifying which strategic business processes must be executed in a way superior to competitors.

Second, the value chain analysis provides a tool for identifying the key human capital pools that must be effectively managed in order to build the required capability. Lepak and Snell (1999) were among the first to suggest that different human capital pools require different HR systems. Their framework suggested that the strategic value and uniqueness of the skill sets determine the overall strategic importance of a given human capital pool. Becker and Huselid (2006) suggest that rather than focusing on the skills, a focus on jobs enables a clearer link to business processes. For instance, they argued that computer programming skills may be the same, but the strategic importance of those skills differs between the computer programmer job in strategic software development relative to the computer programmer job in support function.

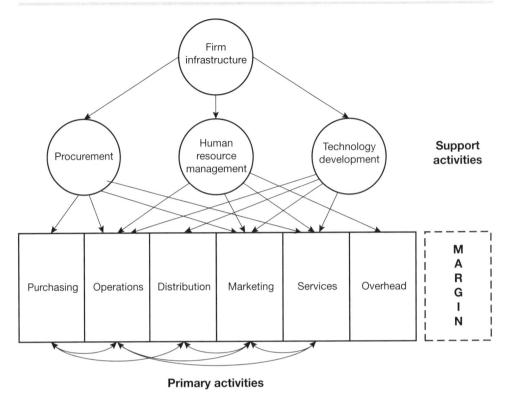

Figure 9.1 Complete value chain

By examining the value chain, one can identify the strategic job families (and consequently skill sets) that are critically paired with the execution of strategic business processes. It is important to note that this does not imply that only one job would be critical to the execution of a particular business process; often these processes require the coordination and cooperation of individuals within two or more jobs.

Once the key human capital pools have been identified, this framework enables the analysis of the skills and behaviors that are required in the execution of the business processes. As Wright and Snell (1998) noted, employee behavior is the most proximal and important HR outcome in the execution of strategy. Business processes require key behaviors of employees, both in the actual execution of the process as well as the tacit and explicit sharing of knowledge in the process of learning.

However, the exhibition of employee behavior entails possessing requisite skills and abilities that must be selected into or developed within employees in the focal jobs. The human capital skills and knowledge encompass the tacit and explicit knowledge necessary for the execution of these processes. Thus, Figure 9.2 illustrates the critical interdependence of business processes, human capital skills and knowledge, and employee behaviors that constitute a capability.

Finally, this analysis leads to the design of the HR system necessary to assure the right number and type of employees required to execute and improve key business processes that underlie core capabilities for drive value creation. Kaplan and Norton (2006), in fact, delineate a measure of "human capital readiness" that calibrates the gap between the human capital requirements relative to the current number of employees who are currently qualified for strategic jobs. This assessment is then used to inform HR investment decisions directed at developing or acquiring skills and abilities of individuals in key jobs, eliciting key behaviors from these individuals, and designing work that provides the requisite level of participation, communication, and knowledge exchange.

This leads into an examination of HR practices. Past research in HR practices has often operationalized the HR system as a single scale of HR practices (Dhatta et al., 2005; Guthrie, 2001) or sometimes an empirically derived multidimensional scale (e.g., Huselid, 1995). However, a number of SHRM researchers have noted that human resource systems can be described along three common dimensions (Appelbaum et al., 2000; Delery, 1998; Dyer and Holder, 1988).

First is the degree of investment in HR practices intended to improve the knowledge, skills, and abilities of the companies' employees. These include recruiting, training, selection, socialization, and any other practice functioning to enhance the workplace competencies of the employees. Such practices seek to build specific relevant skills, or increase the level of those skills among the focal human capital group. With regard to capabilities, this category of practices can aim to ensure that the organization has the skills and skill levels required by those employees key to the execution of business processes.

The second dimension is the degree of investment in HR practices functioning to motivate employee behavior. In general, HR practices can seek to elicit task-related behavior (that is necessary to perform the basic job), encourage employees to exhibit discretionary behavior (i.e., go outside the expected job behaviors to positively impact organizational effectiveness), or to discourage counterproductive behavior (actions that negatively impact the firm such as theft, sabotage, etc.) Practices such as incentive pay plans, performance bonuses, gain sharing, and performance management systems primarily aim at managing employee behavior. Because business processes require certain behaviors of key employee groups, one focus of the HR system has to be on eliciting the positive behaviors and inhibiting the negative ones.

Finally, HR practices function to provide opportunities to participate in substantive decision making regarding work and organizational outcomes. These include such practices as quality circles, suggestion systems, granting discretion and authority on the job, information sharing about the service or production process, and opportunities to communicate with employees and managers in other work groups. This is one area where differentiation may be seen across a variety of business processes. For instance, Starbucks, the coffee retailer, seeks operational excellence in the processes used to make a cup of coffee. Figure 9.2 shows the composition of the value chain in Starbucks Coffee.

A number of training programs within Starbucks teach specific procedures for exactly how much of each ingredient should be used, in what order, etc. In these processes there is little opportunity for employees to deviate from the prescribed behavior. However, in terms of serving customers, Starbucks employees have great latitude to deviate from prescribed behavior, or share ideas and suggestions for certain aspects of the operation.

While the practice can be subcategorized within the AMO framework, Lepak et al. (2003) note that the framework does not preclude overlap among the practices. For instance, training programs may primarily aim at building the requisite skill base, but may also communicate a commitment to the employee that elicits motivation as well. Similarly, participation programs provide opportunity, but may also help build the knowledge and motivation of employees.

In summary, an analysis of capabilities broadens SHRM beyond an exclusive focus on human capital or HR practices as direct or independent resources that drive performance or competitive advantage toward a more comprehensive understanding of how those resources are aligned with processes and technologies. This is consistent with the argument of Mahoney and Pandian (1992) that "[a] firm may achieve rents not because it has better resources, but rather the firm's distinctive competence involves making better use of its resources" (p. 365).

	Sourcing and SCM*	Coffee operations	Sourcing and SCM	Regulatory and environment
PROCESS • Cost • Quality • Speed	Procurement	Roasting and blending	Order fulfillment	Conservation 'C.A.F.E.'
SYSTEMS	e-procurement systems	Roasting curves	POS inventory and CRM	Scientific certification system
PEOPLE	• Coffee trader	• Coffee master • Roaster	• Barista • Floater	• Agronomy • Compliance
OBJECTIVE • Competencies • Behavior • Engagement	• Reduce suppl/ chain risk through long-term re;ations	• Identify house blend combos • Assess sourcing value	• Increase store throughout capacity and fix bottlenecks	• Develop farmer yield capacity • Ensure local development
INVEST	• Experience hire • Technical training • LT incentives	• Job security • Education • Rotation/assign	• Team-based • Time incentives • Share/suggest	• Experience hire • Local knowledge • License/certify • CSR scorecard

* Supply chain management

Figure 9.2 Starbucks coffee

Dynamic capabilities

While capabilities distinguish a firm positively, over time the capabilities can serve as a constraint as well. For instance, Peteraf suggested,

> These resources can provide both the basis and the direction for the growth of the firm. For example, there may be a natural trajectory embedded in a firm's knowledge base. Current capabilities may both impel and constrain future learning and investment activity.
>
> (1993: 181–2)

Such a concern with the "core rigidity" that may stem from capabilities led to the concept of dynamic capabilities.

Teece and his colleagues defined dynamic capabilities as "the subset of the competencies/capabilities which allow the firm to create new products and processes and respond to changing market circumstances" (Teece and Pisano, 1994: 541) and later as "the firm's ability to integrate, build, and reconfigure internal and external competencies to address rapidly changing environments" (Teece et al., 1997: 516). Eisenhardt and Martin suggested that dynamic capabilities "are the organizational and strategic routines by which firms achieve new resource configurations as markets emerge, collide, split, evolve, and die" (2000: 1107). Some have argued that even dynamic capabilities can become rigid, impeding a firm's ability to adapt to a changing environment. Our purpose here is not to debate the concept itself, but rather to note that in addition to specific capabilities such as being able to distinguish a firm's value creation strategy at a given point in time, firms often must also find ways to transform or develop new capabilities in the face of environmental change. This has important implications for SHRM.

Milliman et al. (1991) were early authors examining the concept of HR flexibility, exploring it within the multinational HRM environment. Wright and Snell (1998) proposed a more specific and formal conceptualization for exploring HR flexibility, positing that such flexibility consisted of skill flexibility, behavior flexibility, and HR practice flexibility.

Wright and Snell defined the flexibility of employee skills as the "number of potential alternative uses to which employee skills can be applied" (1998: 764) and "how individuals with different skills can be redeployed quickly" (1998: 765).

Flexibility of employee behavior refers to the degree to which employees are able to exhibit adaptable as opposed to routine behaviors. It deals with the extent to which they possess a broad repertoire of behavioral scripts and can adapt those scripts to specific situations.

Flexibility of HR practices refers to the extent to which HR practices can be adapted and/or applied across a variety of situations or sites within the firm, and the speed with which these adaptations can be applied.

Implications of resources, capabilities, and dynamic capabilities for SHRM

The more recent emphasis on aligning HR practices with strategy through a focus on capabilities has some important implications for HR research. First, as Becker and Huselid (2006) noted, while some HR practices are differentiated across jobs within the firm, there may also be some general HR practices or principles that are part of the larger HR architecture. For instance, during the 1990s IBM sought to transform its "entitlement" culture into a "performance-based" culture. Part of this transformation required implementing more performance-based rewards and even shifting employees to cash-balance pension plans to move the risk from the company to the employees. While the specifics may have differed across jobs, the basic principle began to infiltrate the HR systems across all jobs.

Second, the kinds of practices that have been measured in the past seem to be more of the larger HR architecture (e.g., "On average, how many hours of training do employees get per year?" or "What is the average merit increase for a high performer? For a low performer?"). As researchers began to focus more on core jobs (Delery and Doty, 1996; MacDuffie, 1995) the research began to recognize that certain jobs are more central to a firm's success, and that it is the practices in regards to these jobs that may be most important. This was more explicitly recognized by Lepak and Snell's (1999) HR Architecture that articulated a framework for understanding which jobs were most critical. Thus, future research needs to (a) identify the key job(s) within the firm and (b) focus on the HR practices covering those jobs.

Third, identifying the key jobs will likely entail understanding the core capabilities that the firm is attempting to create or exploit. Differing customer strategies require different capabilities within the firm's value chain, and understanding the key capabilities will lead to better identifying the most critical jobs.

Finally, this leads to a more specific set of tools for tying HR to strategy. Past attempts have usually assessed overall HR practices within the firm and sought to see if those practices "fit" with the firm's strategy to determine performance (c.f., Huselid, 1995). However, a more realistic approach suggests that the key to fit is through understanding the core capabilities inherent in implementing the strategies, and the core jobs within those capabilities, and then focusing an effective set of HR practices to maximize the performance of individuals in those key jobs. Thus, alignment of HR and strategy will best be understood in the context of capabilities, and not global fit with strategy.

References

Amit, R. and Schoemaker, P.J.H. 1993. Strategic assets and organizational rent. *Strategic Management Journal*, 14, 33–46.

Appelbaum, E., Bailey, T., Berg, P. and Kallenberg, A.L. 2000. *Manufacturing advantage. Why high-performance work systems pay off*. New York: Cornell University Press.

Barney, J. 1991. Firm resources and sustained competitive advantage. *Journal of Management*, 17(1), 99.

Becker, B. and Gerhart, B. 1996. The impact of human resource management on organizational performance: Progress and prospects. *Academy of Management Journal*, 39(4), 779.

Becker, B.E. and Huselid, M.A. 1998. High performance work systems and firm performance: A synthesis of research and managerial implications. *Research in Personnel and Human Resource Management*, 16, 53–101.

Becker, B. and Huselid, M. 2006. Strategic Human Resources Management: Where do we go from here? *Journal of Management*, 32(6), 898–925.

Boselie, P., Dietz, G. and Boon, C. 2005. Commonalities and contradictions in HRM and performance research. *Human Resource Management Journal*, 15, 67–94.

Capelli, P. and Singh, H. 1992. Integrating strategic human resources and strategic management. In D. Lewin, O.S. Mitchell and P.D. Sherer (Eds), *Research frontiers in industrial relations and human resources* (pp. 165–192). Madison, WI: IRRA.

Combs, J., Ketchen, D., Jr., Hall, A. and Liu, Y. 2006. Do high performance work practices matter? A meta-analysis of their effects on organizatonal performance. *Personnel Psychology*, 59, 501–28.

Datta, D., Guthrie, J. and Wright, P. 2005. Industry as a moderator of the HR–firm performance relationship. *Academy of Management Journal*, 48(1), 135–45.

Delery, J.E. 1998. Issues of fit in strategic human resource management: Implications for research. *Human Resource Management Review*, 8(3), 289.

Delery, J.E. and Doty, D.H. 1996. Modes of theorizing in strategic human resource management: Tests of universalistic, contingency, and configurational performance predictions. *Academy of Management Journal*, 39, 802–35.

Delery, J. and Shaw, J. 2001. The strategic management of people in work organizations: Review, synthesis, and extension. *Research in Personnel and Human Resources Management*, 20, 165–97.

Dell, M. and Fredman, C. 1999. *Direct from Dell: Strategies that revolutionized an industry*. New York: John Wiley.

Dierickx, I. and Cool, K. 1989. Asset stock accumulation and sustainability of competitive advantage. *Management Science*, 35, 1504–11.

Dyer, L. and Holder, G. 1988. A strategic perspective of human resources management. In L. Dyer and G. Holder (Eds), *Human Resources Management: Evolving roles and responsibilities*. Washington, DC: American Society for Personnel Administration.

Eisenhardt, K. and Martin, J. 2000. Dynamic capabilities: What are they? *Strategic Management Journal*, 21, 1105–21.

Guthrie, J. 2001. High involvement work practices, turnover, and productivity: Evidence from New Zealand. *Academy of Management Journal*, 44, 180–92.

Hatch, N. and Dyer, J. 2004. Human capital and learning as a source of sustainable competitive advantage. *Strategic Management Journal*, 25, 1155–78.

Hitt, M., Bierman, L., Shimizu, K. and Kochar, R. 2001. Direct and moderating effects of human capital on the strategy and performance in professional service firms: A resource-based perspective. *Academy of Management Journal*, 44, 13–28.

Huselid, M.A. 1995. The impact of human resource management practices on turnover, productivity, and corporate financial performance. *Academy of Management Journal*, 38, 635–72.

Lado, A.A. and Wilson, M.C. 1994. Human resource systems and sustained competitive advantage: A competency-based perspective. *Academy of Management Review*, 19(4), 699–727.

Lepak, D.P. and Snell, S.A. 1999. The human resource architecture: Toward a theory of human capital development and allocation. *Academy of Management Review*, 24(1), 31–48.

Lepak, D.P. and Snell, S.A. 2002. Examining the human resource architecture: The relationships among human capital, employment, and human resource configurations. *Journal of Management*, 28(4), 517–43.

Lepak, D.P. and Snell, S.A. 2004. Managing the human resource architecture for knowledge-based competition. In S. Jackson, M. Hitt and A. DeNisi (Eds), *Managing knowledge for sustained competitive advantage: Designing strategies for effective Human Resource Management*, SIOP Scientific Frontiers Series, (pp. 127–54). San Francisco: Jossey-Bass.

Lepak, D.P., Takeuchi, R. and Snell, S.A. 2003. Employment flexibility and firm performance: Examining the moderating effects of employment mode, environmental dynamism, and technological intensity. *Journal of Management*, 29(5), 681–705.

MacDuffie, J.P. 1995. Human resource bundles and manufacturing performance: Organizational logic and flexible systems in the world auto industry. *Industrial and Labor Relations Review*, 48, 197–221.

Mahoney, J. and Pandian, J. 1992. Resource-based view within the conversation of strategic management. *Strategic Management Journal*, 13, 363–80.

Miles, R. and Snow, C. 1994. *Fit, failure, and the Hall of Fame*. New York: Free Press.

Milliman, J., Von Glinow, M. and Nathan, M. 1991. Organizational life cycles and strategic international human resource management in multinational companies. *Academy of Management Review*, 16, 318–39.

Newbert, S. 2007. Empirical research on the resource-based view of the firm: An assessment and suggestions for future research. *Strategic Management Journal*, 28(2), 121–46.

Penrose, E. 1959. *A theory of the growth of the firm*. Oxford: Oxford University Press.

Peteraf, M. 1993. The cornerstones of competitive advantage: A resource-based view. *Strategic Management Journal*, 14, 179–91.

Porter, M. 1996. What is strategy? *Harvard Business Review*, 74, 61–78.

Prahalad, C.K. and Hamel, G. 1990. The core competence of the corporation. *Harvard Business Review*, 68(3), 79–91.

Priem, R.L. and Butler, J.E. 2001. Tautology in the resource-based view and the implications of externally determined resource value: Further comments. *Academy of Management Review*, 26, 57–66.

Ray, G., Barney, J. and Muhanna, W. 2004. Capabilities, business processes, and competitive advantage: Choosing the dependent variable in empirical tests of the resource based view. *Strategic Management Journal*, 25, 23–37.

Rubin, P. 1973. The expansion of firms. *Journal of Political Economy*, 84, 936–49.

Schuler, R.S. and Jackson, S.E. 1987. Linking competitive strategies with human resource management practices. *Academy of Management Executive*, 1(3), 207–19.

Sherer, P.D. 1995. Leveraging human assets in law firms: Human capital structures and organizational capability. *Industrial and Labor Relations Review*, 48: 671–91.

Snell, S.A. 1992. A test of control theory in strategic human resource management: The mediating effect of administrative information. *Academy of Management Journal*, 35(2), 292–327.

Snell, S.A. and Youndt, M.A. 1995. Human resource management and firm performance: Testing a contingency model of executive controls. *Journal of Management*, 21(4), 711–37.

Teece, D. and Pisano, G. 1994. The dynamic capabilities of firms: An introduction. *Industrial and Corporate Change*, 3(3), 537–56.

Teece, D.J., Pisano, G. and Shuen, A. 1997. Dynamic capabilities and strategic management. *Strategic Management Journal*, 18(7), 509–33.

Wernerfelt, B. 1984. A resource-based view of the firm. *Strategic Management Journal*, 5(2), 171–80.

Wright, P.M. and Snell, S.A. 1991. Toward an integrated view of strategic human resource management. *Human Resource Management Review*, 1, 203–25.

Wright, P.M. and Snell, S.A. 1998. Toward a unifying framework for exploring fit and flexibility in strategic human resource management. *Academy of Management Review*, 23, 756–72.

Wright, P.M., Dunford, B.B. and Snell, S.A. 2001. Human resources and the resource based view of the firm. *Journal of Management*, 27, 701–21.

Wright, P.M., Gardner, T.M. and Moynihan, L.M. 2003. The impact of HR practices on the performance of business. *Human Resource Management Journal*, 13, 21–36.

Wright, P.M., McMahan, G.C. and McWilliams, A. 1994. Human resources as a source of sustained competitive advantage: A resource-based perspective. *International Journal of Human Resource Management*, 5, 301–26.

Wright, P.M., Smart, D.L. and McMahan, G.C. 1995. Matches between human resources and strategy among NCAA basketball teams. *Academy of Management Journal*, 38, 1052–74.

Wright, P.M., Gardner, T.M., Moynihan, L.M. and Allen, M.R. 2005. The relationship between HR practices and firm performance: Examining causal order. *Personnel Psychology*, 58, 409–46.

10

Linking human resource management and customer outcomes

David E. Bowen and S. Douglas Pugh

Linking human resource management and customer outcomes

How do a firm's human resource management (HRM) practices affect customer outcomes? We answer this question by examining the linkages across business strategy, employees' perceptions of their human resource management practices, the organizational climates that are shaped considerably by these HRM perceptions, and customer outcomes such as satisfaction, quality perceptions, loyalty, and even profitability.

Consistent with a *strategic* human resource management (SHRM) perspective, the links in the chain begin with business strategy, i.e. leadership's crafted formula for how to win in the marketplace (see Figure 10.1). A common premise of SHRM is that organizations must horizontally align their HRM practices toward their strategic goal and that practices must complement one another for successful strategy implementation (e.g. Schuler & Jackson 1987; Wright & Snell 1991). To drive the remaining linkages, it is essential that HRM professionals can deliver an "HR value proposition" (Ulrich & Brockbank 2005) for each of its key stakeholders – employees, managers, customers, and shareholders. Value is delivered when the work of HRM professionals helps those stakeholders reach their goals, e.g. contribute positively to employee and customer satisfaction. In order for HRM to be of value to customers, HRM professionals must begin with a line of sight to the marketplace (Ulrich & Brockbank 2005), a prerequisite for becoming a true strategic partner.

Despite widespread acceptance that HRM contributes to firm performance, the question has remained as to what "intermediate linkages" drive the connection (Ferris et al. 1998: 394). We describe how an organization's practices, particularly HRM, can create "strong climates" (Bowen & Ostroff 2004; Schneider et al. 2002) which clearly signal to employees what strategic goals are important and how they are expected to behave consistently with them.[1] In turn, we draw upon the growing body of "linkage research," pioneered and continued by Schneider and his colleagues (e.g., Schneider et al. 1980; Schneider & Bowen 1985; Schneider et al. 2005), and also popularly known in the form of the "service profit chain" (Heskett et al. 1997), which reveals that what employees experience in their work worlds is associated with the experiences they provide for customers, and that these experiences translate into important customer outcomes (see Pugh et al. (2002), Schneider & White (2004) for reviews), even linking to profitability.

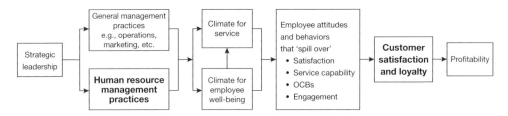

Figure 10.1 A model linking HRM practices and customer outcomes in services

We begin by describing the forces that have contributed to HRM professionals taking customer linkages more seriously. Next, we overview the emergence of thinking and research on the linkages between employee perceptions of their workworld and customer outcomes, and the role of HRM practices in creating those linkages. Then we describe our linkage model (Figure 10.1). The focus is on *service* employees and customers since that is where most linkage research has been conducted. However, this is still a broad focus, since 80 percent of U.S. employees are employed in the service sector (Ford & Bowen, 2008). Additionally, numerous "goods-producing" firms have been increasingly shifting to a services emphasis, with GE generating 70 percent of its revenues from services and IBM 50 percent, as just two examples. Our discussion will also highlight some of the HRM practices in selection, training, and so on, that appear to link to customer satisfaction.

We close by summarizing how HRM needs to be managed strategically, contingently, scientifically, and cross-functionally in order to best link HRM practices and customer outcomes. The discussion throughout is based upon a mix of theory, research and applied examples – the mix we think should guide both HR professionals and scholars as they attempt to understand and manage the HRM–customer relationship.

Assessing management practices from a *customer* perspective

Organizational/management scholars have a long history of failing to examine organizational dynamics and even outcomes through the eyes of customers. This lack of attention to customer outcomes was well captured by Danet (1981) years back when she observed that organization theorists have viewed organizations from the top looking down (management's perspective) and the inside looking around (employees' perspective) but rarely from the outside looking in (which would include the customer's perspective). The customer's absence in the management field is still largely true today, as indicated by how seldom the "customer" appears in management and organizational behavior textbooks and journal articles in our field (Ford & Bowen, 2008).

These general conclusions about not viewing management practices from the customers' perspective have been true of HRM practices, historically, as well. As Schneider (1994) observed, HRM has tended to adhere to an industrial revolution-oriented model with an almost exclusive focus on performance against internally set and internally relevant standards. Effectiveness criteria for HRM practices such as selection have been dominated by internal standards such as employee attendance or number of products and services produced, not against external standards such as customer perceptions of quality.

Forces that encourage a customer focus in HRM

The TQM Movement

In 1987, Congress established the Malcolm Baldridge Quality Award which energized the advancement of the Total Quality Management Movement (TQM). The first and foremost principle of TQM is customer focus; that the central objective of a firm's management practices, such as HRM, to improve quality, is to satisfy customers. The primary endgame of TQM was to improve quality for external customers, but TQM practices were also to be applied to internal customers, such as line managers, and employees.

In short, TQM helped foster thinking and practice about the linkages between internal management practices and customer outcomes. Indeed, TQM proponents advocated viewing organizations not as closed, self-contained systems, but instead as open systems (Bowen & Waldman 1999) not unlike the idea of boundaryless organizations (Ashkenas et al. 1995). This more open view, inclusive of the customer, has been reinforced with the advent of multidimensional assessments of effectiveness such as the "Balanced Scorecard" (Kaplan & Norton 1992).

An emphasis on "customer literacy" in HR professionals

To be able to "score" well on customer criteria, HRM professionals must possess "customer literacy" (Ulrich & Brockbank 2005). This starts with HR professionals really knowing their organization's customers and their buying criteria. They must have their target customers clearly in mind, and what valued and unique benefits they hope to obtain. What bundle of low-cost, personalized service, innovation, product features, etc. drives customer attraction and retention? Only if HRM professionals are customer literate can they then effectively work through the process of specifying the employee behaviors necessary to deliver those benefits, and the HRM practices necessary to enable and reward those behaviors. The goal is to build a strong linkage between the HRM value proposition and the customers' value proposition (Ulrich & Brockbank 2005).

The growth of services

Many services are still labor intensive in their delivery and often that delivery occurs in real-time encounters with customers. Consequently, employees are often close to their customers, both physically and psychologically (Parkington & Schneider 1979) which allows the organization's climate to "show" not only to employees, but to customers as well (Schneider et al. 1980). HRM practices shape organizational climates that employees perceive as customer-oriented, or not.

Real-time encounters between employees and customers means that quality control cannot be exercised via supervision that can "stop production" in-progress or error detection techniques that can remove defects even before they reach the consumer. Instead, in services, quality control is very much a HRM activity (Bowen & Schneider 1988). HRM activities help get the right people in place and make sure they have the appropriate skills via selection and training. Service and sales reps out in the field with customers cannot be subject to direct, personal supervision; quality control must come from HRM practices in hiring and training.

The rise of an employee branding perspective

Employee branding is the process by which employees internalize the desired brand image and are motivated to project that image to customers and other stakeholders (Miles & Mangold

2004). Brand image refers to the conceptualization that an organization wants its customers to have of it – the set of benefits that customers would obtain by doing business with the company. A number of authors have recently positioned employees as the "living brand" (Bendapudi and Bendapudi 2005) or focused on "employee branding" (Miles & Mangold 2004) with the message of generating a bond between the employees and the brand, which in turn forges loyalty between customers and the brand and company. This requires that the firm sends many messages to employees that embed the meaning and core values of the brand within employees. HRM practices that signal the company's priorities and competitive positioning are an important source. Companies that have been mentioned as effective in doing so include the typical service role models such as Southwest Airlines and Ritz-Carlton, but employee branding has also been described in other firms such QuikTrip and Wawa-run convenience stores.

The emergence of research on the linkages between how employees experience their workplace and customer outcomes

The conceptual and empirical origins of what would become linkage research, as labeled by Wiley (1996), are to be found some 25 years ago when Schneider, Parkington and Buxton (1980) asked front-line bank employees about a number of aspects of organizational functioning, such as personnel support, managerial functions, and equipment support, that had emerged from interviews with employees as suggesting to them that service in the bank branch was important. They found that what front-line employees in bank branches reported about service climate predicted with statistically significant accuracy the satisfaction of the customers at the branches. The relationships between the employee service climate dimensions and customer perceptions of service quality suggested that the things employees experienced in the workplace (for example, a lack of management support of service delivery) impacts customers' service experiences.

The 1980 results were then replicated and extended by Schneider and Bowen (1985) who found that dimensions of customer perceptions of service quality were positively related to employees' perceptions of a number of HRM dimensions. They concluded that service organizations in which employees have positive perceptions of human resource practices will be those in which employees can devote their energies to serving customers. That is, when employees perceive that their organization uses rewards to let them know when they have done good work, creates work conditions that facilitate their ability to perform, helps them with career progression, provides orientation and training for new assignments, and the like – i.e., their own needs have been met – they are then more able to concentrate on meeting the needs of their customers – what the authors labeled a "spillover effect." In sum, the same set of human resource management practices helped satisfy two stakeholders, employees and customers, essentially linking the "value propositions" of both.

Building upon this, the "service-profit chain" further developed the organizational practices that forge these employee–customer linkages and extended them to their economic consequences (Heskett et al. 1994; Heskett et al. 1997) In the service profit chain, customers' service experiences are linked directly to employees, specifically, employee productivity, which is in turn affected by employees' service capability. Service capability is an employee's ability, authority, and latitude to meet customer needs. Employee satisfaction and loyalty drive service capability, and satisfaction are determined by a number of factors all related to the internal quality of work-life employees experience. The front-end of the chain begins with the operating strategy and service delivery system (also labeled "internal service quality"), which includes HRM elements such as job design, decision-making latitude, selection and development, rewards and recognition, and providing training so that employees have the tools to serve customers. These HRM elements contribute to employee service capability and, ultimately, customer satisfaction and organizational performance. Additional research has repeatedly confirmed that HRM practices help frame climate perceptions and how, in turn, employees then relate to customers (Pugh et al. 2002; Rogg et al. 2001).

Disney theme parks are a good applied and well-known example of such a chain in practice. First, Disney invests considerable energy in selecting the right person for the job even for their part-time park employees. By "right," this refers to particular characteristics of education, physical features, grooming, and appearance (physically fit, attractive, conservatively groomed college students). Second, they invest in training. While some of this training involves technical aspects of the job, a very large part involves teaching the norms, language, roles, and scripted emotional expressions necessary to produce an outstanding experience for the customer (Van Maanen 1991). As a service, Disney is fundamentally selling an experience to customers, and that experience cannot be controlled and monitored by management as could the production of a car or TV set. The shape of the experience is largely at the discretion of the employees, and the climate and culture of Disney shape the employee behaviors.

As the Disney example illustrates, the experiences employees are having at work are going to show to the customers with whom they interact. We now cover this in more depth in our linkage model that follows.

A model of the linkages between HRM practices and customer outcomes

Strategic leadership

As shown in Figure 10.1, which builds upon the preceding linkage research, our model begins with strategic leadership from the top, but also leadership *throughout* the organization. Recalling our discussion of "customer literacy," what is the customer's value proposition? How can the firm link to that in crafting its hoped-for winning formula in the marketplace? The answers to these strategic leadership questions should then drive efforts through HRM practices to create "strong" organizational climates, in which employees *share* an understanding of strategic goals and what is expected of them.

These statements about building the linkage between strategy and organizational climates in which employees have shared perceptions is only prescriptive! Often, employees are not as clear on these linkages as management assumes. In fact, one of the key assumptions of linkage research is that if you want to find out how the strategy is working in *reality*, not theory, ask front-line employees, e.g., climate surveys and their perceptions of customer outcomes, to discover how the strategy is really playing out (Macey & Schneider 2006).

Management practices and climate formation: the "strength" of the HRM system

Employees form climate perceptions from how they see the organization carrying out its day-to-day business, and the goals the organizations appear to be pursuing (Schneider & White 2004). Employee perceptions of management practices, both general and HRM-focused, are important.

The "strength" of the HRM system is a critical factor in determining whether strong organizational climates are created that signal to employees what is important to management, and rewarded in the organization (Bowen & Ostroff 2004). This refers to the characteristics of how HRM practices operate as an overall *system*. HRM strength is found in system characteristics such as: "agreement among principal HRM decision makers" as to the strategic HRM message to convey; "consistent HRM messages," e.g., practices that all send the same strategic signal; "validity," practices that accomplish what they are supposed to; and "instrumentality," employees see favorable consequences, a compelling value proposition, for behaving consistent with signals. HRM practices, in the form of a "strong" HRM system, together with other management practices, influence the creation of two interrelated organizational climates relevant to customer outcomes.

Climate for service

Organizational climate is typically conceptualized, and managed, around a specific strategic objective, e.g., innovation, safety, service, as opposed to its being treated as a set of shared employee perceptions of management practices, in general (e.g., Schneider 2000). That is, there is a climate *for* some type of strategic referent, as opposed to climate as some generic, global shared set of employee perceptions. Our focus is on the *climate for service* (which, itself, can assume different climate *for* refinements, depending upon the customers' value propositions) referring to employees' shared perceptions of the practices, procedures, and behaviors that are rewarded, supported, and expected by the organization with regard to customer service and customer service quality (Schneider et al. 1998). When employees perceive an abundance of cues from a setting's management practices that highlight service quality, they are experiencing a climate for service.

What general management practices can contribute to a climate for service? As one example, Schneider and Bowen (1985) found that a climate for service emerged via management practices in the areas of: (a) logistics, e.g., the availability of equipment, supplies, tools to deliver service; (b) systems support, e.g., marketing, operations, etc.; (c) efforts to retain customers; and (d) general managerial behavior, such as planning, coordinating, and establishing goals and routines to serve customers. Later work has focused on similar themes; for example, Schneider et al. (1998) found that work facilitation and inter-departmental service directly contributed to overall service climate, and Johnson (1996) found that information seeking, training, and rewards and recognition were the major themes that contributed to service climate and, through climate, to customer satisfaction.

Climate for employee well-being

Managers in pursuit of service quality and customer satisfaction need to create two different, but interrelated climates: a climate for service and also a climate for employee well-being, which is a climate focused on meeting the needs of employees (Schneider & Bowen 1993). As indicated by the arrow upward from climate for well-being to climate for service, the climate for employee well-being is an important foundation on which a climate for service can be built. Employees need to feel that their own needs have been met before they can truly focus on meeting the needs of others, e.g., customers. Similar findings have been shown by Borucki and Burke (1999), who found that employee climate perceptions could be classified into two categories: management concern for customers (equivalent to service climate) and concern for employees (equivalent to climate for well-being). *Both* of these climates contributed to sales personnel service performance.

These two climates are interrelated. Work facilitation, assessed as an HRM dimension in Schneider and Bowen (1985), is a dimension that also correlated significantly with climate for service. Although interrelated, it is important to state again that they are still different – they are only moderately intercorrelated, and emerge as distinct factors (Borucki & Burke 1999). As such, they involve different organizational dynamics, and both climates are necessary to fully drive subsequent linkages toward customer outcomes. HRM professionals must design practices to support employees both in their general roles as organizational members as well as in their specific roles as service providers.

HRM practices that link to climate for service and customer outcomes

The HRM practices we highlight next are those that have demonstrated some effectiveness in influencing customer satisfaction. Again, the "validity" of HRM practices contributes to the strength of the HRM system and its ability to create a strong climate. Here are some approaches to various HRM practices that appear to send all the right "signals" about a climate for service and create the service capabilities necessary to satisfy customers.

Selection

Heskett and colleagues (1997) stress that the best service companies hire for attitudes, not skills. More fully, the focus should be on hiring for positive attitudes toward customer service, with training complementing this hiring. Recent research suggests that this attitude can be measured effectively through personality-based measures of customer orientation (Frei & McDaniel 1998; Ones & Viswesraran 2001; Ones et al. 2005). Ones and colleagues have described customer orientation as a compound personality trait, containing elements of the "Big 5" personality factors. Most important, they have shown that customer orientation significantly predicts not only managerial ratings of performance, but also other dimensions of performance including counterproductive workplace behavior. Moreover, customer orientation measures add incremental validity beyond the effects of cognitive ability.

Another aspect of service-oriented selection has become known as the preferred employer in an industry – which builds a more favorable selection ratio to find those employees who fit well the needs of the targeted market segment. As Zeithaml, Bitner and Gremler (2006) report, Rosenbluth International, a corporate travel agency, has acquired such a reputation, likely owing to President Hal Rosenbluth's philosophy, "We don't believe the customer can come first unless our people come first. If our people don't come first, then they're not free to focus on our clients; they are worried about other kinds of things." This point of view reinforces another service management maxim "Treat Your Employees the Way You Would Like Them to Treat Customers."

Another approach that builds linkages is found at Southwest Airlines which often includes frequent flying customers as part of the interviewer panel screening applicants for flight attendant positions. Strategically, Southwest strives to differentiate itself in the marketplace by being a fast, fun, and loving airline. Customers have the best sense of what that competitive edge looks like in flight attendant behavior, so they are afforded a voice in hiring. And this certainly also leverages customer loyalty to the airline.

Employee performance measurement

"What gets measured gets done," so it would seem that having customers provide feedback on employee performance would inform management whether employees are living the brand

and whether the climate for a particular type of service is strong enough to influence desired employee behaviors. Customers, then, could be included as raters in a 360-degree appraisal process (Waldman & Bowen 1998). Given employee concerns about the validity of surprise customer appraisals, one middle course used with some frequency is to alert both employees and customers that the service encounter is being monitored, e.g., "being recorded for quality purposes" (Schneider & White 2004).

Customers could be allowed to view the employee appraisal form to see if the behaviors and outcomes align with their own expectations (Ulrich & Brockbank 2005). Also, customer and service quality criteria should be included upward through the organization, from supervisors to senior managers. Sometimes there is a tendency to emphasize customer care criteria only for front-line employees (Schneider et al. 2005b).

Training

Training can deliver value to both employees and customers. Salanova et al. (2005), for example, found that training impacted service climate directly, and also had an impact on employee engagement. Liao and Chuang (2004) found in a sample of 25 restaurants that manager rankings of the extent to which service-related elements were emphasized in training (e.g., providing quick service, introducing customers to menu items and ingredients, being sensitive to customers' individual needs and wants) were significantly associated with employee perceptions of service climate. Again, employees form perceptions of what is important to the organization based on the signals they receive in training.

General Electric links employee and customer value propositions by inviting certain customers to attend training programs being run at Crotonville – for employees (Ulrich & Brockbank 2005). For example, leadership development programs on change management may include both executives and customer representatives, leveraging HRM practices to create strategic unity between otherwise internal and external stakeholders.

Employee reports about what they know of customer perceptions, attitudes, preferences, and the like should help frame the content of training programs. Linkage surveys can be used to ask employees where they need the development of skills and abilities to better serve customers, and the connections between these responses and customer outcomes suggest that employees can accurately identify training needs (Schneider & White 2004). And this customer-driven training content should be used in training and development throughout organizational levels, not just at the front-line (Schneider et al. 2005a).

Finally, this closeness between employees suggests that employees need to be trained in the skills necessary to perform "emotional labor" – i.e., how to deal with the ongoing press of customer demands and angry customers. Many training programs still focus on technical or interpersonal skills necessary to be effective with other *internal* members of the organization.

Rewards and recognition

Service climate is defined as perceptions of what is *rewarded*, supported, and expected with regard to service delivery, and as such, reward systems are powerful communications of what is important to management. If management says that quality service is important, but rewards quantity over quality, employee service climate perceptions will reflect what behaviors are actually rewarded, not what behaviors management says are important. Unfortunately, the "folly of rewarding A, while hoping for B" (Kerr 1975) appears to be a common malady in services.

162

Many leading companies tie aspects of compensation to customer satisfaction metrics. For example, at PeopleSoft, the performance evaluations of account managers are based on customer satisfaction and customers' ability to use the company's software (Webber & Row 1997). Johnson (1996) found that employee perceptions that the organization rewarded and recognized employees who provide superior service and take a personal interest in solving customer problems contributed significantly to service climate, and this dimension was strongly related to customer satisfaction.

Another example is offering customers the opportunity to reward employees whom they view as deserving. At least one airline provides some of its best, frequent-flying customers $50 coupons on which they can write an employee's name, sign it, and return it to be given to the employee (Ulrich & Brockbank 2005).

Employee empowerment

Empowerment is often recommended as an effective management practice for delivering service quality and satisfying customers. Empowerment has been defined as sharing with employees: more decision-making power and autonomy; information on strategy, business plans, competitor information, customer data; skills and knowledge via training in under-standing business information, effective teamwork skills, customer complaint management; and rewards based upon performance (Bowen & Lawler 1992, 1995). Empowerment, then, requires more of an HRM investment in employees than the low-cost, production-line approach to service delivery as found in fast-food, convenience stores, in which customer expectations are simple and stable, and technology is routine. The added HRM investment from empowering employees delivers a return with more complex services in less predictable environments such as airline travel and consulting.

Seeking customer information for the design of HRM practices

Many of the HRM practices we have mentioned require seeking out information from customers and feeding that information back to employees. A highly consistent finding across linkage research is that organizations which develop strong service climates and deliver excellent customer service actively seek out information about customers *and* relate that information back to employees.

Unfortunately, customer data are often overcollected and underutilized (Schneider & Bowen 1995). Many organizations collect customer information, but the act of providing that information to employees to enhance service performance communicates the importance of service delivery to top management. Unfortunately, the task of collecting and using customer information is often associated with units or functions in the organization other than Human Resources, but it should not be. HR *should* have a role in the strategic management of this information because of its powerful signaling function in the design of HRM practices.

Linking climate and customer outcomes: the spillover effect

Of the many possible employee attitudes and behaviors that might spill over to affect customer outcomes, the most frequently mentioned are employee satisfaction and service capability-based behaviors (from the service-profit chain). We will focus on two others that are more recent in receiving attention. One is a set of behaviors, organizational citizenship behaviors (OCBs), including employee displays of altruism, courtesy, sportsmanship, conscientiousness, and civic virtue that can enhance customer satisfaction and loyalty. The other is employee engagement.

163

Organizational citizenship behaviors

When employees are treated fairly, they, in turn, are more likely to display organizational citizenship behaviors (OCBs) toward customers, resulting in their satisfaction (Bowen et al. 1999; Masterson 2001; Maxham & Netemeyer 2003). Fair treatment of employees can consist of many aspects, such as supervisor displays of interactional fairness, e.g., communicating respectfully with employees, that can drive employee displays of OCBs (Cropanzano et al. 2007). Fair treatment can also be evidenced by HRM practices which employees perceive as fair. The idea that employees evaluate HRM practices is based on a "user reactions" perspective on HR, which advocates that *internal* customer satisfaction, i.e., employees' own evaluation of how they feel treated by HRM practices, should be included among technical criteria, such as reliability and validity that dominate assessments of HR effectiveness (Cardy & Dobbins 1994; Gilliland 1993). Examples of fair HRM would include designing and conducting performance appraisals with input from employees and communicating ratings to employees in a timely manner; in rewards, setting salaries internally equitably among employees in the organization and, if any inequities are necessary, explaining why to employees.

Employee engagement

A recent perspective that is generating great enthusiasm in the academic and applied literatures and in practice is employee engagement (Harter et al. 2002; Macey & Schneider, 2008; Salanova et al. 2005; Schneider et al. 2005). Engagement moves beyond traditional ideas of job satisfaction in that it has a strong affective tone suggesting passion for the work and organization, involvement of the self, absorption in the work, and a high degree of energy. Unique to the idea of engagement is vigor: feelings of physical strength, cognitive liveliness, and emotional energy that employees tie directly to the work and workplace (Shirom 2003). Engaged employees also demonstrate behaviors including organizational citizenship, role expansion, and initiative, all of which serve organizational goals (Macey & Schneider 2008).

As a newer construct, there is debate over engagement as to where it fits into a linkage model connecting the organization, employees, and customers (see Macey & Schneider, 2008), but research leaves little doubt that engagement affects outcomes important to the organization (Harter et al. 2002; Salanova et al. 2005). Salanova et al. (2005), for example, view engagement as a motivational state that is directly influenced by organizational resources. They developed their measure of organizational resources through a grounded theory method of front-line service employees, and identified three categories with direct bearing on HRM issues: training, job autonomy, and technology. In their model, engagement, along with organizational resources, predict service climate, and service climate directly impacts employee performance as rated by customers. As such, engagement is cast by Salanova and colleagues as similar to the foundation issues (Schneider et al. 1998) that need to be present for a climate for service to develop. What does seem clear from the research is that engagement attitudes and behaviors begin with an organization that provides resources and leadership, and these behaviors spill over to customers, affecting employee perceptions of the quality of service provided and customer loyalty (Salanova et al. 2005). Harter and colleagues (2003), for example, report that in a study of more than 7,000 business units, there was a mean difference of 2.9 percent in ratings of customer loyalty between those units in the lowest quartile on employee engagement and the units in the highest quartile. The revenue impact of that 2.9 percent difference between units with lower and higher levels of employee engagement will of course depend on factors such as the type of service, size of business unit, and sales per customer, but the impact of a 2.9 percent gain in customer loyalty is probably substantial for many service organizations.

Customer outcomes . . . and profitability

It is now very well established in the literature that an organization's service climate matters: it is related to various indicators of customer attitudes including customer satisfaction, perceptions of service quality, ratings of service employee performance, and customer loyalty (see Pugh et al. (2002) for a review). Most service climate research studies end the story there, using research in marketing and consumer behavior to make the point that these customer outcomes matter because they, particularly customer loyalty, ultimately have a positive impact on organizational profitability. This is a compelling argument because the evidence is indeed there that customer satisfaction drives customer loyalty and ultimately organizational profitability (Heskett et al. 1997). But, it is interesting that the body of research tying service climate to organizational financial performance is relatively sparse (note, however, that there is a larger body of linkage research tying more general attitudes such as employee satisfaction or morale, rather than service climate, to organizational financial performance, e.g., Harter et al. 2002).

The linkage between customer satisfaction and financial performance is complex, to say the least. Although there are a few studies linking service climate to organizational financial performance (e.g., Borucki & Burke 1999; Schneider et al. (2005) on unit sales) there are other studies showing counterintuitive negative relationships between employee and customer perceptions and financial performance (Wiley 1996). Busy stores, for example, may often perform financially well but have lower customer satisfaction. What we are best able to conclude, however, is that service climate impacts customer satisfaction, and to the extent customer satisfaction is important to an organization, service climate is a lever that can be used to influence it with favorable returns on organizational performance, across various measures and time.

Final thoughts on linking HRM and customer outcomes

We close with four overarching perspectives on how to manage the relationship between HRM practices and customer outcomes. Connecting to customer outcomes is leveraged in these four areas.

Strategically

Sharpen strategic focus

One message that sometimes comes out of the strategic HRM literature is simply that organizations should "do HRM better" (Schneider & White 2004). That is, the advice is rather generic: good organizations do a good job at strategically selecting, training, and rewarding. But with HRM being *strategic*, it suggests that some HRM practices should be better suited to particular organizational purposes than others. In order for climate for service to set in motion the strongest linkages to employee behavior and customer outcomes, the strategic focus should be sharpened from just generic service to a more market-segmented climate for certain types of service. For example, a low-cost business strategy geared to customer expectations of low-frill, standardized service offerings at a Red Roof Inn obviously requires a different mix of HRM practices to create a climate for that type of service versus that of a Four Seasons. An obvious point, perhaps, but one that should not obscure the less obvious notion of strategically designing internal HRM practices to focus on *your* customers' value proposition.

165

Compete on intangibles

HRM professionals and HRM practices can help build organizational climates and shape employee behaviors that customers view as valuable and rare, and competitors view as difficult to copy. This is the *sustainable* competitive advantage of the pantheon of service role models such as Southwest Airlines, Toyota and Lexus dealerships, and Four Seasons hotels around the world. HRM can build *relationships* within the firm, and between the firm and its customers, built on emotional ties, trust, and fairness linking to customer loyalty and even profits (Bowen et al. 1999; Ulrich & Brockbank 2005).

Create high-performing customers as a competitive advantage

Involve customers as partners in designing and co-producing the services they consume; stay involved with them in the ongoing co-creation of value. Customers help co-produce many services from simple examples of ATM or online banking to business-to-business examples of business customers helping to co-design, operate, and maintain information systems with firms such as EDS. To accomplish this is difficult, and thus difficult for competitors to copy. To do so, firms must work with their customers as important human resources of the firm (Bettencourt et al. 2002; Bowen 1986; Tax et al. 2006). Creating high-performance customers requires selecting customers to work with who possess the necessary competencies, training them in how to perform as expected, and rewarding them for doing so.

Contingently

Determine the conditions under which climate linkages are the strongest

Before HRM professionals dedicate resources to building service climates, they should assess where and when service climate will be strongly linked to customer outcomes. Here are some research-based insights on relevant conditions.

CUSTOMER CONTACT

The core argument in the service climate literature is that service climate is important because of the physical and psychological closeness of employees and customers (Parkington & Schneider 1979). But what of organizations where there is less physical and psychological contact? Increasingly, some organizations are moving to take the human element out of service delivery (e.g., ATMs, kiosks at airports). Where there is less contact, does service climate become less relevant for shaping customer attitudes? A study by Dietz et al. (2004) suggests that the answer is yes. In their study, they found typical positive relationships between service climate and customer satisfaction, but they found that these associations were significantly weaker in bank branches characterized by lower levels of customer contact. This implies that the employees who have the greatest degree of customer contact should be the ones with the best information about customers and the organizational practices that affect them. These employees should be the primary focus of survey efforts.

FREQUENT SHOPPERS

In one study it was found that in a video rental chain, frequent customers valued high-quality service interactions (Kendall & Barker 1999). For these customers, employee perceptions of service climate affected customer satisfaction (these were the customers who expected high-quantity and quality interactions with employees). Low-volume customers (occasional renters), on the other hand, were primarily interested in price, not employee expertise. Their satisfaction was not related to employee attitudes.

STORE PACE

Several studies have shown that when stores are busy, customers expect employees to focus on the core aspects of service delivery, and their expectations for pleasant emotional displays by employees are less (Rafaeli 1989; Rafaeli & Sutton 1990). These authors found that training to increase friendly service at checkout in convenience stores correlated negatively with store profits. Also, in busy retail environments, aggregated employee perceptions of their work environment were more weakly related to customer satisfaction than in more slow-paced environments (Goldberg-Siderman et al., unpublished manuscript).

OTHER BOUNDARY CONDITIONS? DIRECTIONS FOR FUTURE RESEARCH

What are the dynamics and strengths of the linkages among HRM practices, climate, and customer outcomes in firm–customer relationships other than B2C services? For example, certainly, there is psychological closeness in B2B settings between firm reps and firm agents/buyers – how do the linkages operate in such settings? This question has not received serious research attention.

Scientifically

Invest in HRM practices based on data – not on intuition or trend chasing

Linkage research should be used by practitioners to discover the important drivers of customer satisfaction, in their own unique strategic and organizational context (e.g., Macey & Schneider 2006; Wiley & Campbell 2006). These drivers provide valuable information for how to predict and improve customer satisfaction. By validating HRM practices against *external* customer criteria, it becomes possible to make informed choices about which HRM practices to emphasize the most in pursuit of customer satisfaction. Data-driven linkage research searches not just for correlations between HRM practices and customer outcomes, but for the most *important* correlations. For example, which HRM investments, e.g., upgrades to selection or training, will yield the highest return on a variety of customer outcomes of interest? And statistically significant linkage data support reliance upon employees as valid reporters of how customers perceive the "internal" organizational climate and customer perceptions of service quality.

Consider "new" performance data to utilize

Many business performance measures are capital based and, consequently, inadequate for assessing the unique economics of people-businesses (Barber & Strack 2005). These authors emphasize the need to focus on factors such as how employees create value directly for customers. Therefore, economic profit is more appropriately calculated using a people rather than a capital denominator as is used in economic value added (EVA) or cash value added (CVA).

Cross-functionally

Avoid the "HR Trap"

Senior management must not mistakenly think that if they take care of employees, and have the right HRM mix, customer satisfaction will follow – and if it does not, employees are to blame.

Customer satisfaction requires marketing making attractive customer value propositions, management setting reasonable prices, operations creating service delivery systems that allow both employees and customers to accomplish what they are trying to do. Effective service requires a seamless, integrated approach across different organizational functions with which the customer interacts. As a final word, HRM links most fully and positively to customer outcomes when HRM professionals partner with their colleagues in other functions to implement business strategies that create value for stakeholders, both internal *and* external.

Note

1. We should note that there has been some discussion in the academic literature on the differences between the constructs of climate and culture (e.g., Dennison 1996). Climate is generally regarded as the perceptions of organizational imperatives, as captured by what is rewarded, supported, and expected in the organization, whereas culture refers to the "deeper" beliefs and values that underlie these practices. For our purposes, we are focusing mainly on climate – and the HRM practices that shape employees' perceptions of them – but both ideas capture the notion of what is important, valued, and rewarded in the organization.

References

Ashkenas, R., Ulrich, D., Jick, T. & Kerr, S. (1995). *The Boundaryless Organization: Breaking the Chains of Organizational Structure.* San Francisco, CA: Jossey-Bass.
Barber, F. & Strack, R. (2005). The surprising economics of a 'people business'. *Harvard Business Review,* June, 81–90.
Bendapudi, N. & Bendapudi, V. (2005). Creating the living brand. *Harvard Business Review,* May, 1–7.
Bettencourt, L., Ostrom, A.L., Brown, S.W. & Roundtree, R.I. (2002). Client co-production in knowledge intensive business services. *California Management Review,* 44(4), 100–28.
Borucki, C.C. & Burke, M.J. (1999). An examination of service-related antecedents to retail store performance. *Journal of Organizational Behavior,* 20, 943–62.
Bowen, D.E. (1986). Managing customers as human resources in service organizations. *Human Resource Management,* 25, 371–83.
Bowen, D.E. & Lawler, E.E. (1992). Total quality-oriented human resource management. *Organizational Dynamics,* 20, 29–41.
Bowen, D.E. & Lawler, E.E. (1995). Empowering service employees. *Sloane Management Review,* 36, 73–84.
Bowen, D.E. & Ostroff, C. (2004). Understanding HRM–firm performance linkages: The role of 'strength' of the HRM system. *Academy of Management Review,* 29, 203–21.
Bowen, D.E. & Schneider, B. (1988). Services marketing and management: Implications for organizational behavior. *Research in Organizational Behavior,* 10, 43–80.
Bowen, D.E. & Waldman, D.A. (1999). Customer-driven employee performance. In D.R. Ilgen & E.A. Pulakos (Eds), *The Changing Nature of Performance: Implications for Staffing, Motivation, and Development* (pp. 154–91). San Francisco, CA: Jossey-Bass.
Bowen, D.E., Gilliland, S.W. & Folger, R. (1999). HRM and service fairness: How being fair with employees spills over to customers. *Organizational Dynamics,* 27, 7–24.
Cardy, R.L. & Dobbins, G.H. (1994). *Performance Appraisal: Alternative Perspectives.* Cincinnati, OH: South-Western.
Cropanzano, R., Bowen, D.E. & Gilliland, S.W. (2007). The management of organizational justice. *Academy of Management Perspectives,* 21(4), 34–48.
Danet, B. (1981). Client-organization relationships. In P.C. Nystrom & W.H. Starbuck (Eds), *Handbook of Organizational Design* (pp. 382–428). New York: Oxford University Press.

Dennison, D.R. (1996). What is the difference between organizational culture and organizational climate? A native's point of view on a decade of paradigm wars. *Academy of Management Review*, 21, 619–54.

Dietz, J., Pugh, S.D. & Wiley, J.W. (2004). Service climate effects on customer attitudes: An examination of boundary conditions. *Academy of Management Journal*, 47, 81–92.

Ferris, G.R., Arthur, M.M. & Berkson, H.M. (1998). Toward a social context theory of the human resource management–organization effectiveness relationship. *Human Resource Management Review*, 8, 235–64.

Ford, R. & Bowen, D.E. (2008). Service-dominant management education: It's about time. *Academy of Management Learning & Education*, 7, 224–43.

Frei, R.L. & McDaniel, M.A. (1998). Validity of customer service measures in personnel selection: A review of criterion and construct evidence. *Human Performance*, 11, 1–27.

Gilliland, S.W. (1993). The perceived fairness of selection systems: An organizational justice perspective. *Academy of Management Review*, 18, 694–734.

Goldberg-Siderman, L., Grandey, A. & Pugh, S.D. (undated). *Linking Leader Behavior to Employee Attitudes to Customer Service Outcomes: Business-Unit-Level Mechanisms and Constraints*. Unpublished manuscript.

Harter, J.K., Schmidt, F.L. & Hayes, T.L. (2002). Business-unit-level relationship between employee satisfaction, employee engagement, and business outcomes: A meta-analysis. *Journal of Applied Psychology*, 87, 268–79.

Harter, J.K., Schmidt, F.L. & Keyes, C.L. (2003). Well-being in the workplace and its relationship to business outcomes: A review of the Gallup studies. In C.L. Keyes & J. Haidt (Eds), *Flourishing: The Positive Person and the Good Life* (pp. 205–24). Washington, D.C.: American Psychological Association.

Heskett, J.L., Sasser, W.E., Jr. & Schlesinger, L.A. (1997). *The Service Profit Chain*. New York: The Free Press.

Heskett, J.L., Jones, T.O., Loveman, G.W., Sasser, W.E., Jr. & Schlesinger, L.A. (1994). Putting the service–profit chain to work. *Harvard Business Review*, March–April, 164–74.

Johnson, J.W. (1996). Linking employee perceptions of service climate to customer satisfaction. *Personnel Psychology*, 49, 831–51.

Kaplan, R.S. & Norton, D.P. (1992). The balanced scorecard – Measures that drive performance. *Harvard Business Review*, 70(1), 71–9.

Kendall, S.D. & Barker, L. (1999). When does service matter? Linking employee service emphasis to customer satisfaction within heavy, lapsed, and light customer segments. Paper presented as part of a symposium at the 14th Annual Conference of the Society of Industrial and Organizational Psychology, Atlanta, GA.

Kerr, S. (1975). On the folly of rewarding A, while hoping for B. *Academy of Management Journal*, 18, 769–83.

Liao, H. & Chuang, A. (2004). A multilevel investigation of factors influencing employee service performance and customer outcomes. *Academy of Management Journal*, 47, 41–58.

Macey, W.H. & Schneider, B. (2006). Employee experiences and customer satisfaction: Toward a framework for survey design with a focus on service climate. In A.I. Kraut (Ed.), *Getting Action from Organizational Surveys* (pp. 53–75). San Francisco, CA: Jossey-Bass.

Macey, W.H. & Schneider, B. (2008). The meaning of employee engagement. *Industrial and Organizational Psychology: Perspectives on Science and Practice*, 1(1): 3–30.

Masterson, S.S. (2001). A trickle-down model of organizational justice: Relating employees' and customers' perceptions of and reactions to fairness. *Journal of Applied Psychology*, 86, 594–604.

Maxham, J.G. III & Netemeyer, R.G. (2003). Firms reap what they sow: The effects of shared values and perceived organizational justice on customers' evaluations of complaint handling. *Journal of Marketing*, 67, 46–62.

Miles, S.J. & Mangold, G. (2004). A conceptualization of the employee branding process. *Journal of Relationship Marketing*, 3, 65–87.

Ones, D.S. & Viswesvaran, C. (2001). Integrity tests and other criterion-focused occupational personality scales (COPS) used in personnel selection. *International Journal of Selection and Assessment*, 9, 31–39.

Ones, D.S., Viswesvaran, C. & Dilchert, S. (2005). Personality at work: Raising awareness and correcting misconceptions. *Human Performance*, 18, 389–404.

169

Parkington, J.P. & Schneider, B. (1979). Some correlates of experienced job stress: A boundary role study. *Academy of Management Journal*, 22, 270–81.

Pugh, S.D., Dietz, J., Wiley, J.W. & Brooks, S.M. (2002). Driving service effectiveness through employee–customer linkages. *Academy of Management Executive*, 16, 73–84.

Rafaeli, A. (1989). When cashiers meet customers: An analysis of the role of supermarket cashiers. *Academy of Management Journal*, 32, 245–73.

Rafaeli, A. & Sutton, R.I. (1990). Busy stores and demanding customers: How do they affect the display of positive emotion? *Academy of Management Journal*, 33, 623–37.

Rogg, K.L., Schmidt, D.B., Shull, C. & Schmitt, N. (2001). Human resource practices, organizational climate, and customer satisfaction. *Journal of Management*, 27, 431–49.

Salanova, M., Agut, S. & Peiro, J.M. (2005). Linking organizational resources and work engagement to employee performance and customer loyalty: The mediation of service climate. *Journal of Applied Psychology*, 90, 1217–27.

Schneider, B. (1994). HRM – a service perspective: Toward a customer-focused HRM. *International Journal of Service Industry Management*, 5, 64–76.

Schneider, B. (2000). The psychological life of organizations. In N.M. Ashkanasy, C.P.M. Wilderson & M.F. Peterson (Eds), *Handbook of Organizational Culture and Climate* (pp. 17–21). Thousand Oaks, CA: Sage.

Schneider, B. & Bowen, D.E. (1985). Employee and customer perceptions of service in banks. *Journal of Applied Psychology*, 70, 423–33.

Schneider, B. & Bowen, D.E. (1993). The service organization: Human resources management is crucial. *Organizational Dynamics*, 21, 39–52.

Schneider, B. & Bowen, D.E. (1995). *Winning the Service Game*. Boston, MA: Harvard Business School Press.

Schneider, B. & White, S.S. (2004). *Service Quality: Research Perspectives*. Thousand Oaks, CA: Sage.

Schneider, B., Macey, W.H. & Young, S.A. (2005). The climate for service: A review of the construct and implications for achieving CLV goals. *Journal of Relationship Marketing*, 3, 111–32.

Schneider, B., Macey, W.H. and Young, S.A. (2005). Corporate service intelligence. *Technical Report/Newsletter*. Rolling Meadows, IL: Valtera Corporation.

Schneider, B., Parkington, J.J. & Buxton, V.M. (1980). Employee and customer perceptions of service in banks. *Administrative Science Quarterly*, 25, 252–67.

Schneider, B., Salvaggio, A.N. & Subirats, M. (2002). Climate strength: A new direction for climate research. *Journal of Applied Psychology*, 87(2), 220–9.

Schneider, B., White, S.S. & Paul, M.C. (1998). Linking service climate and customer perceptions of service quality: Tests of a causal model. *Journal of Applied Psychology*, 83, 150–63.

Schneider, B., Ehrhart, M.G., Mayer, D.M., Saltz, J.L. & Niles-Jolly, K. (2005). Understanding organization–customer links in service settings. *Academy of Management Journal*, 48, 1017–32.

Schuler, R.S. & Jackson, S.E. (1987). Linking competitive strategies and human resource management practices. *Academy of Management Executive*, 1(3), 207–19.

Shirom, A. (2003). Feeling vigorous at work? The construct of vigor and the study of positive affect in organizations. In D. Ganster & P.L. Perrewe (Eds), *Research in Organizational Stress and Well-being* (Vol. 3, pp. 135–65). Greenwich, CN: JAI Press.

Tax, S.S., Colgate, M. & Bowen, D.E. (2006). How to prevent your customers from failing. *Sloan Management Review*, 47, 30–8.

Ulrich, D. & Brockbank, W. (2005). *The HR Value Proposition*. Boston, MA: Harvard Business School Press.

Van Maanen, J. (1991). The smile factory: Work at Disneyland. In P.J. Frost, L. Moore, M. Louis, C. Lundberg & J. Martin (Eds), *Reframing Organizational Culture*. Beverly Hills, CA: Sage Publications.

Waldman, D.A. & Bowen, D.E. (1998). The acceptability of 360 degree appraisals: A customer–supplier relationship perspective. *Human Resource Management*, 37, 117–31.

Webber, A.M. & Row, H. (1997). Four who know how: Best-practice answers to the four key customer service questions. *Fast Company*, October, 130–1.

Wiley, J.W. (1996). Linking survey data to the bottom line. In A.I. Kraut (Ed.), *Organizational Surveys: Tools for Assessment and Change* (pp. 330–59). San Francisco, CA: Jossey-Bass.

Wiley, J.W. & Campbell, B.C. (2006). Using linkage research to drive high performance: A case study in organizational development. In A. Kraut (Ed.), *Getting Action from Organizational Surveys: New Concepts, Technologies, and Applications*. San Francisco, CA: Jossey-Bass.

Wright, P.M. & Snell, S.A. (1991). Toward an integrative view of strategic human resource management. *Human Resource Management Review*, 1, 203–25.

Zeithaml, V.A., Bitner, M.J. & Gremler, D.D. (2006). *Services Marketing: Integrating Customer Focus Across the Firm* (4th edn). New York: McGraw-Hill Companies.

Index